Refugees as Immigrants

Refugees as Immigrants

Cambodians, Laotians, and Vietnamese in America

EDITED BY
David W. Haines

Rowman & Littlefield Publishers, Inc.

8-91

#16832535

ROWMAN & LITTLEFIELD PUBLISHERS, INC.

Published in the United States of America in 1989.
by Rowman & Littlefield Publishers, Inc.
81 Adams Drive, Totowa, New Jersey 07512

Library of Congress Cataloging-in-Publication Data

Refugees as immigrants

  Bibliography: p.
  Includes index.
    1. Refugees—Indochina. 2. Refugees—United States.
3. Indochinese—United States—Cultural assimilation.
4. Indochinese Americans. I. Haines, David W.
HV640.5.I5R42   1987   362.8'7'089959   87-26637
ISBN 0-8476-7553-X

5   4   3   2   1

Printed in the United States of America

Contents

Tables

Preface

The purpose of this volume is to provide the reader with access to an important body of information, taken from surveys on the initial adaptation of Southeast Asian refugees to the United States. The material is an expansion of the findings presented at a panel on the experiences of Southeast Asian refugees, held in May 1986 at the annual meeting of the American Association for the Advancement of Science. My concern, in organizing the panel, was that this information was being grossly underutilized by both the academic and policy-oriented communities. This concern was shared by the contributors, who were willing to take on the unenviable task of providing a concise overview of their otherwise widely scattered writings on the surveys for which they had responsibility.

The central purpose has dictated much of the form of the individual chapters. In order to provide an adequate introduction to each of the projects, the authors have addressed a common set of questions. Thus, each chapter provides information on the basic structure of the research, the major descriptive findings about the socioeconomic status of the sampled population, more specific findings of the research project (either in terms of its depth of data or the specific theoretical interests of the investigator[s]), and reflections on the use of the research within the rapidly shifting historical context of the resettlement of Southeast Asian refugees. This commonality is meant to facilitate the cross comparison of the different studies. As I argue in the introduction, this body of research is far stronger (and has far wider potential) when approached in its totality than when approached as a disconnected series of studies—important though the individual efforts are on their own terms.

It is often helpful to provide at the outset some general warnings about what a book does *not* attempt to do. This volume is, for example, not an introduction to the experience of those Southeast Asian refugees who have been resettled in the United States. Rather, it is an introduction to a specific kind of research on the adaptation of these refugees as one recent set of immigrants to the United States—albeit one with unique features in its premigration and exodus experiences. Nor is the volume intended to contribute to a particular theoretical position, to demonstrate normative state-of-the-discipline methodologies, or even to contribute to theory per se—

indeed, several of the contributors would argue strongly for the need for descriptive work. Finally, this volume is not intended to be an easily digested, terminal summary of this body of research. Rather, it aims only to introduce a body of work, illustrate its value, and thus encourage its further use.

Volumes of this kind hinge largely on the willingness of the contributors to sacrifice some of their own specific interests and approaches to the attainment of joint goals. That those represented here have been willing to make such an effort is encouraging. The book has also benefitted from the encouragement of a sympathetic general editor at Rowman and Littlefield. Paul Lee, who resolved issues of publication that would otherwise have been time-consuming, and from the efforts of production editor Mary Simmons, who helped solve the many editorial problems posed by this collective social science effort. Comments from Linda Hodge at the original panel and from Karen Rosenblum subsequently have helped clarify aspects of the general approach in the chapters and the collective argument about the need to better utilize this body of research. Mary Speer was instrumental in ensuring completion of the manuscript, particularly regarding adequate quality control in tabular presentations and computations, and in the references. I am indebted as well to the Rockefeller Foundation, which provided support for a review of the research on Southeast Asian refugees during 1985 to 1986 that led me to organize the originating panel, and to the Foundation as well for a supplemental grant to cover certain aspects of the technical preparation of the manuscript.

1

Introduction

David W. Haines

The research on Southeast Asian refugees in the United States is important for three reasons. First, and most directly, it documents and illuminates the process of adjustment among a diverse refugee population that has come to the United States in large numbers during a remarkably short period of time. Second, concerned as the research is with the early adjustment of a particular set of newcomers, it has a significant role in the broader investigation of immigrant adaptation to American society. Third, since refugee resettlement involves the interaction of refugees and a complex, detailed program designed to aid them, this research provides a rare window on the effects—intended and unintended, positive and negative—of social programs.

The surveys described in this volume reflect this diversity of focus as the authors move back and forth among concerns specific to refugees (loss of kin in exodus, the effects of camp residence); those shared by other immigrants (jobs available in specific localities, the effects of socioeconomic background, shifts in fertility rates); and those that reflect the extensive and detailed involvement of public and private organizations in refugee resettlement (use of assistance and services, migrations putatively in response to policy changes). It is the relative mix of such concerns, coupled with varying coverage of different components of the overall Southeast Asian refugee population at different times in their adjustment, and with the rapidly shifting economic, political, and programmatic context at the time of interviewing, that gives each survey its unique place within the overall body of research.

With the necessary warning about the extent of simplification needed to describe complex sets of data in a relatively small space, the chapters that follow speak for themselves. However, for those lacking previous exposure to the research on Southeast Asian refugees in the United States, there may be value in a brief introduction to this population, to the shifting contexts in which refugee resettlement has taken place in the United States, and to the

1

research on that resettlement of which the survey research presented here
is one crucial element. This chapter provides such an overview, and then
turns to a brief introduction to the surveys and some of the methodological
and analytic themes that run through them.

General Characteristics of the Population

By the end of September 1987 (the federal government's fiscal year), 846,000
refugees from Cambodia, Laos, and Vietnam had been resettled in the
United States. To establish total population size, however, this figure needs
to be adjusted for children subsequently born in the United States to these
refugees (probably around 200,000 [see Rumbaut and Weeks 1986]), those
persons from Vietnam, Laos, and Cambodia already in the United States in
1975 (about 20,000), and those who have arrived in recent years as immigrants rather than legally defined refugees (about 50,000). By the end of
1987, this total population of well over a million was a major element within
the general Asian American population.

In looking at the experience of Cambodians, Laotians, and Vietnamese in
the United States, it is essential to note the radical shifts in arrival rates over
the years. The entry of 130,000 refugees in 1975 was followed by very small
numbers of arrivals in 1976 and 1977, growing to 20,000 in 1978, quadru-
pling to 81,000 in 1979, doubling to 167,000 in 1980, and falling modestly
to 132,000 in 1981. In 1982, the number of arrivals roughly halved to 72,000,
nearly halved again in 1983 to 39,000, and has since then been about 40,000
to 50,000 each year, with additional numbers entering as normal immigrants
rather than as legally defined refugees. It is the two crests of flow, in 1975
and in 1980–1981, that are the origin of the designation of "first wave" and
"second wave" Southeast Asian refugees.

These shifts in flow, however, are more complex when viewed in terms of
the composition of arrivals by country of origin (Table 1.1). It is clear from
the data that increases and decreases in flows have been far from uniform
for the three national groups. Vietnamese have maintained a majority
position throughout, but this has become quite nominal as the arrivals of
Cambodians and Laotians increased both absolutely and as a proportion of
the total flow in the late 1970s. Refugees from Laos, in particular, not only
arrived in widely varying numbers each year, but also constituted a widely
shifting proportion of arrivals, jumping from 15.4% of all arrivals in 1977 to
39.2% the following year, holding at roughly that level in 1979 and 1980 and
then falling to under 15% for the years thereafter. Within these national
origin groups there were, as well, shifting proportions of different subseg-
ments of the population—the continuing majority of refugees from Vietnam
throughout these years masks the swell in the number of ethnic Chinese in
the late 1970s.

Table 1.1   National Origins of Refugees by Year of Arrival (Fiscal years 1975-1987)

	Number of arrivals			Percentage of arrivals		
	Cambodia	Laos	Vietnam	Cambodia	Laos	Vietnam
1975	4,600	800	125,000	3.5	.6	95.9
1976	1,100	10,200	3,200	7.6	70.3	22.1
1977	300	400	1,900	11.5	15.4	73.1
1978	1,300	8,000	11,100	6.4	39.2	54.4
1979	6,000	30,200	44,500	7.4	37.4	55.1
1980	16,000	55,500	95,200	9.6	33.3	57.1
1981	27,100	19,300	86,100	20.5	14.6	65.0
1982	20,100	9,400	42,600	27.8	13.0	59.1
1983	13,200	2,900	23,000	33.8	7.4	58.8
1984	19,900	7,200	24,900	38.2	13.8	47.9
1985	19,200	5,300	25,400	38.5	10.6	50.9
1986	10,100	12,900	22,400	22.2	28.4	49.3
1987	1,900	15,500	22,400	4.8	38.9	56.3

Note: All numbers are rounded to the nearest hundred. Totals will thus vary from overall arrival rates provided in other sources.

Source: Gordon (1987:156); ORR (1987a, 1987b).

Within the United States, this diverse population, arriving in ever-shifting numbers and composition, has been spread out throughout the country. As indicated in the data provided in Table 1.2, this was particularly true of the 1975 arrivals. In 1976, 29 states were home to at least 1% of the Southeast Asian refugee population. Even by 1984 (and the combined effects of shifts in initial resettlement and considerable secondary migration), 22 states still had at least 1% of the total Southeast Asian refugee population; this was less than the 33 states that had at least 1% of the total U.S. population in 1980, but more than the 15 states in that same year that had at least 1% of the Asian-origin population, as indicated by the 1980 census.

Despite this impressive overall dispersion, the refugee population has consistently shown concentrations in specific states. The proportion of refugees in California has steadily climbed from an initial 21.6% in 1976 to 32.6% in 1980, passing 40% in 1984, exceeding the proportion of Asian Americans in that state. Other states with relatively high concentrations of Southeast Asian refugees (over 3% of the total) have, through the years, included Texas (consistently the second state to California), Illinois, Washington, Minnesota, New York, Pennsylvania, and Virginia, as well as Florida and Louisiana for the initial 1975 arrivals. These relatively large numbers reflect a mix of factors. In some cases the number of refugees is consistent with the state's overall size (e.g., Illinois, New York); in other cases with the relative predominance of Asian Americans (e.g., Washington as well as California); and in yet other cases with the specific effects of the resettlement

Table 1.2   Geographic Distribution of Refugees by State (in percent) (1976, 1980, 1984)

	Southeast Asian refugees			U.S. population	
				Total 1980	Asian 1980
	1976	1980	1984		
Alabama	1.0	.5	.4	1.7	.3
Alaska	.1	.1	—	.2	.2
Arkansas	1.5	.7	.6	1.0	.2
Arizona	1.0	.6	.3	1.2	.7
California	21.6	32.6	40.1	10.4	35.2
Colorado	1.7	1.8	1.5	1.3	.9
Connecticut	.9	.9	.9	1.4	.6
Delaware	.1	—	—	.3	.1
D.C.	.4	.7	.2	.3	.2
Florida	3.9	2.0	1.6	4.3	1.7
Georgia	1.1	1.0	1.2	2.4	.7
Hawaii	1.5	1.4	.9	.4	15.9
Idaho	.3	.2	.2	.4	.2
Illinois	3.1	3.7	3.3	5.0	4.6
Indiana	1.5	.9	.5	2.4	.7
Iowa	2.0	1.6	1.2	1.3	.4
Kansas	1.4	1.3	1.3	1.0	.5
Kentucky	.7	.4	.3	1.6	.3
Louisiana	3.0	2.5	1.9	1.9	.7
Maine	.3	.1	.2	.5	.1
Maryland	2.1	1.1	1.2	1.9	1.8
Massachusetts	1.1	1.6	2.7	2.5	1.4
Michigan	2.1	1.8	1.4	4.1	1.7
Minnesota	3.0	3.4	3.2	1.8	.9
Mississippi	.4	.3	.2	1.1	.2
Missouri	2.4	1.0	.9	2.2	.7
Montana	.2	.2	.1	.3	.1
Nebraska	1.0	.5	.3	.7	.2
Nevada	.4	.4	.3	.4	.4
New Hampshire	.1	—	—	.4	.1
New Jersey	1.4	1.0	.9	3.3	2.9
New Mexico	.7	.5	.3	.6	.2
New York	3.3	2.9	3.5	7.8	8.9
North Carolina	.9	.9	.7	2.6	.6
North Dakota	.3	.1	.1	.3	.1
Ohio	2.4	1.4	1.4	4.8	1.4
Oklahoma	2.7	1.5	1.2	1.3	.5
Oregon	1.7	2.9	2.4	1.2	1.1
Pennsylvania	5.9	4.1	3.4	5.2	1.9
Rhode Island	.2	.5	.7	.4	.2

Table 1.2 (Continued)

	Southeast Asian refugees			U.S. population	
				Total	Asian
	1976	1980	1984	1980	1980
South Carolina	.7	.4	.3	1.4	.4
South Dakota	.4	.2	.1	.3	.1
Tennessee	.8	.8	.6	2.0	.4
Texas	7.9	8.7	7.2	6.3	3.6
Utah	.6	1.3	1.1	.6	.5
Vermont	.1	—	—	.2	—
Virginia	4.1	2.8	3.0	2.4	1.9
Washington	3.7	4.4	4.6	1.8	3.0
West Virginia	.2	.1	—	.9	.2
Wisconsin	1.5	1.4	1.5	2.1	.6
Wyoming	.1	—	—	.2	.1
Guam	.6	.1	—		
Unknown	.3	—			
Other	—	—			

Notes: Data on Southeast Asian refugees derive from reports to the Congress of the Office of Refugee Resettlement and its predecessors; data on the overall U.S. population and the overall Asian and Pacific Islander are estimates derived from a sample of cases from the 1980 Census (see original sources). Columns may not sum to 100 percent because of rounding. "—" indicates less than .5 percent. The population of U.S. territories is not included in the calculations for the overall or the Asian and Pacific Islander population.

Sources: HEW Refugee Task Force (1976:24); ORR (1981a:22–23, 1985:A-14-15); Johnson and others (1983:8).

program itself—the numbers in Pennsylvania and in Florida reflect the presence in those states of reception centers used to accommodate the Vietnamese influx in 1975.

While the comparison of refugees with the general Asian-origin population is an instructive one, the Asian-origin population is in itself very diverse. Table 1.3 provides data on the geographic distribution of specific Asian-origin populations from the 1980 census, both by region, and by state for the Western region. While the data are limited to the Vietnamese (and there are differences among the Southeast Asian groups [Gordon 1980, Strand and Jones 1985:149–59]), they provide some reflection on the extent to which the geographic distribution of refugees is predictable in terms of the experience of other immigrant groups. In some ways this distribution appears to be similar to that of the wider Asian American population: Vietnamese are relatively unrepresented in New England and the Eastern Central states (those states in the band from Michigan through Alabama), and overrepresented in the Pacific region. In other ways, however, their

Table 1.3   Regional Distribution of Vietnamese Refugees and Asian-Americans (1980)

	Total		Specific countries of origin					
	U.S.	Asian-origin	China	Philip-pines	Japan	India	Korea	Viet-nam
Regions								
New England	5.5%	2.4%	4.1%	1.1%	1.0%	4.4%	2.6%	2.1%
Middle Atlantic	16.2	13.7	22.7	8.8	5.5	29.8	16.5	6.9
East North Central	18.4	9.0	7.3	8.9	5.0	19.4	13.4	7.0
West North Central	7.6	2.7	1.9	1.4	1.5	3.8	4.7	6.4
South Atlantic	16.3	7.5	6.2	7.5	3.6	12.9	12.6	11.0
East South Central	6.5	1.2	.9	.7	.7	2.5	2.0	2.2
West South Central	10.5	5.0	4.1	2.7	2.3	8.0	5.4	18.3
Mountain	5.0	3.1	2.5	1.8	4.1	1.9	3.7	3.9
Pacific	14.0	55.4	50.3	67.0	76.2	17.4	39.2	42.3
Pacific region only								
Alaska	.2%	.2%	.1%	.4%	.2%	.1%	.5%	.1%
California	10.4	35.2	40.1	45.8	37.5	15.4	28.7	34.8
Hawaii	.4	15.9	6.9	16.9	33.5	.2	4.9	1.4
Oregon	1.2	1.1	1.0	.6	1.2	.6	1.4	2.3
Washington	1.8	3.0	2.2	3.3	3.8	1.1	3.8	3.6

Notes: Columns for the regional totals may not sum to 100 percent because of rounding; entries for the Western region may not sum to the total presented in the regional list for the same reason. The order of the populations is in terms of overall size in 1980, estimated to be 812,178 (Chinese), 781,894 (Filipino), 716,331 (Japanese), 387,223 (Asian Indian), 357,393 (Korean), and 245,025 (Vietnamese). See Gardner, Robey, and Smith (1985:5) for estimates of the size of these populations as of September 1985, The total Asian-American figure includes Pacific Islanders (approximately 260,000 of the total of 3.7 million persons). The states by region are as follows: New England (Connecticut, New Hampshire, Maine, Massachusetts, Rhode Island, and Vermont); Middle Atlantic (New Jersey, New York, and Pennsylvania); East North Central (Illinois, Indiana, Michigan, Ohio, and Wisconsin); West North Central (Iowa, Kansas, Minnesota, Missouri, Nebraska, North Dakota, and South Dakota); South Atlantic (Delaware, District of Columbia, Florida, Georgia, Maryland, North Carolina, South Carolina, Virginia, and West Virginia); East South Central (Alabama, Kentucky, Mississippi, and Tennessee); West South Central (Arkansas, Louisiana, Oklahoma, and Texas); Mountain (Arizona, Colorado, Idaho, Montana, Nevada, New Mexico, Utah, and Wyoming); and Pacific as listed in the lower portion of the table.

Source: Percentages are computed from estimates of state and regional Asian-American populations from the 1980 Census (Johnson and others 1983:8–9).

distribution is more unusual: the large proportion in the West Central states differs from the pattern for either the general population or for the Asian American population, reflecting specific aspects of the resettlement program in such states as Texas, Louisiana, Minnesota, and Iowa. In yet other cases, the Vietnamese distribution is similar to some but not all segments of the Asian American population: thus the proportion of Vietnamese in the

Middle Atlantic region is lower than for most of the other Asian American populations but not lower than for all of them; the proportion in the South Atlantic region is higher than for most but not all of the other Asian-origin groups; and the proportion in the Pacific region is lower than for most—but again not all—of the other groups.

The Southeast Asian refugee population is thus a large one that has grown in surges and has been dispersed across the United States in patterns that are partially similar, and partially dissimilar, to other Asian-origin segments of the U.S. population. It is also an internally diverse population, and contrary to much public comment, has been so since the earliest arrivals in 1975. Thus, as indicated in Table 1.4, the overall shifts in the aggregate educational background of refugees are significant but relatively modest. Except for the effects of the presence among the 1975 arrivals of an important segment of the well-educated, the average educational level remains in the range of seven to seven and a half years throughout. Data on the ability to speak good English also show a break between the initial arrivals and later ones, though data on refugees arriving after 1980 show some amelioration of inability to speak English (reflecting the effects of English language training in the processing centers in Southeast Asia through which most refugees after that time were going). Throughout such aggregate changes, however, the more important point is the continuing range of diversity within the arriving refugee population.

Table 1.4   Educational Background and English Ability of Southeast Asian Refugees by Year of Arrival

	Average years of education			Percent speaking no English			Percent speaking good English		
	(S-1)	(S-2)	(S-3)	(S-1)	(S-2)	(S-3)	(S-1)	(S-2)	(S-3)
1975	9.5	9.4	9.4	30.6	30.4	40.6	25.2	32.1	27.2
1976–77	7.1	7.6	7.5	31.8	25.1	49.3	26.8	23.1	10.9
1978	8.2	7.5	7.3	53.7	35.1	54.3	9.0	5.5	18.6
1979	7.6	7.9	7.4	41.9	37.1	67.8	19.0	7.2	6.2
1980	6.8	7.4	7.0	57.1	37.7	67.6	6.0	9.7	6.9
1981	7.0	6.8	6.7	52.3	36.8	61.9	8.4	7.1	7.0
1982	6.8	7.5	7.0	42.3	29.9	54.7	17.4	8.5	4.9
1983		7.7	6.5		29.4	48.9		12.2	8.6
1984			7.4			40.3			9.2

Notes: Numbers in parentheses at the tops of the columns refer to the specific survey from which the retrospective information is gathered: S-1 is the 1982, survey, S-2 is the 1983 survey, and S-3 is the 1984 survey; findings for the respective surveys appear in the listed sources of the succeeding calendar year. "Good" English includes those who reported that they could speak English well or fluently. All figures refer to the situation at time of arrival in the United States as retrospectively assessed by the respondents.

Source: ORR (1983:25, 1984:108, 1985:96).

Indeed, the very construct "Southeast Asian refugee" is a tenuous one. Better, though still inadequate to the diversity of this population, is the now usual division into five distinct "ethnic" populations: ethnic Chinese (mostly from Vietnam), Hmong, Khmer, Lao, and Vietnamese—though there are other, smaller populations as well. As indicated in the data presented in Table 1.5, each of these groups not only has its own distinctive cultural, social, and linguistic background but also has clear differences in its pre-arrival history and in its experience in its early years in the United States. Thus, these selective data suggest that the Vietnamese are the best edu-cated, the most fluent in English, and the most experienced in professional/technical occupations prior to exodus (true for men and particularly so for women). The group closest to them in these characteristics, and exceeding them in numbers from an urban background, are the Chinese. These two groups, to the extent the San Diego data are representative, also have the smallest households, the lowest fertility, and the least extensive aftereffects of exodus (e.g., less loss of kin, shorter periods in refugee camps). The Hmong, on the other hand, are the most rural, the least educated, and spend the most time in refugee camps; they also have the largest households and the highest fertility. The Khmer and the Lao lie between these two poles, each has significant urban and rural components; each averages a little over two years in refugee camps and about five years of education (reflecting sizable numbers with no education balancing out many with extensive education). As well, each has an occupational profile that shows significant proportions of both white collar and farming/fishing occupations. For the Khmer, however, there is the added residue of the ravages of the Pol Pot regime that took power in 1975 and the continuing warfare since the Vietnamese invasion that toppled that regime in 1978. Among the results for refugees are a very frequent loss of kin (including large numbers of widows) and lingering psychological problems.

The Contexts of Refugee Adaptation

The adaptation of this disparate population to the United States has hinged on a complex set of factors: some relating to the specific experiences that refugees bring with them, others to the specific environments they find in the United States, yet others to the effects of the programs designed to facilitate their transition into American society. Since one of the key challenges to the research described in this volume is precisely the need to sort out the relative effects of these divergent sets of factors, they deserve a brief review here.

The first of the major contexts for understanding refugee adaptation involves the social and personal histories of the refugees themselves. One component of these complex, layered histories is the web of social behavior

Table 1.5   General Characteristics by Ethnicity

	Chinese	Hmong	Khmer	Lao	Vietnamese
California, 1977					
Mean education (years)	5.9		8.0	3.6	9.7
Some or better English:					
Speaking	48%		49%	49%	74%
Reading	47%		49%	50%	74%
Five sites, 1982					
(1978–82 arrivals only)					
Household averages:					
Overall size	4.5			5.5	4.7
Children under 16	1.6			2.5	1.7
Education:					
At least some college	3.6%			5.1%	13.8%
No formal education	6.5%			21.0%	1.6%
Households with at least one person who knew "some" English at arrival	47%			46%	68%
Percent in camps for longer than one year	38.5%			53.2%	19.2%
San Diego, 1983					
Percent illiterate in native language	17.6%	70.8%	34.2%	26.6%	1.0%
Years of education	6.7	1.6	5.0	4.9	9.8
Percent urban	95.4%	8.3%	46.3%	79.1%	94.0%
Years since migration	4.6	6.6	5.3	5.9	4.8
Months in refugee camps	10.3	34.3	25.5	23.0	7.8
Years in the U.S.	3.6	3.6	2.8	3.6	4.1
Household size	5.8	8.7	8.3	6.3	5.5
Close family members lost	.5	1.0	1.7		.6
Percent widowed	2.3%	3.5%	12.2%		1.0%
Total fertility rate	4.7	11.9	7.4	6.6	3.4
National sample (1983)					
Occupational background in country of origin					
Males					
Professional/technical workers	7.7%	6.2%	17.4%	9.9%	19.4%
Sales/clerical workers	46.7	19.1	38.0	29.6	34.3
Craftsmen/foremen	17.5	3.1	3.6	20.8	16.7
Operatives	10.0	0.0	6.3	6.8	7.3
Laborers	3.2	0.0	1.1	3.5	2.5

Table 1.5   (Continued)

	Chinese	Hmong	Khmer	Lao	Vietnamese
Males (Continued)					
Service workers	6.0	18.2	9.6	10.3	6.0
Farmers/fishers	8.9	53.5	24.2	19.1	13.7
Females					
Professional/technical workers	3.5%	0.0%	8.5%	6.0%	19.2%
Sales/clerical workers	60.7	4.3	36.5	39.4	60.8
Craftsmen/foremen	15.9	0.0	3.1	5.4	5.2
Operatives	9.4	0.0	2.5	1.2	3.3
Laborers	3.3	0.0	1.5	1.8	0.4
Service workers	3.6	3.2	5.1	9.5	3.1
Farmers/fishers	3.6	92.5	42.8	36.7	7.9

Notes: Figures are generally limited to adults except for such variables as household size and number of children. The ISR survey did not include Hmong and Khmer and these columns are thus blank; for the California survey, there was no separate category for Hmong. For the ISR survey, Chinese means only Sino-Vietnamese; for the California survey this is true for the figures on education, but not for those on language (for which Chinese from Vietnam and from Cambodia are combined). For the San Diego data, "Khmer" includes ethnic Chinese from Cambodia as well; for the California data "Lao" includes all Laotions.

Sources: San Diego derive from Rumbaut (1985a:441–442) and Rumbaut and Weeks (1986:445); the 1982 five-site survey data are from Caplan, Whitmore, and Bui (1985:46, 48,57,70); the data for California are from Aames et al. (1977:16,106,107); and the national data on occupation are from ORR's 1983 survey of Southeast Asian refugees (as compiled in Haines [1986:73], cf. ORR [1984:101–112]).

and cultural values that are often designated as "traditional." In addition, Southeast Asian refugees have very particular histories within their societies of origin that leave them with clusters of characteristics that may, at times, distinguish them as much from their compatriots as from those of other nationalities. Refugees are, after all, rarely "typical" members of the societies from which they come. Further complicating their histories are the events of exodus: these provide similarities of experience to some refugees and differences to others. Thus there are, for example, some pervasive differences between so-called first and second wave refugees in the extent to which the latter have three distinct layers to their personal histories that the first lack: they have generally been exposed to life under communist regimes (often including reeducation camps); they have experienced protracted and dangerous escapes, often after several attempts; and they have usually spent lengthy periods in refugee camps both before and after acceptance by the United States.

The refugees continue to have divergent experiences after arrival in the

United States. Even the simple arrival rates of different national-origin groups suggest the varying dynamics of ethnic community structure and formation that different refugees must face. Thus, as indicated by the data provided in Table 1.6, and setting aside the further complications of ethnic variation within the national groups, a Vietnamese arriving in 1980 was part of an arrival cohort that faced, for better or for worse, a large established Vietnamese refugee community, most of its members having arrived in 1975. A Cambodian arriving in the same year (1980), however, was part of an arrival cohort bigger than the total of all previous arrivals; the same was true of an arriving Laotian.

The second major context involves the society in which refugees find themselves, a society that is itself neither homogeneous nor stable over time. One critical aspect of the ever-changing recipient society is the state of its economy. As the arrival of refugees was at its peak, for example, the availability of jobs was declining due to the recession of the early 1980s. The existing research shows not only the poor employment situation of refugees arriving during this period, but also a declining situation for even the earlier arrivals—those whom survey efforts in the late 1970s had suggested were more frequently in the labor force, experienced a lower unemployment rate, and worked longer hours than the general U.S. population. If recession had such a noticeable effect on even those most acclimated to the U.S. labor market, it inevitably had both immediate and long-term effects on those who were entering the U.S. labor market for the first time, or who, as relatively recent arrivals, were especially vulnerable to lay-offs.

Table 1.6   The Demographic Dynamics of Ethnic Community Formation (Fiscal years 1975–1985)

	Percent of total national-origin arrivals		
	Cambodian	Laotian	Vietnamese
1975	3.6	.5	25.9
1976	.9	6.8	.7
1977	.2	.3	.4
1978	1.0	5.4	2.3
1979	4.7	20.2	9.2
1980	12.4	37.1	19.7
1981	21.0	12.9	17.8
1982	15.6	6.3	8.8
1983	10.2	1.9	4.8
1984	15.5	4.8	5.2
1985	14.9	3.6	5.3

Note: Columns may not sum to 100 percent because of rounding.
Source: Table 1.1.

In addition, the adaptation of Southeast Asian refugees is conditioned by the presence of other recent newcomers to American society. Large numbers of other immigrants are often located in the same localities as are refugees. While none (except undocumented migrants from Mexico and possibly El Salvador) have grown in number at the rate of Southeast Asian refugees, nevertheless such other immigrants draw on many of the same, sometimes limited resources. In particular, many other Asian-origin populations have expanded rapidly since the immigration reforms of 1965. Some have grown in number nearly as rapidly as Southeast Asian refugees, but through regular immigration quotas and the subsequent arrival of family members of citizens—perhaps most notably those from Korea. Other refugee groups, whether or not so designated by the government (e.g., Cubans and Haitians arriving during or subsequent to the Mariel exodus in 1980 who were classified as "entrants" or Salvadorans the vast majority of whose claims to asylum are denied), affect the context in which resettlement occurs as well.

The third key context for resettlement involves the refugee program itself. Refugees are not only unlike other immigrants in the nature of their migration, they are also unlike in terms of the kinds of assistance made available to them in the United States. Their adjustment is, to some extent, the effect of programmatic intervention. One key question to which much of the research on refugees has been directed is whether such assistance has, in fact, aided refugees. Like the characteristics of the refugees and of the environments in which they resettle, this programmatic context is complex, diverse, and subject to change often over very short periods of time.

Consider, for example, the provision of cash assistance to Southeast Asian refugees. Such cash assistance to refugees has generally been provided through two mechanisms: first, through existing state AFDC (Aid to Families with Dependent Children) programs, the normal state portion of which is reimbursed by the federal refugee program; and, second, through an AFDC-like program (liberalized in its eligibility criteria), state costs for which are entirely reimbursed by the federal refugee program. Among its many provisions, the Refugee Act of 1980 stipulated that, effective April 1, 1981, such cash (and medical) assistance specially for refugees would be available for only the first 36 months of a refugee's residence in the United States, and that refugee program reimbursement of normal state costs for AFDC provided to refugees would likewise terminate at the end of 36 months of residence. This change in policy made it of great concern to states whether refugees continued to use AFDC assistance after the 36-month period. One year later, the period of eligibility for refugee-specific cash assistance was reduced to 18 months. This change became effective less than a month after the regulation had been published. While limiting the specific refugee cash assistance program, the federal government continued to reimburse states for AFDC costs for 36 months of residence, and opted to reimburse state and local GA/GR costs (general assistance and general relief) for eligible refugees in the United States for over 18 months but no longer than 36 months. This brought the federal government into direct involvement with these exceedingly varied programs, a national description of which had not been published for several years.

Such changes have continued. Finding refugees still too frequently receiving assistance, the federal government moved forward with demonstration projects (the major one in California) designed to separate refugees from the AFDC program in favor of the special refugee assistance program, thus changing the long-standing policy of assessing refugee eligibility for AFDC first, with the eligibility for the special refugee assistance program to be decided thereafter for those not eligible for AFDC. In early 1986, as one effect of the Gramm-Rudman-Hollings legislation, the period of federal reimbursement for AFDC (and other normal assistance programs) was reduced to 31 months due to a lack of sufficient funds. In early 1987, the administration proposed to further reduce the time period for which it would reimburse state costs to 24 months, and reduce the period of eligibility for the special refugee cash assistance program to 12 months. Throughout, it is hard to see how refugees could have kept track of such changes, much less understood the complex motives for budget reductions as well as the ideologically complex and often diffuse discussions of "welfare mentality," "dependency rates," "entitlement" versus "discretionary" programs, and the basic workings of the U.S. welfare system in general, including the disparate and complicated roles of the states on the one hand and the federal government on the other.

In assessing the interactions of these three distinct contexts for resettlement, it is worth reiterating the extent to which each is specific to particular localities at particular times. It is, after all, specific economic opportunities in specific localities that lead to jobs for refugees—e.g., electronics work in California or fishing along the Gulf Coast. It is locally distinct housing markets that determine where refugees will live and how others will react to them—thus the availability of a new and vacant housing complex on the outskirts of New Orleans led to a dense Vietnamese concentration that a few years later (when such housing was more sought after) led to complaints of favoritism toward the Vietnamese (Finnan and Cooperstein 1983). It is the political structure of particular states and localities that determines the benefits and assistance available to refugees—thus the 1982 reduction of refugee-specific cash assistance to an eighteen-month period left refugees in such states as Washington and Oregon suddenly without support, while those in New York and Pennsylvania needed to do little more than shift to existing state general assistance programs (the eligibility criteria for and benefits of which were virtually the same as the discontinued refugee-specific assistance).

Research on Southeast Asian Refugees

The development of research on Southeast Asian refugees has mirrored the course of refugee resettlement in the United States. In dealing with the initial 1975 exodus, the research reflected the perception that the exodus was a one-time event. Work in the staging areas in the Pacific tended to be concerned with the mechanics of camp maintenance (e.g., Shaw 1977; Mattson and Ky 1978) while that regarding the situation of refugees in the reception centers in the United States was topically broader. Most important in the latter category are the work of Kelly (1977) on Fort Indiantown Gap, Pennsylvania, and the work, mostly concerned with psychological aspects of resettlement, at Camp Pendleton, California (e.g., Harding and Looney 1977; Rahe and others 1978; and Liu, Lamanna, and Murata 1979). There was for this initial period, as well, considerable program data (e.g., numerous military and civilian "after-action" reports on camp operation) and demographic data that provide both an overview of the population and the basis for comparative work on the subsequent adjustment of the refugees. Justus's (1976) comments on how refugees responded to requests for such data (e.g., exaggeration of occupational background), also at Camp Pendleton, provide a useful reminder of the assumptions that lie, often hidden, within such quantitative data.

In 1975 a series of surveys focusing on the economic adaptation of the refugees was initiated. Funded by the federal government and conducted by Opportunity Systems, Incorporated (OSI), the surveys were initially conducted several times a year, and eventually shifted to an annual basis. With modifications, these surveys have continued until the present (Gordon discusses the more recent ones in Chapter 2). There was also a particularly useful survey in California in 1977 (Aames et al. 1977) that, unlike the OSI surveys, provided information not only on Vietnamese but also on Cambodians and Laotians, and, in some tabulations, ethnic Chinese as well. Such key survey sources were complemented by clinical research and small-scale survey work such as that in Seattle in 1975 to 1976 (Lin, Tazuma and Masuda 1979; Masuda, Lin, and Tazuma 1980), which began to help define key elements of psychological adjustment. Anthropologists turned to various facets of the social and cultural dynamics of refugee adaptation (e.g., Skinner and Hendricks 1977, Silverman 1977, Barger and Truong 1978).

What distinguished this early research was, at least in general, an emphasis on Vietnamese refugees and on the relatively positive and linear pattern of economic success they were experiencing. By the late 1970s, however, the situation in Southeast Asia had dramatically changed with the growing exodus by boat from Vietnam and the Vietnamese invasion of Cambodia. The research was changing too. The large numbers of arrivals were yet to come, but the decisions for these arrivals had been made, and the number of arrivals was, in any case, well above that of the hiatus years of 1976 and

1977. It was also clear that the rapid economic adjustment of the early arrivals had not been without its psychological problems, and that there were some within the refugee population whose economic situation remained poor. One result of these changes was a quantum leap in the volume of the research; another result was the increasing attention to diversity within the refugee population regarding both background characteristics and alternative patterns in adaptation.

By 1979, there was a reasonable amount of raw program and survey information available; published material was available as well on the 1975 exodus and on the research conducted during the 1975–77 period, especially various considerations of refugee economic adjustment that drew heavily on the series of government-funded OSI surveys conducted since 1975 (e.g., Stein 1979; Montero 1979; subsequently Marsh 1980; and Bach and Bach 1980). In addition, new data collection activities held great promise for expanding the ability to document specific aspects of resettlement. The first results from the work of Starr and Roberts appeared in 1979 (Starr et al. 1979); an extensive survey was in process in Illinois that would provide data on adjustment (and the perceptions of it) with better attention to distinctions among ethnic groups (Kim 1980, Kim and Nicassio 1980); the Social Security Administration funded the three-site survey of Vietnamese refugees that Dunning discusses in Chapter 4 (the only survey to be stratified for year of entry from 1975 to 1979); and a wide variety of "needs assessment" type surveys were providing useful information, albeit of varying rigor and focus (e.g., Sedanko and Tutchings 1978; Tutchings 1979; Human Resources Corporation 1979; Pennsylvania Department of Public Welfare 1979). To reflect the new situation, the OSI surveys were expanded to include more recent arrivals, and also Cambodians (in 1978) and Laotians (in 1979).

The continuing interest in refugees reflected not only the rise in refugee influx from Southeast Asia (and relatively high levels of Soviet Jewish emigrés during the late 1970s as well) but also work on the 1979 bill that became the Refugee Act of 1980. Congressional action spurred official attention to research, ensured circulation of key articles, was the reason for the funding of an influential overview of U.S. refugee programs (Taft, North, and Ford 1979), and was to have an enormous direct and indirect effect over the succeeding years in the funding of evaluation work by the federal government as well as in extensive improvements in basic demographic and program data. The increase in materials is well-documented in bibliographies of this period (e.g., Frankel 1980, ORR 1981b, Stein 1980, Church World Service 1980, and, subsequently, Ashmun 1983). The appearance of a 1981 special issue of *International Migration Review* on refugees, and the 1980–1981 publication of the *Journal of Refugee Resettlement* gave support to the idea of "refugee studies" as a coherent area of research. In addition, the initiation of the evaluation and research agenda by the federal government (including the five-site survey by the Institute for Social Research, discussed in Chapter 7) ensured an increasing amount of quantitative and qualitative research. During this period, the issues of refugee resettlement became the bases for conferences such as those on the Hmong held at the University of Minnesota (Downing and Olney 1982; Hendricks, Downing, and Deinard 1986), and a staple at national and regional professional meetings.

The net result was a cumulative breakthrough by the mid-1980s in the understanding of the rudiments of the processes underlying resettlement, including such now-frequent topics as the nature and effects of diversity within the population, the complexities of labor market phenomena at local levels, and the importance of the structure of domestic groups in all aspects of resettlement. Yet what is perhaps the most essential feature of the research at this point was its breadth. Given a rapidly expanding field of inquiry with ample funding, particularly for efforts that could be construed to be "policy-relevant," there was inevitably the possibility of dealing in detail with more and more specific topical areas and refugee groups than would otherwise have been the case.

It is worth stressing the rapidity with which very substantial sets of data were becoming available: the final report of the Bureau of Social Science Research survey became available in late 1982 (Dunning 1982); a follow-up on the economic progress of 1975 arrivals based on government records appeared in 1984 (Baker and North 1984); the final report of the Institute for Social Research (ISR) survey appeared the next year (Caplan, Whitmore, and Bui 1985)—and was followed by an important extension of that work regarding the scholastic achievement of refugee children (Caplan et al. 1985b); initial results from NICHD-funded survey work appeared at roughly the same time (IHARP 1984, Rumbaut 1985a, Rumbaut and Weeks 1986); and comparative analysis of Vietnamese refugees and other recent Asian immigrants based on the 1980 Census was also published in 1985 (Gardner, Robey, and Smith 1985). Throughout the period, there were also continuing annual surveys of refugees by the federal government (overviews of which were published in the annual reports of the Office of Refugee Resettlement) and continually improving demographic and program data. Other kinds of research also developed rapidly, whether involving the structure of refugee neighborhoods (Rynearson and DeVoe 1984), the social organization of refugee research (Nguyen Manh Hung 1984), general anthropological studies of adjustment (Howell 1982), clearer distinctions about diversity in the refugee population (e.g., Peters et al. 1983), or the issues of refugee health and mental health (the latter well represented in Owan 1985).

This rapid expansion in research on Southeast Asian refugees was not without its problems: the advantages of the eclecticism of research on refugee resettlement continue to be partially offset by the lack of a clear disciplinary foundation; the rapid growth of the field may have overridden the ability to synthesize the emerging data and analysis; the strong boost given by the relevance of the research to specific public policies may well have undermined its internal logic and integrity; and the internal politicization of the potential research community may have atomized and thus undermined the total research effort. Indeed, the sheer volume of the research may have assured disattention to key elements of it. One necessary task, then, is the reexamination of this impressive body of research. And it is to that task for one specific component of the research, that based on survey work, that this volume is directed.

The Survey Research

Within the overall context of Southeast Asian refugee resettlement in the United States, the surveys described in this volume cover differing segments of the overall population at specific times, in specific places, and with specific methodological and topical approaches. In Chapter 2, Gordon provides a description not only of the federal government's basic data system on refugees, but also the more recent of the now annual federal government surveys of the Southeast Asian refugee population. These surveys have generally been based on simple random samples of the entire resident population throughout the United States, samples drawn separately each year; in the mid-1980s, however, the surveys were restricted to the most recent five years of arrivals and gradually converted to a panel design. In order to meet such a fully national design at a feasible cost, the surveys have been based on telephone interviews, with a necessarily restricted topical focus. These surveys provide the best national data across the complete period of Southeast Asian refugee resettlement, and thus provide an appropriate introduction to the general patterns in refugee adjustment.

While the federal government's surveys have consistently focused on economic issues, other surveys have had different foci, and, without the burdens of fully national samples, have been able to focus on more in-depth, face-to-face, interviewing approaches. In Chapter 3, Roberts and Starr describe their panel study of Vietnamese refugees with initial interviews in 1979 and subsequent reinterviews one and then two years later. Reflecting the situation at the time of funding, the study (like early federal government surveys) focused on Vietnamese refugees (in two regions) all of whom had arrived in 1975. Reflecting their disciplinary interests, what Roberts and Starr set out to do had less to do with the dynamics of early economic adjustment—always the federal government's central concern—and more with the social and cultural dynamics of Vietnamese refugee life within the broader framework of immigrant adaptation and acculturation. Correspondingly, and as demonstrated in their analysis in this volume, their work provides the first documentation of the postcrisis adjustment of the initial 1975 Vietnamese refugees. The particular strengths of the study lie in this general theoretical emphasis and in the panel design; the limitations lie precisely with that focus on 1975 arrivals in two particular regions.

The survey described by Dunning in Chapter 4 provides a necessary counterpoint to the work described by Roberts and Starr. The survey, with interviewing in late 1980, accomplished a general broadening of the survey research in three key ways. First, by collecting retrospective data from the interviewees at the study's three sites (the New Orleans, Houston, and Los Angeles metropolitan areas), it was possible to address the cumulative process of adjustment since arrival, rather than being restricted to the interviewees' activities at the time of interview. Second, the study attempted to address the by then obvious fact that 1975 arrivals were only one segment, and were eventually to be a minority one, of the overall Vietnamese refugee influx. The stratification of the sample by year of arrival (1975 to 1979) makes the study unique in providing data on entry cohorts inadequately represented in other survey work. Third, though focused on economic issues, the study—as ably demonstrated by Dunning's discussion—was topically very broad, including data on psychological perceptions, religious change, and background social information not available from other surveys.

As these surveys of Vietnamese were in process, however, the arriving flows of refugees were increasingly heterogeneous in national and ethnic origin. The federal government had added separate components to its own surveys for Cambodians and Laotians in the late 1970s; but the published findings made no distinction, in particular, between the two widely different segments of the Laotian population: the ethnic (lowland) Lao, and the various highland Laotian groups, particularly the Hmong. The 1979 Illinois survey described by Kim in Chapter 5 provides the first large set of data that covers not only the different Vietnamese arrival cohorts, but also the other nationalities as well, including the necessary distinction between the two major segments of the Laotian population. With this coverage and the size of the samples used (and with separate samples to provide as much reliability as possible), the study makes possible a consideration of adjustment as it affects different components of the population by nationality and ethnicity, at least with regard to Laotians. The topical breadth of the survey, with strong attention to social, economic, and psychological issues, reflects as well the merging of the economic and social/psychological threads of the research existent at that time.

Strand's discussion in Chapter 6 of the 1981 survey in San Diego provides another example of this switch to a multiethnic framework, again with separate profiles of Hmong, Lao, Khmer, and Vietnamese. As seen in the data he presents, the simple description by such categories readily documents the different situations of the different ethnic populations in the United States. It is appropriate that such a survey is conducted in a single locality since the attempt to provide adequate numbers of each of the groups over differing years of arrival is a demanding methodological prerequisite: to add additional sites to such a design poses distinct problems.

The surveys described by Kim and Strand bracket an important period in the history of the survey research on Southeast Asian refugees. They point forward in addressing the distinct ethnic populations (although excluding ethnic Chinese as a separate category) but still maintain attention to all years of arrival. To provide an equivalent approach at the national level was a forbidding task. The work described by Whitmore, Trautmann, and Caplan in Chapter 7 represents the most sustained effort to accomplish that task. Attempting in their initial work to provide a deeper understanding of the dynamics of refugee economic adaptation, they focused on three of the five populations (Vietnamese, Sino-Vietnamese, and Lao) in five key sites (Seattle, Houston, Chicago, Boston, and Orange County, California). The sample was further restricted to relatively recent arrivals, forsaking what had been the common practice of including in surveys all those who had arrived since 1975. The result, based on interviewing in 1982, is the most detailed analysis available of income dynamics among Southeast Asian refugeess, and the work remains a crucial piece of the existing research on those grounds alone. Their subsequent examination of academic achievement, based on a linking of the original data set with both more detailed information on a subsample and school records, marks an additional, important advance in the scope and potential of the survey research on refugee adaptation.

Chapter 8 returns the volume to San Diego for a separate survey project some two years later than that described by Strand. Lacking the forbidding problems contingent on trying to construct a national sample, Rumbaut and his colleagues were able to return to the broader approach of earlier work, covering the five key ethnic populations (Chinese, Hmong, Khmer, Lao and Vietnamese) over all years of arrival, but with the resources to pursue a panel design (although unsuccessfully for the Lao) with structured interviewing in 1983 and again in 1984, and with additional qualitative interviewing between those two periods. The chapter brings together the kinds of theoretical interests epitomized by Roberts and Starr for the early Vietnamese arrivals, the broad attention to different topical interests so characteristic of Dunning's work, and the requisite sensitivity to ethnic differences. Rumbaut's discussion of refugee youth, including the integrating of school achievement scores with the survey data, serves to pull together threads of analysis from ISR's work on the same subject. It thus provides a fitting conclusion to the volume.

Some Key Themes

Each of the surveys thus has its own particular location in the broader history of research on Southeast Asian refugees, a history in turn interlinked with that of refugee resettlement itself. Each survey sheds light on many of the same aspects of refugee adaptation for overlapping groups of refugees—by nationality, year of arrival, geographical location, and time of interview. Thus while the efforts have individual merit, the potential value of the set is far greater—indeed, it is probably a fair assertion that there is more usable data on the early adjustment of Southeast Asian refugees than on any other immigrant group of comparable size over the course of American history.

As the surveys are partially overlapping in coverage, so also they have a number of commonalities in the difficulties they face in sampling and interviewing a difficult-to-locate population, the kinds of descriptive topics they address, the key analytic dilemmas caused by the complexities of the subject matter, and the difficulties in determining the appropriate framework within which the research is to be seen. These common interests and difficulties—of method, topical focus, analytic complexity, and conceptual framework—run as themes through the research as a whole, and generally through each individual research effort as well. Some brief comments on them conclude this introductory chapter.

In terms of methodology, all authors in the volume spend considerable effort in describing the nature of, and reasons for, the particular design of the surveys for which they had responsibility. The central reason is a simple one: there is no fully adequate way to both sample adequately the Southeast Asian refugee population and provide reliable and detailed information on those sampled. The national surveys that Gordon describes start off with the most complete list of refugees, but the reliability of these lists has varied across the years; the approach used virtually necessitates interviewing by phone; and there are inevitable problems in tracing potential respondents. Local surveys have distinct advantages in interviewing and tracing, but, as both Rumbaut and Strand note for San Diego, the enumeration of the potential respondent universe in even a single urban area is an arduous task. When research teams must work in several different areas, as was the case for the work described by Roberts and Starr, Dunning, and Whitmore, Trautmann, and Caplan, the effort is forbidding.

The difficulties in sampling are compounded by the dictates of data collection in foreign languages, and among a population relatively unaccustomed to survey research and relatively vulnerable to breaches of confidentiality regarding personal relations or economic status. In terms of data collection, the survey work has necessitated not only the complexity of questionnaire translation (and back translation), but also the training of native language interviewers. As the number of languages expands to include Vietnamese, Khmer, Lao, Hmong, and different Chinese dialects, the difficulties multiply. Furthermore, even significant resources of time, effort, and funding do not always resolve the social complexities of this multilingual, multiethnic research process. As Rumbaut notes in Chapter 8, methodological decisions about numbers of interviewers and kinds of supervisory personnel can undermine the very ability to conduct the research. All the surveys share these methodological dilemmas. It is only because, as Gordon accurately points out, there are different survey data in addition to extensive background demographic data that it is possible to have confidence in the representativeness and validity of findings from individual survey efforts.

The surveys also share some similar topical emphases, partially reflecting the nature of refugee resettlement, and partially reflecting both the theoretical and policy-related concerns that lie at the origin of the surveys. There are two basic sets of such topical interests, one having to do with the central, common patterns in refugee adjustment, and the other with the diversity underlying such commonalities. In terms of the first set, survey work on refugees tends to dwell on such subjects as the economic situation of refugees, their general background characteristics (occupation, education, English-language competence), the basic correlates of their current economic situation, and their use of services and assistance in the United States. In terms of the second set of foci, key subjects tend to include (both in text and frequently in table headings) the ethnic composition of the population, the differences among arrival cohorts, geographical location (most recently with emphasis on refugees in California), and basic demographic characteristics (men versus women, old versus young). Together, these two sets of interests coalesce into the familiar inventory of the increasing employment of refugees over time, the importance of English to employment, the differences between "first" and "second" wave refugees, generational strains within families, and so on. It is these kinds of topics that have filtered down (in very diluted form) into the media and into policy discussions (or political arguments) about refugees and refugee resettlement programs.

Beyond such common topical interests and the well-defined descriptive patterns that emerge regarding them, however, this body of research also shares a series of analytic dilemmas. Three of these deserve note since they reappear, sometimes implicitly and sometimes explicitly, with some frequency in the chapters that follow. First is the continuing attempt to sort out within the general patterns of adjustment the respective effects of refugee characteristics at time of entry, length of time in the United States (and all that conveys about the "natural" process of immigrant adaptation), and the specific conditions during different periods of that residence. For example, while it is very clear that by the early 1980s refugees who had arrived in 1975 were doing better than those who had arrived in the late 1970s, it remained difficult to sort out the respective effects of length of residence in the United States and the differing background characteristics of the refugees at the time of arrival. With the recession of the early 1980s, the importance of conditions in the recipient society was underlined: refugees with similar skills arriving before or during the recession faced very different problems. This remains a constant struggle for all of the surveys here, even those with a panel design, since there are no panel data that bridge the tumultuous events in resettlement and in the U.S. economy over this first decade of Southeast Asian refugee resettlement. Again, it is only the surveys as a set that can begin to address this quandary.

A second analytic dilemma involves the diversity within the Southeast Asian refugee population. While no one any longer seriously considers "Indochinese refugee" as a homogeneous category, it is necessary to stress that even the five-fold ethnic categorization now current has its problems. Thus, as is clear from background data on the Khmer and Lao, for example, each of these populations includes distinct urban and rural components. In turn, Rumbaut has found in work on refugee youth, which he discusses briefly in Chapter 8 (see also Rumbaut and Ima 1987), a distinct bimodal distribution of these two groups in terms of educational achievement. Similar diversity exists for Vietnamese whose society is strongly differentiated by class, religion, and regional background. Ethnic differences aside, differing occupational groups, different age groups, men versus women, and adults versus children, partake of distinctive patterns in adjustment. In their examinations of educational achievement, for example, both Rumbaut and Whitmore, Trautmann, and Caplan stress the importance of looking at the varying adaptational patterns of the different generations.

The third dilemma in looking at refugee resettlement has been the continuing uncertainty about the relevant units of analysis. Survey research, almost by definition, takes the individual as the key unit from and about which information is gathered. However, it has been abundantly clear to all researchers working on the dynamics of refugee adjustment that individuals rarely exist as isolated units, and that most aspects of adjustment occur in and through specific group contexts. In economic terms, for example, poverty and the use of public assistance are both functions of households which, in turn, comprise the mutually interimplicated economic roles of the individuals within them. Whitmore, Trautmann, and Caplan are particularly emphatic about the importance and complexity of these household relations. Similarly, in assessing social and cultural adjustment, such social units as the family and the community emerge as central in importance. Roberts and Starr in Chapter 3, for example, point out the way in which the relative acculturation of individual refugees reflects their involvement in refugee and nonrefugee social interactions. The problem lies in the shifting structure and relevance of such units: households are not the same as families—the former fail to include all salient family members and the latter are not the sole basis for household construction. Yet both of these social units are far more precise in structure and boundaries than community or neighborhood. This unit definition problem is greatly exacerbated by the complexity of the social relations of refugees, and by the wide differences in both "traditional" and adjustment-related forms of such relations among the different segments of the refugee population, whether in terms of ethnicity, class, age, or gender.

These persisting analytic problems are matched, and at least partially caused, by a final theme that runs through the survey research represented here: the debate, largely implicit, about the general framework within which the study of refugee adaptation lies. On the one hand lies an emphasis on refugees as refugees. As a programmatic stance, this reflects the extensive public and private involvement in the provision of assistance and services to aid refugees in the transition to a new life for which they are inevitably less prepared than are other immigrants. Since the existence of such an extensive body of survey research largely reflects this programmatic involvement, it is hardly surprising that much research emphasizes the issues of economic adjustment during the very early years of residence in the United States. On the other hand lies an emphasis on Southeast Asian refugees as one of a broader range of recent immigrant groups to the United States, albeit one with certain unique features. Here it is hardly surprising to see emphases on such traditional academic topics regarding immigrant adaptation as the role of the community in ethnic self-identity (e.g., Roberts and Starr on ethnic and nonethnic contacts in Chapter 3); the continuing effects of specific Asian traditions (Whitmore, Trautmann, and Caplan on academic achievement in Chapter 7); general changes in post-migration fertility (Rumbaut in Chapter 8); the ambiguities of becoming a hyphenated American (Dunning in Chapter 4); or the nature of the relationships among the psychological, economic, and social dimensions of adaptation (Kim's argument in Chapter 5 that they are inextricably interlinked).

Whether the interest lies with refugees as refugees, or refugees as immigrants, the sheer volume of the research suggests its importance to analyzing the early years of newcomer adaptation in the United States. In addition, the strong governmental involvement in refugee resettlement suggests the importance of this research for assessing the potential effects of social programs, and the way in which research is, or is not, used effectively in the construction of such programs. What remains to be seen is whether this body of work will receive the attention it is due, thereby providing both extensive documentation for the early years of Southeast Asian refugee adaptation and an unusually broad base from which to conduct further research and analysis.

2

National Surveys of Southeast Asian Refugees: Methods, Findings, Issues

Linda W. Gordon

Since 1975, the federal government has been sponsoring surveys of Southeast Asian refugees on at least an annual basis. These surveys have been national in scope, with an emphasis on employment and social-service use—prime areas of concern to the federal government in helping refugees adjust to the United States. The continuity and scope of these surveys make them a crucial resource in assessing the overall patterns of refugee adaptation. The recent conversion of the surveys to a panel design (with reinterviewing the same persons in succeeding years) provides the potential for a deeper look into the dynamics of economic adaptation.

This chapter describes the annual surveys sponsored by the Office of Refugee Resettlement (ORR) and its predecessors. Emphasis is on those conducted from 1981 to 1985, both for the research techniques employed and for the insights they offer about refugees' adjustment to American life. The chapter begins by reviewing the information base on the Southeast Asian refugee population that government records provide (an unusually complete and comprehensive source of data on a recently arrived population) and then turns to sequential discussions of the structure of the surveys, key cross-sectional findings, and then to some of the longitudinal findings made possible by the conversion of the surveys to a panel design.

The Context for the Surveys

The Refugee Act of 1980 contained detailed and specific requirements for data collection and reporting. In addition, public interest in refugees, as a highly visible component of the nation's immigrant population, has been strong. In this context, the collection and dissemination of statistics on refugees is extensive and has become more institutionalized since 1980. The Refugee Act of 1980 required an annual report to Congress on the progress of refugees who arrived in the United States beginning in 1975.[1] Specific language in the Act provides for "an updated profile of the employment and labor force statistics for refugees," "a description of the extent to which refugees received . . . assistance or services," "a description of the geographic location of refugees," and "evaluations of the extent to which the services provided . . . are assisting refugees in achieving economic self-sufficiency, achieving ability in English, and achieving employment commensurate with their skills and abilities." These legislative reporting requirements are unusually extensive for an immigration-related program and partly explain the volume of research that has focused on refugees. Congress's interest in the collection of policy-oriented data is evident in the wording of the Act.

In partial response to these requirements, the ORR Data System has been developed as a computer file with individual records on refugees; it is the primary source of baseline statistics for the domestic refugee program. Consistent with the reporting requirements originally specified in the Refugee Act, the coverage begins, where possible, with the refugees who arrived in the U.S. in May 1975. The current file represents an upgrade of one that existed under the earlier Indochinese Refugee Program. It is virtually complete for refugees from Southeast Asia, and all other refugees have been included since late 1982. An individual's record is opened at the time of arrival. The major source of the information on the record is the "assurance" form, which serves as a record of voluntary agency sponsorship of the refugee family, listing each family member.[2] These forms are completed during overseas processing.

The ORR Refugee Data System is used primarily to generate both routine and special-purpose statistics characterizing the refugee population. These statistics are used in fulfilling the Congressional reporting requirements described earlier and provide background information needed for planning and managing programs for refugees. For example, reports are produced and updated monthly to show how many refugees of each ethnicity are placed in each state. On a national level, we know that states vary in the ethnic composition of their refugee populations. This has implications for the mix of services needed and the results to be expected from programs.

The existence of good baseline data on the refugee population at the time of arrival has contributed in several ways to the body of survey research on the refugees:

- In the design of research, with regard to site selection, choice of group(s) to be interviewed, and topics of interest.
- In the interpretation of research findings, by providing a context for those findings.

In most survey research funded by ORR, we have used knowledge of the geographic distribution of refugees to choose several major cities in which to conduct face-to-face interviews. This was true of the survey focused on refugee self-sufficiency conducted by the Institute for Social Research (Caplan, Whitmore, and Bui 1985; Whitmore, Trautmann, and Caplan, this volume), and it is true of another study completed in five sites in 1986, which looks at the adjustment of recent refugees from Afghanistan, Ethiopia, Poland, and Romania (Cichon, Gozdziak, and Grover 1986). The ORR Data System is also used as the sampling frame for the Annual Survey of Refugees, to be described below—although the automated file has limitations as a sampling frame, since it does not contain street addresses and is not updated when refugees move.

Because of the practical difficulties of conducting a survey in four or five different languages, knowledge of the ethnic composition of the refugee population has often been used to make decisions about which ethnic groups to include in a survey. For example, it was decided to exclude Cambodians from the ISR survey because in 1981, when the study was being planned, Cambodians were relatively rare in the refugee population. They arrived in greatest numbers in the early 1980s. The history of the arrival of each ethnic group in the U.S. (dates, numbers, locations) is well documented in official program publications.[3] so survey research can build on this knowledge rather than attempt to reconstruct it. Finally, the data indicate that these refugees are a very young population, with a median age upon arrival of 20 or younger. Therefore, a large proportion of refugees are school-age children. This suggests that the performance of these children in school will be a key to the progress of Southeast Asians as a group during the next generation, and explains why ISR chose to pay particular attention to school performance in the survey research described in Chapter 7.

The role of good baseline data in providing a context for the interpretation of survey findings is also worth emphasizing. In the late 1970s, almost all surveys of Southeast Asian refugees were limited to Vietnamese. Since they were nearly 90% of the total, this was appropriate, and generalization of findings to the total refugee population was not seriously misleading.[4] A survey of Vietnamese refugees today, however, would pertain only to about five-eighths of the Southeast Asian refugees in the United States. At the other extreme, a great deal of press attention and official concern has focused on the adjustment of the Hmong refugees from Laos, who comprise only about 7% of this refugee population.

Knowledge of the age-sex structure of the refugee population is also valuable for assessing research findings. For example, Dunning in the BSSR survey (1982 and this volume) was one of the first to describe the particular adjustment problems of older refugees, in terms of difficulties in learning English, maintaining accustomed roles in the household, and coping with social isolation. As difficult as these problems are, we can at least take some comfort in knowing that they characterize a small fraction: only 2% of the arriving Southeast Asian population is aged 65 or older. On the other hand, nearly 20% of the Soviet refugees are in this age group, and similar adjustment problems have been reported for them. To cite another example, we know that the sex ratio is roughly equal in the Cambodian and Lao populations, but that the Vietnamese population contains about 60% males. We also know that this excess of males is concentrated among persons from their mid-to-late teens through their twenties, so that young men outnumber young women by two or three to one in some age groups. Furthermore, this sex ratio imbalance has increased with the arrival cohorts of the mid-1980s compared to those arriving earlier (Gordon 1985). With this background, the findings of Caplan, Whitmore, and Bui (1985) about the role of single adults in the economic adjustment of complex refugee households take on added importance. Such information also provides a context, if not a full explanation, for recent news reports of gang activity among young Vietnamese men.

The Annual Survey: Its History and Changing Methodology

The first of the government-sponsored surveys of Vietnamese refugees in the United States was conducted in late 1975, about six months after the first group of refugees arrived. The early surveys were carried out under the auspices of the Indochinese Refugee Program and were conducted more often than once a year, so that the October 1985 survey was the fourteenth of the series.[5] All surveys have been conducted by telephone by native language speakers from a previously translated questionnaire. The first several surveys were confined to Vietnamese refugees, but as the numbers of the other Southeast Asian groups in the United States grew, they were added to the sample. In the late 1970s and again in early 1985, some on-site tracing and interviewing was done, to assess the effect of nonresponse on the survey findings.

In 1981 the survey was redesigned in several significant ways. The questionnaire was revised and has remained essentially the same to the present time. It focuses on issues of economic adjustment: employment and labor force participation, and use of assistance or services, in keeping with the reporting requirements of the Refugee Act of 1980. Stratified sampling with oversampling of the smaller nationality groups was dropped in favor of a simple random sample, since the smaller groups had grown large enough to be adequately represented this way. The annual alien registration program of INS had been suspended and was no longer available to provide a recent sampling frame. Therefore, ORR began using its Refugee Data System as the sampling frame for persons who arrived after January 1980, relying on the INS alien registration of that date for sampling earlier arrivals. As time went on, the proportion of the refugee population that arrived after that date grew, and the Refugee Data System became the more important sampling frame. Since 1981, the surveys have been conducted in the fall of each year, centering on the month of October.

In 1984, ORR began to convert the Annual Survey into a panel study. The sample first selected in 1983 was recontacted, and a new sample of persons arriving in 1983–1984 was drawn. Likewise, a new group of 1984–1985 arrivals has been added to the sample and was interviewed for the first time in late 1985; future surveys will continue to add new arrivals. Since late 1984, the procedure has been to sample new arrivals in the month after they arrive and to initiate tracing soon thereafter. The panel study design was in part a solution to the practical difficulties of drawing a new sample each year and tracing it from an ever-aging sampling frame—particularly since the 1980 alien registration was producing as few as one-third of the sample as successful interviews for some arrival cohorts. The panel design also provides, for the first time, the ability to distinguish changes over time from period and cohort effects in the adjustment process.

Finally, beginning in 1985, ORR restricted the coverage of the survey to refugees who arrived during the most recent five years instead of attempting to cover all Southeast Asians who have arrived since 1975, and the legislative change of 1986 ratified this decision. The change was made for several reasons, one of which was the problem with the 1980 sampling frame mentioned above. Another was the conviction that, at some point, refugees should be allowed to graduate to the status of "former refugees." Indeed, interviewers began to get this response from the refugees themselves, especially those who had become naturalized citizens. While it was necessary to record some of these as "refused interview," the response may be an excellent indicator of assimilation. Since five years is the minimum waiting period for naturalization, it is a logical cutoff point. It is also reasonable that official refugee program attention should concentrate on the early years of U.S. residence, and this change stopped survey resources from being progressively diluted by the need to represent an ever-growing universe. There is an obvious loss of information about the earlier cohorts, which could usefully be filled by independent survey work and later by U.S. Census data.

In summary, the Annual Survey of Refugees is now a panel study of Southeast Asian refugees who are interviewed annually during their first five years in the United States. Recent arrivals have averaged about 50,000 yearly, from which a sample of about 200 persons is drawn. Therefore, the ongoing sample will approach a panel of 1,000, slightly reduced from the levels of the early 1980s, when about 1,200 were interviewed. Since the sampling frame contains records on individuals, individuals are sampled and their households contacted. Interviews are then conducted with an adult member of the household, who may be the sampled person, the household head, or another person who is able to speak for the household. Interviewers obtain some information about all household members, including labor force data on all persons aged 16 and over, and more detailed information on the respondent.

In 1985, by restricting the survey to the more recent arrivals, ORR was able to concentrate more resources on tracing hard-to-locate persons in the sample. This led to an unusual result for a longitudinal survey: instead of the usual panel attrition, more respondents were gained who were initially selected in 1983 or 1984 and not located in 1984, than the number lost between 1984 and 1985. While 67 persons were lost to nonresponse in 1985, 175 nonrespondents from 1984 were interviewed. Also interviewed were 91.4% of those interviewed the previous year. (As one test of the effect of nonresponse, we tabulated answers to key questions in the 1985 survey by persons who were interviewed in 1984 separately from the 175 sampled earlier but not found in 1984, and found no differences in response patterns.)

A telephone survey, of course, has advantages and disadvantages. On the plus side, it is the only way to conduct interviews of a truly national sample, reaching people in small cities and rural areas as well as in the large cities with concentrations of refugees. Using a telephone bank staffed by persons speaking all the refugee languages, it is possible to interview a member of any language group in any location. On the minus side, the sacrifice of the rapport of a face-to-face interview limits the time and depth of the interview. Telephone surveys of this population have been criticized for the presumed bias of missing households unable to afford telephones. Actually, very few sampled refugee households were without telephones, only 6 in 1985, and they were outnumbered by the 18 households that were not contacted due to unlisted phone numbers—perhaps another indicator of assimilation. A more serious shortcoming is the possible bias engendered by failing to locate people sampled from a central data base. Many of these cases are lost due to secondary migration, often to a new community. It is quite likely that these lost cases have characteristics different from those that are easier to trace. However, the two groups match on basic characteristics such as country of origin, and as noted above, the 1985 response patterns of 1984 respondents and nonrespondents did not differ. The changes in research design adopted in 1984 and 1985 have improved the overall response rate which, in the 1985 survey, was 82% for persons who arrived in 1984 and 1985. While the possibility of bias still exists, the advantages of a nationwide longitudinal study are substantial, and the findings can contribute to an understanding of the adjustment process.

Cross-sectional Findings

Perhaps the most stable finding of the Annual Survey from 1981 through 1984 was that indicators of economic adjustment show improvement as length of time in the United States increases. This finding has also characterized other survey research on refugees and immigrants and is consistent with theories of assimilation. Table 2.1 illustrates the nature of the results from past cross-sectional surveys. In any given year (shown in the table columns), the longer refugees had lived in the United States, the higher was their labor force participation and the lower their unemployment rate. (The 1976–77 cohort has always been somewhat anomalous, and the few variations from the pattern were rather easily dismissed as insignificant.) For each arrival cohort (the table rows), labor force participation was low and unemployment high in the first year after arrival, but this picture improved greatly during the first two or three years. Unemployment rates followed the general U.S. trend, peaking in the 1982 survey when unemployment was high and improving thereafter, while remaining more than twice as high as U.S. rates. Finally, examination of the diagonals (lower left to upper right) of Table 2.1 shows a standard progression for each cohort: labor force participation rates of only 20 to 30% in the first year, rising to a range of 41 to 53% in the second year, and so on.

While time in the United States is not subject to policy intervention, people who work with refugees could at least take comfort from the finding that basic indicators of economic adjustment moved in the desired direction. However, as the peak years of refugee admissions receded into the past,

Table 2.1   Unemployment and Labor Force Participation among Southeast Asian Refugees, 1981–1984

Year of entry	Labor force participation (in percent)				Unemployment (in percent)			
	1981[a]	1982[a]	1983[a]	1984[a]	1981[a]	1982[a]	1983[a]	1984[a]
1984	—	—	—	30.0	—	—	—	41.0
1983	—	—	20.7	41.6	—	—	55.0	35.6
1982	—	25.2	40.9	45.4	—	62.5	30.4	12.5
1981	22.8	41.5	46.5	51.4	45.2	40.7	16.8	16.4
1980	52.8	51.3	55.3	54.5	27.1	32.1	21.1	11.6
1979	49.2	60.2	60.5	60.1	8.1	19.3	17.8	9.8
1978	48.8	67.6	68.2	66.2	5.0	19.0	19.7	2.6
1976–7	70.7	74.3	79.5	76.1	3.5	9.4	17.2	4.6
1975	76.0	72.1	69.7	67.3	6.4	12.7	12.1	6.3
Total sample	55	56	55	55	13	24.1	18.0	14.6
U.S. rates[b]	64.0	64.1	64.1	64.6	7.5	9.9	8.4	7.0

[a]The 1981, 1982, and 1983 samples were drawn independently. The 1984 sample encompassed persons interviewed in 1983, nonrespondents originally sampled in 1983, and 1983–84 arrivals sampled in 1984.
[b]October unadjusted figures from the Bureau of Labor Statistics, U.S. Department of Labor.

Note: Survey statistics refer to all household members aged 16 and over.

Source: Annual Surveys of Refugees as reported in ORR (1982:18; 1985:91).

resulting in an increase in the average time in the United States of the refugee population, the expected improvement in overall indicators of economic adjustment failed to appear. The stable figure for the total sample of 55% for labor force participation across four survey years is one example. Another is the persistence of rather high rates of use of public cash assistance by refugee households. The Annual Survey and general program data in the early and mid-1980s have shown more than half of refugees to be living in households receiving cash assistance.

As Bach (1984) points out in his analysis of the Annual Survey data, examination of labor force participation rates or unemployment rates in a single cross-sectional survey leads to an interpretation emphasizing rapid improvement in these indicators during the first few years of residence. Examination of the experience of a single cohort in successive years also tends to show rapid improvement during the first year or two of residence. However, the changes have not all been in one direction. Particularly among the cohorts in residence for the longest time, labor force participation was stable or declining from 1982 to 1984. Finally, the success of these refugees in finding work was very adversely affected by the general rise in unemployment in 1982. Unemployment rates for all but the 1981 cohort peaked in 1982 and did not approach their earlier levels until 1984. Bach has argued that the emphasis on length of residence in the United States as a primary predictor of labor force participation has led to overly optimistic conclusions. In addition, the analytical meaning of time in the United States is unclear, and research should begin to examine what happens to refugees during that time.

With the shift to interviewing the same sample in consecutive years, adding one year's worth of arrivals and dropping those of longer than five years' residence, the cross-sectional findings of the Annual Survey began to change. Table 2.2 shows the basic indicators of economic adjustment from the 1983 through the 1985 surveys for persons arriving in 1980 and later; a substantial proportion of the persons covered appeared in the survey in two or all three years. For this reason, the findings no longer represent independent cross-sectional samples. Examination of labor force participation or unemployment rates in a single year for successive cohorts (the columns of Table 2.2) still yields an impression of steady improvement over time. However, this table shows to a greater extent than does Table 2.1 a leveling-off or even a deterioration in these indicators in the experience of a single cohort (the rows of Table 2.2) after about the second year. The direct impact on the overall sample statistics of dropping sampled persons who arrived more than five years earlier can be seen in the reduced labor force participation rate for the total sample, from 55% in the 1981–1984 surveys to 44% in the 1985 survey.

Other cross-sectional findings from the Annual Survey deserve a brief review (ORR 1986: 98–112). The surveys have consistently shown substantial

Table 2.2   Unemployment and Labor Force Participation among a Longitudinal Sample of
             Southeast Asian Refugees, 1983–1985

Year of entry	Labor force participation (in percent)			Unemployment (in percent)		
	1983	1984[a]	1985[a]	1983	1984[a]	1985[a]
1985	–	–	28	–	–	50
1984	–	30.0	42	–	41.0	36
1983	20.7	41.6	41	55.0	35.6	17
1982	40.9	45.4	45	30.4	12.5	16
1981	46.5	51.4	46	16.8	16.4	12
1980	55.3	54.5	56	21.1	11.6	18
Total sample	55[b]	55[b]	44	18[b]	15[b]	17

[a] The 1984 sample encompassed persons interviewed in 1983, nonrespondents originally
sampled in 1983, and 1983–84 arrivals sampled in 1984. The 1985 sample included
persons sampled in 1983 or 1984 and interviewed previously, nonrespondents from 1983–
1984, and persons sampled as they arrived in 1984–85 and first interviewed in 1985.
[b] The total sample in 1983 and 1984 included persons who arrived in the 1975–1979 period.

Note: Survey statistics refer to all household members aged 16 and over.

Source: Annual Survey of Refugees as reported in ORR (1986:102).

changes between the types of jobs held in the refugee's country of origin
and the employment obtained in the United States. In the 1985 sample,
38.7% of the employed adults had held white collar jobs originally, but only
16.4% held white collar jobs at the time of the interview. This substantial
amount of downward occupational mobility may be responsible for considerable dissatisfaction among the refugees. The proportion in blue-collar jobs
(skilled, semi-skilled, or laborers) had gone from 20.5% before migrating to
61.3% at the time of the interview. The proportion in farming and fishing
fell from 35.0% to 1.1%.

Since 56% of the refugees aged 16 and over reported not being in the
labor force in 1985 (compared to 35% of the U.S. population), their reasons
for not seeking employment are of interest. Substantial variation by age
exists. Of persons in the 16–24 age category, 83.1% were obtaining more
education before entering the labor force. Since this age category encompasses about one-third of the refugee population over age 16, their activities
contribute heavily to the overall survey results. Persons in the 25–34 age
category were most likely (35.2%) to cite family responsibilities as prevent-
ing them from seeking work, with another 33.9% saying they were pursuing
education. Family responsibilities were also most important (35.2%) for
those aged 35–44, while health problems predominated for persons over 44
(43.5%). For the total sample, as age increased, fewer persons were pursuing
education rather than employment, but more cited limited English ability
and health problems as barriers to employment.

In these and other surveys, English language ability has been linked strongly to indicators of economic adjustment. In the 1985 survey, for example, persons who characterized their own English as fluent had a labor force participation rate of 62.3%, nearly as high as that for the overall U.S. population. Refugees who reported they spoke no English, however, had a labor force participation rate of 14.6% and an unemployment rate of 41.4%. For those refugees who were employed, average weekly wages were higher for every level of self-assessed English proficiency.

However, Bach and Carroll-Seguin (1986) have argued that the effect of English language proficiency on refugees' economic adjustment has received undue emphasis, perhaps because it is one of the few background characteristics or skills amenable to program intervention. In their regression analysis of the pooled 1982 and 1983 Annual Survey samples, they found English ability *at arrival* to be related to *current* (1982–1983) labor force participation for persons who had arrived before 1980, but not for those who arrived in 1980–1983. Perhaps English language proficiency is more meaningful as an indicator of social position in the country of origin than as a skill in itself; the same argument has been made for the strong relationship of years of foreign education to labor force participation in this refugee population (Bach and Carroll-Seguin 1986).

Finally, gender has the expected relationship to labor force participation in the Annual Survey: men are more likely to be in the labor force than women. In an analysis of the 1983 Annual Survey, Bach (1984:21–22) showed that while 58% of men and 42% of women over 16 were in the labor force, this 16 percentage point difference was reduced to 10 percentage points when differences in background and training were taken into account. This contrast is repeated in the general U.S. population; it is of particular concern in a refugee population because of the important role played by refugee and immigrant women in the economic adjustment of their households (Bach and Carroll-Sequin 1986:387–88).

In reviewing some typical cross-sectional findings from the Annual Survey, emphasizing those that pertain to economic adjustment, the role of time in the United States has received particular attention, as has a number of personal characteristics of the refugees that are also related to economic adjustment. Regression analysis of the type performed by Bach (1984; see also Bach and Carroll-Seguin 1986) makes an important contribution toward sorting out the importance of the various personal characteristics. For an introductory effort at disentangling the various effects of time, it is necessary to return now to the longitudinal analysis.

Longitudinal Findings

The findings presented in Table 2.3 begin to show what changes in the employment experiences of individual refugees are reflected in aggregate

Table 2.3   Changes in the Employment Status of Individual Refugees from 1983 to 1984, Based on Linked Records from the ORR Annual Survey

Employment status in October 1983	Employment status in October 1984 percent of refugees having:	
Total sample:	No job	Job
No job	76.9	23.1
Job	16.6	83.4
Men:		
No job	72.7	27.3
Job	15.2	84.8
Women:		
No job	80.5	19.6
Job	18.9	81.1

figures such as those displayed in Tables 2.1 and 2.2. Table 2.3 shows the results of linking the records of all adults represented in both the 1983 and 1984 Annual Surveys and examining a simple measure: whether or not they held a job in each year at the time of the survey. (This measure combines persons not participating in the labor force with persons who are unemployed but seeking work.) We have seen in Table 2.1 that labor force participation was stable (for the total sample including those not interviewed in both years) while unemployment dropped from 1983 to 1984. Table 2.3 shows that this net finding masked significant gross change: 23.1% of all adults who did not have jobs in 1983 were working in 1984, but 16.6% of all adults who had held jobs in 1983 were not working in 1984. Clearly, changes over time are not all positive, even during a period of economic improvement.

While this type of analysis of the Annual Surveys is just beginning, it illustrates what can be learned from a longitudinal analysis. The differentials between men and women presented in Table 2.3 indicate just one of many possible directions. Consistent with the persistent differential in labor force participation identified by Bach, Table 2.3 shows that men were more likely than women to get jobs between 1983 and 1984 (27.3% of men versus 19.6% of women began working). The contrast was not as great, but was still present, for those moving from having jobs to not having them in consecutive years (18.9% of women ceased working while 15.2% of men did so). These findings show the power of the longitudinal data base to improve our understanding of the experiences of recently arrived refugees in the U.S. labor market. However, it would be most valuable to know *why* these refugees are no longer working, and we did not ask the question. This may indicate a certain blind spot on the part of refugee program officials: we act as if a single job placement solves a refugee's employment problem.

Caplan, Whitmore, and Bui (1985) found that women they interviewed in 1982 were less likely than men to have received services in the United States to prepare them for employment. Refugee program officials reacted with concern to this finding and launched some initiatives to see that women received needed services. Despite these efforts, the 1985 Annual Survey showed a persisting contrast: 36% of the adult male refugees were enrolled in a job training program at some time in the four weeks preceding the interview, while 22% of the adult females were so enrolled. The probability of being enrolled in English language training was the same for both sexes, 21%.

Closely related to the employment issue is another issue of paramount importance to refugee program officials: the use made by refugees of public assistance programs. It is recognized that many refugee families will need assistance immediately upon arrival, since they usually arrive without resources, but programs are designed to move refugees into employment as quickly as possible, thereby reducing their dependence on public assistance. Over the past three years, the proportion of refugees living in households receiving assistance has been rather stable, despite intensified program efforts to reduce dependence. The movement of refugees out of as well as into employment that was described above explains some of this apparent lack of change of the aggregate measures. Another comparison over time, using households rather than individuals as the unit of analysis, is shown in Table 2.4.

Examination of the marginals in Table 2.4 shows the kind of information routinely collected: in 1983, 60.8% of the households sampled were receiving public assistance, while in 1985, 55.9% of the same households (that is, the household containing the person initially sampled) were receiving assistance. This improvement of about 5 percentage points over two years is

Table 2.4   Changes in the Recipient Status of Refugee Households from 1983 to 1985, Based on Linked Records from the ORR Annual Survey

Recipient status in October 1983	Recipient status in October 1985		
	Number of Households		
	Not receiving assistance	Receiving assistance	Total sample
Not receiving assistance	240	146	386 (39.2%)
Receiving assistance	194	404	598 (60.8%)
Total sample	434 (44.1%)	550 (55.9%)	984 (100.0%)

in the desired direction, if not of striking size. Examination of the cells shows considerably more movement within the sample. Of the households receiving assistance in 1983, 32.4% were no longer receiving it in 1985; but 37.6% of those *not* receiving assistance in 1983 were receiving it by 1985. This dynamic picture is much more complicated than the picture of steady improvement suggested by cross-sectional findings.

Future Directions for Research and Analysis

Clearly, changes in the employment status of individual refugees are one explanation of changes in household dependency. As the longitudinal analysis develops, it should be possible to see this effect directly. Some preliminary findings from the 1985 survey point to another influence. In 1985, 59.9% of all the households surveyed had at least one wage earner, and 39.7% of even the households receiving assistance had at least one wage earner. This paints a more positive picture than the dependency figures, and it seems to result from several factors. First, refugee households are large, averaging about six persons. If such a household has one wage earner at entry-level wages, it will still qualify for partial public assistance under many state and federal programs. Second, the majority of refugees arriving in recent years have been "family reunification" cases. We see a significant number of households in the Annual Survey whose members arrived in different years. Although the 1985 Annual Survey was based on a sample of persons who arrived between May 1, 1980, and April 30, 1985, some of them lived in households with persons who arrived earlier. In this way, a household may encompass recent arrivals who are likely to be unemployed and qualified for assistance as well as persons of several years' residence who have found employment. Changes in household composition, particularly through the arrival of new members from overseas, may play a role in the apparent persistence of dependency in refugee households. Finally, a substantial minority of the households show changes in composition from one year to the next other than new arrivals from overseas, as children are born, older children leave home, and other relatives move in and out as their circumstances change. Analysis of the complicated and shifting nature of refugee households is continuing from the longitudinal data base.

In these Annual Surveys and in other survey research on this refugee population, analysts have chosen at different times to emphasize different measures of economic well-being. The choice of the measure is crucial in determining whether positive or negative aspects of the refugees' economic situation will be highlighted. Table 2.5 pictures three household measures simultaneously as seen in the 1985 survey: whether the household is above or below the poverty level, whether or not it contains a wage earner, and whether or not it receives any public cash assistance.

Table 2.5   Sources of Income by Poverty Status of Households

Poverty status	Earned income, no assistance	Earned income, with assistance	No earned income, assistance only
Above poverty level	23.7%	17.4%	0.4%
At or below poverty level	9.8%	9.0%	39.7%

Note: Four households reported no earned income and assistance payments totaling more than the appropriate poverty line. Table is based on the full sample of 1,056 households.

Source: Annual Survey of Refugees, 1985.

As Table 2.5 shows, the households interviewed in 1985 can be characterized in the following ways: 66.5% receive public cash assistance (the most common characterization); 58.5% have incomes below the poverty level; 40.1% have no earned income. The key to understanding these very different characterizations is the sizable middle group, 26.4% of the households, that subsists on a *combination* of earned income and public cash assistance. With a large household and only one entry-level wage earner, this is a plausible scenario, and Table 2.5 shows that 9% of the sample remained below the poverty level despite having both types of income. Future analyses will examine several related issues: to what extent does household composition determine economic well-being? Does the middle "partially dependent" group represent a transition phase from total dependency to complete self-sufficiency? Does persistent dependency result in part from newly arriving refugees joining existing households or from other household changes? The longitudinal data base will be particularly valuable in addressing these questions.

From analysis of the age structure of the arriving refugee population, it is clear that it is a very young population, with evidence of high fertility in the recent past (Gordon 1985). This is especially true of the Cambodians and Lao, while the Hmong have the highest fertility of all. Some survey research indicates continued high fertility among refugees in the United States (Rumbaut and Weeks 1986). This points to the persistence of large refugee households that are likely to qualify for assistance based on the presence of young children. Knowing this, it is important to learn more about how high fertility contributes to the movement of refugee households on and off of cash assistance. The behavior of the very large cohort of young adults with regard to family formation will also play a key role in the refugees' future. Will they continue their record of scholastic achievement at the college level, postponing marriage and childbearing to become established in careers? Or will they continue to rely in part on cash assistance to support large families? The five-year time frame of the Annual Survey may not be enough to address this longer-term issue in refugee adjustment.

In conclusion, a few observations are in order about the relevance of research for policy development and intervention. The few findings presented above indicate that the picture with regard to refugee employment and use of cash assistance over time is both better and worse than is often thought: worse, because it demonstrates that not all change is improvement, and better, because it shows that dependency is often partial rather than complete. Policy and program development needs to take this complicated reality into account. Perhaps refugee employment programs should place more emphasis on job retention in addition to job placement. With family reunification as a basic principle of the refugee program and large, complex households common, resettlement strategies must be geared to such households. Finally, the research shows that refugee employment is especially sensitive to adverse economic conditions, an aspect of the larger context for refugee resettlement over which refugee program officials have no control.

Notes

1. The Refugee Assistance Extension Act of 1986 changed the wording of this requirement to "the five fiscal-year period immediately preceding the fiscal year within which the report is to be made and for refugees who entered earlier and who have shown themselves to be significantly and disproportionately dependent on welfare."
2. The arrival record is designed to contain the following data elements:
   - Name
   - Alien number (assigned by INS)
   - Date of birth
   - Country of birth
   - Country of citizenship
   - Date of arrival in the U.S.
   - Sex
   - Marital status
   - Family status
   - Sponsoring voluntary agency
   - Agency case number
   - City and state of initial resettlement
   - Education
   - Occupation
   - English language ability

   The file records created originally did not contain much useful information for the last three elements on this list. However, improved coding of these elements has been included in the records kept by a State Department-funded agency, the Refugee Data Center, since July 1983, and these codes are being added to the ORR file. With regard to the other data elements, the records are generally complete for the refugees who arrived in 1975, because they were processed in U.S. camps where detailed records were kept, and for the refugees who have arrived since early 1981, because ORR has handled the creation of the records according to file specifications since that time. Records for refugees arriving from 1976 through 1980 were pieced together from several sources and are most likely to contain missing data elements. At a minimum, all records contain the alien number, year of birth, and date of arrival.
3. The basic reference is the *Report to the Congress, Refugee Resettlement Program*,

published annually on January 31 and covering the fiscal year ending on the previous September 30. It is published by ORR with contributions from other federal agencies and the voluntary agency resettlement community. The "Annual Report" contains a summary in narrative and statistical form on refugee program activities and events during the year. See also Gordon (1987) for a summary of the history of the arrival of the groups within the Southeast Asian population.

4. It is interesting that official program publications in the early years after 1975 made little or no reference to the ethnic differences within this refugee population.

5. The major descriptive findings from each year's Annual Survey have been presented in the *Report to the Congress* (see Note 3). More detailed analyses of the survey findings appear in several works by Robert Bach. See especially Bach (1984) and Bach and Carroll-Seguin (1986).

3

Differential Reference Group Assimilation among Vietnamese Refugees

Alden E. Roberts and Paul D. Starr

Since the fall of Saigon in 1975, thousands of Vietnamese refugees have emigrated to the United States. The Vietnamese as well as other Indochinese refugees faced numerous problems involving their adaptation and assimilation. They also encountered the antipathy of many Americans.

To study the potential problems of 1975 arrivals, a three-year panel study of Vietnamese refugees was conducted from 1978 to 1981 in Northern California and the central Gulf Coast. The refugees were questioned about economic adjustment and related problems, attitudes toward American and Vietnamese culture, health problems, discrimination, and a host of other topics. Besides providing a "snapshot" of the adaptational problems of the refugees, the panel design also enabled us to measure change in the socioeconomic and cultural conditions of the refugees' lives.

While several other survey research projects have focused upon the adjustment and adaptation of Indochinese refugees, most of these surveys have included all Southeast Asian refugee groups and multiple arrival cohorts. Most of these surveys have also been cross-sectional in nature as opposed to the longitudinal design of panel research on the same respondents. Our data set differs from most others because it focuses exclusively on early Vietnamese refugee arrivals and does so on the basis of a panel design.

This research was supported by a grant from the National Institute of Mental Health (IRO1MH30029). We are grateful to Thai Ngoc Nguyen, Rebecca G. LeNoir, De Nguyen, M.D., Hy Truong Nguyen, Bai An Tran, Nhung Thi T., and Bao Duc Truong for their assistance.

Adjustment

Migrants in general and refugees in particular undergo a tremendous number of both undesirable and desirable life changes in the process of their geographical and social uprooting. Compared with immigrants, refugees are typically better educated, earn more income, and have higher-status occupations than their fellow countrymen (Kunz 1973, 1981). Since it is often difficult or impossible to transfer occupational skills and status to a new country, refugees often experience downward mobility (Montero 1979; Stein 1979) in the United States. In time, some refugees become upwardly mobile and achieve or surpass previous statuses. However, other refugees may never attain positions equal to their former statuses.

One crucial indicator of economic adjustment is monthly income. In our sample, the mean family income in 1978 was $755 a month with a standard deviation of $504. The distribution of income was skewed toward the upper incomes as evidenced by the median family income of $600. About one-third of the respondents were receiving food stamps and about three in ten were receiving some form of welfare (Starr et al. 1979). By 1981, the mean family income had increased to $1220 a month with a standard deviation of $516. These income figures are comparable to other refugee surveys. For example, Strand's and Jones's San Diego survey (1985:84) found that about 50% of their Vietnamese respondents had monthly household incomes of $1000 or less.

Another key element in socioeconomic adjustment is occupation. In our survey, 68% of the Vietnamese respondents were employed. This is comparable to the Strand and Jones survey (1985:117), which found that 60% of the Vietnamese refugee respondents were in the labor force. About 80% of the employed respondents in our survey worked at either lower-working-class or upper-working-class occupations. The most common occupations were semiskilled employees or machine operatives (Starr et al. 1979; Roberts 1983). These economic adjustment data are again comparable with other surveys of Indochinese refugees. Stein (1979:29) reported that after two years in the United States, over 72% of the employed refugees were upper or lower working-class.

Several other descriptive findings from the survey help indicate the sometimes shifting social and economic situation of these Vietnamese refugees. Looking at Table 3.1, we see that the mean age increased slightly from 42.32 to 43.62 during the time of the study. The mean educational level increased from 4.49 to 4.64 (4 indicates respondent completed high school, and 5 indicates completion of some college). Psychological distress, as measured by the Lengner 22-item scale, decreased from 7.58 symptoms in year one to 5.43 in year three. This last is an encouraging finding.

Nevertheless, while such findings help place our work in context with the

Table 3.1   Changes in Key Respondent Characteristics

	1978–1979	1979–1980	1980–1981
Age (in years)	42.32	42.96	43.63
Education[a]	4.49	4.58	4.64
Monthly Income	$754.95	$987.09	$1220.01
Psychological distress[b]	7.58	6.03	5.43

[a] The figures on education refer to a scale in which 4 indicated completion of high school, and 5 completion of some college.
[b] The scores on psychological distress derive from the Lengner 22-item scale.

other survey work presented in this volume, our major concern has been with social and cognitive assimilation of these refugees to American society, and it is to those issues that the remainder of this chapter is directed.

Assimilation

Besides the socioeconomic adjustment of refugees, a major adaptational process is assimilation. The social integration and social solidarity of any migratory or refugee group is crucially affected by the existence or degree of their assimilation into the dominant culture. While various dimensions of the assimilation process coexist, one key aspect is an individual's cognitive perspective. In negotiating the new social order, does the migrant or refugee look to his or her own culture or ethnic group or to the new culture for a correct normative stance? Does the refugee's reference group change over time for the group in general or for just certain role occupants? Several studies of the social psychological aspects of migration (Ex 1966; Portes 1968; Kuo and Lin 1977) have shown that individuals differ in their orientation toward both their former culture and the way of life found in the host country. For the refugee, the possibilities range from remaining as traditional as social circumstances allow to becoming as "native" as the receiving community will permit.

A useful concept in analyzing a migrant's cultural orientation is that of the reference group. A "reference group" is a group or grouping an individual looks to for standards or norms. A reference group may also serve a comparative function for a person's evaluation of self or other (Hyman 1942; Newcomb 1952). According to Merton (1957), the term "reference group" is actually a misnomer. The sociological concept of group refers to a number of people who interact according to some pattern and define themselves as members of the group. The theory doesn't specify that a "reference group" necessarily has to be a group. A reference "group" can also be a collectivity or category. Shibutani (1955) felt that reference groups are basically group perspectives assumed by an individual. Turner (1956) saw reference groups as closely related to role-taking. In role-taking, an individual attempts to perceive as others perceive. For Turner, a reference group can operate as a relevant generalized other through the process of the individual taking the role of the group and, in turn, orienting himself in line with that perception. Similarly, Eisenstadt (1954) treated the concept of reference group as synonymous with norm orientation. Thus, a reference group can be either a group the person actually belongs to or a group (real or imagined) that the individual would like to belong to (Merton 1957).

The incorporation of a migrant or immigrant group can take various paths (Gordon 1964). One possible strategy is for the ethnic group to form an ethnic enclave within the host society. An ethnic enclave can serve various functions for its members such as a sharing of information on how to cope with the new culture, providing a somewhat familiar social life, and protecting the refugee or immigrant from cultural shock. Under certain situations, an ethnic subculture can also preserve tradition and cultural continuity. However, if assimilation is taking place, the ethnic enclave can serve as a positive reference group, providing new norms, values, beliefs, and standards of proper behavior. The key element is the amount of assimilation that is taking place. Three logical possibilities exist, all of which have precedents (Van den Berghe 1981). The first and probably most common possibility is for the group to be slowly changed through the process of assimilation. New and old behaviors and norms become gradually interspersed. A second path is for the ethnic group to have as little contact as possible with the host society and to attempt to remain as traditional as possible. The final possibility is for the ethnic group to attempt to be even more traditional than they were in their former country.

The most common process is assimilation. Most ethnic groups that entered the United States tended to be integrated gradually, through the slow and often incomplete process of cultural and structural assimilation (Gordon 1964; Park 1964; Montero 1981); the Vietnamese are not exceptions (Montero 1979; Stein 1979; Starr et al. 1979). For an immigrant or refugee, assimilation is synonymous with social integration into the dominant society. Refugees differ considerably in their potential for assimilation. The refugees most likely to be assimilated are those with the greatest potential for cultural compatibility (highly dependent on the ability to speak English); those with high-level skills and better education are more likely to be rewarded with good jobs. Refugees with little education, minimal occupational skills, and poor English are more likely to live on the fringes of American society. In addition, they are also most likely to have a weak or nonexistent Vietnamese community to which to turn, because one of the expressed aims of the nationwide dispersal sponsorship program was to avoid the concentration of Vietnamese in any one section of the country (Liu, Lamanna, and Murata 1979; Montero 1979).

The amount of contact that an immigrant has with his or her fellow ethnics, together with the path that the group as a whole has taken in the assimilation process, crucially affects the individual's reference group. We have a fair amount of evidence that proximity and interaction are interrelated as are interaction and similarity, and proximity and similarity (Newcomb 1952; Homans 1961; Starr and Roberts 1982b). Durkheim (1933) argued that the dynamic density of societies (and supposedly subcultures) is related to the amount of interaction or social solidarity. Immigrants who interact more with American society should be more assimilated. Since similarity and interaction are related, Vietnamese who have more interaction with Americans would become similar to Americans in a variety of ways, including their reference groups.

The effects of an immigrant's interaction with fellow immigrants are more complex and depend upon what is happening with the ethnic group as a whole. If the ethnic group is becoming more Americanized, then the immigrant who interacts more with fellow ethnics (friends, neighbors, family, and fellow workers) should become more Americanized. If the ethnic group is becoming more traditional, then the high interacter should become more traditional. If the ethnic group is retaining the status quo, the immigrant with a great deal of interaction with fellow ethnics is predicted to have little change in his or her reference group. Hypotheses about the social isolate are based upon the principle of social inertia. With little or no outside stimulation from either Americans or fellow Vietnamese, the social isolate is predicted to remain about the same. Only if the group as a whole is retaining the status quo will the social isolate remain in step with the group.

The final hypothesis deals with how well a refugee is doing in American economic life. Because of the rewards involved, those individuals who earn more money and have higher-status occupations in America are predicted to have a more Americanized reference group. The cause/effect relationship for this hypothesis, as well as for several previous hypotheses, is difficult to determine. Just as interaction can lead to similarity, similarity can lead to interaction. In the same vein, would financial and occupational success lead to an Americanized reference group, or would a migrant with an initial Americanized orientation be more likely to be financially successful?

Methods

During the summer and fall of 1978, interviews were completed with a sample of Vietnamese refugee heads-of-household in two regions of the United States that have attracted large numbers of refugees—the central Gulf Coast and Northern California. The nine cities in which a total of 349 refugees were interviewed included Dothan (12) and Mobile (22) in Alabama; Panama City (22) and Pensacola (27) in the Florida Panhandle; New Orleans

(97); and San Francisco (72), Oakland (18), San Jose (64), and Stockton (16) in California.

Sampling was accomplished in five of the cities by using master lists of refugees taken in each location from organizational rosters, public directories, and community groups, and then randomly selecting individuals from these lists. In the four large urban areas (New Orleans, San Francisco, Oakland, and San Jose) for which up-to-date information about the size and nature of the refugee population was less reliable, the same sources were used but with greater reliance upon the extensive knowledge of local informants in those parts of each city known to have refugee residents. Because of the influx of new arrivals from camps of first asylum in Asia, the secondary migration of those initially located in other communities and the extensive mobility of some types of refugees (particularly single males), it was not possible to completely adhere to conventional sampling procedures developed for the study of more established populations. The sampling employed here, however, obtained responses from a cross-section of refugees, those of different ages, family situations, and statuses, residing in emerging ethnic enclaves as well as living in relative isolation in both urban and suburban areas.

The interviews were accomplished by Vietnamese refugee assistants in their native language and were based upon a questionnaire that had been developed, translated, and back-translated with the help of a team of four translators, two of them experienced Vietnamese physicians. In addition to asking for considerable biographical information, interviewers inquired about economic adjustment, attitudes regarding Vietnamese and American culture, perceptions of the environment and quality of life, use of social services, health and well-being, encounters with discrimination, past migration, future plans, and other topics. Most interviews took about two hours, with a range of from one to four hours. The refusal rate was low, under 6%, and did not significantly vary by community or known demographic characteristics.

The panel's initial interviews were followed by another set of interviews in late 1979 and early 1980, and a third set in late 1980 and early 1981. As is typical with panel studies, there was some attrition. The sample size for the second set was 260 and for the third set was 209. Various questions were asked about changes in lives of the refugees as well as follow-up questions on attitudes, behavior, and health.

Since single questions do not typically measure complex concepts very well, several scales were constructed. To indicate how well a refugee had a command of the language of his new country, an important factor in assimilation, respondents were asked specific questions about how well they judged their ability to read, speak, and write English, and how much English they spoke outside their homes. A highly reliable English usage scale was then developed (Cronbach's (1951) alpha = .980).

The primary dependent variable of concern in this paper is reference group assimilation. Gordon (1964) delineated three categories of assimilation: first, cultural assimilation, which is the acquiring of the dominant group's culture; second, structural assimilation, which involved both integrating with occupational, educational, political, and other institutions, and establishing close intergroup personal relations; and third, marital assimilation. Gordon's cultural assimilation was measured by a thirty-three item reference group assimilation scale (see Appendix). The items are a combination of Vietnamese and American attitudes, behaviors, beliefs, and values scored or recoded in the direction of assimilation to American culture. The scale had moderate reliability (alpha = .579). The same items were also used in panel waves two and three to measure potential change in the reference group orientation of the respondents. The reliability of the scale in wave two was improved (alpha = .748) and was further improved in wave three (alpha = .770).

To examine how a respondent's social contact might affect his or her reference group orientation, questions were asked about the number of persons in the refugee's household, the number of close friends (both Vietnamese and American) the respondent had, and if there were other Vietnamese where he or she worked. Structural assimilation was measured in terms of occupational prestige and income. Occupational prestige was measured using the occupational scale of Hollingshead's (1957) two-factor index of social position. Monthly income was measured as the average monthly household income. Perceived social status in Vietnam, sex, age, marital status and education were used as control variables.

Results

The first key hypothesis is that Vietnamese refugees will be more assimilated and hold a more American reference group as time passed. To test this idea, we did a T-test of difference between the means of the reference group assimilation scale at times one, two, and three. There was a slow but consistent increase in the summated scale scores from years one to two, and from two to three. The most significant increase occurred between the second and third year ($T = 3.905$, $p < .001$). The increase between years one and two was insignificant ($T = .796$, n.s.), with the increase between years one and three also significant ($T = 4.745$, $p < .001$).

An alternative hypothesis would be that the increase was a methodological artifact due to attrition in the panel. If the most traditional Vietnamese were less likely to answer the survey at times two and three, then the increase in the reference group assimilation scale would be due to the differential attrition of traditional Vietnamese. To test this ideal, we performed an F test of difference for the reference group assimilation scale between refugees who answered only the first wave of questions and those who participated in subsequent waves. The difference between the groups was insignificant (F = .856, n.s.) and tends to rule out the alternative hypothesis of differential attrition due to methodological artifact.

While the refugees as a whole were being slowly assimilated, there was a good deal of stability of reference group orientation from year to year. Looking at the bivariate correlation coefficients in Table 3.2 we see the correlations were quite substantial from year to year indicating considerable reference group stability. However, the positive but not perfect relationships, and the strength of the most recent relationships, reflect both stability and change in the refugee's reference group orientation.

Since the Vietnamese refugee population as a whole was slowly assuming a more American reference group, the prediction of the second hypothesis was that those Vietnamese with more social interaction would become more assimilated. Looking at the bivariate associations in Table 3.2, we see that amount of assimilation tends to depend upon type of interaction. Number of members of the household is consistently negatively related to reference group assimilation for all three sets of interviews. Number of close Vietnamese friends is negatively related to reference group assimilation for each set of interviews (i.e., all nine of the possible correlations are negative). Number of close American friends is usually positively associated with reference group assimilation (i.e., eight of the nine correlations are positive). The evidence for other Vietnamese at work is mixed. Four of the six associations with reference group assimilation are negative and two are positive.

Finally, at the bivariate level, occupational prestige and monthly income are positively related to reference group assimilation, lending some evidence to the hypothesis that these two sets of variables would be positively related.

To control for various possible spurious effects, reference group assimilation in year three was regressed on earlier reference group assimilation scores, the social contact variables, the occupational success variables, perceived social status in Vietnam, the English usage scale, and various demographic variables. While autoregression can be a problem in panel data, ordinary least squares regression gives conservative estimates of the coefficients (Chase-Dunn 1975:727).

Looking at the effects of social contact in Table 3.3, we see that two of the three significant coefficients involve the negative association between number of close Vietnamese friends and reference group assimilation. While the number of close American friends was positively related to reference group assimilation score in two of the three years, the second year coefficient was negative, and in no case does a coefficient reach statistical significance. It should be noted that while numbers of close Vietnamese and close American friends are positively associated, the refugees typically had two to three times as many Vietnamese friends as they did American friends.

The final significant social contact coefficient is the positive association

Table 3.2 Means, Standard Deviations and Correlation Coefficients of Research Variables

Variables

Variables	(1)	(2)	(3)	(4)	(5)	(6)	(7)	(8)
(1) Number of Members in Household — Year 1								
(2) Number of Close Vietnamese Friends in U.S. — Year 1	−.032							
(3) Number of Close American Friends in U.S. — Year 1	−.006	.582						
(4) Number of Close Vietnamese Friends in U.S. — Year 2	−.009	.254	.163					
(5) Number of close American Friends in U.S. — Year 2	−.032	.121	.234	.465				
(6) Other Vietnamese at Work — Year 2 (0-No, 1-Yes)	.050	.041	.001	.049	.086			
(7) Number of Close Vietnamese Friends in U.S. — Year 3	.079	.225	.123	.282	.060	.091		
(8) Number of Close American Friends in U.S. — Year 3	−.049	.212	.301	.269	.401	.018	.403	
(9) Other Vietnamese at Work — Year 3 (0-No, 1-Yes)	.140	.067	−.014	.069	.113	.403	.098	.008
(10) Reference Group Assimilation — Year 1	−.031	−.106	−.089	.069	.153	−.107	−.074	−.021
(11) Reference Group Assimilation — Year 2	−.105	−.089	.022	−.026	.180	−.046	−.295	.074
(12) Reference Group Assimilation — Year 3	−.067	−.134	.002	−.033	.108	−.060	−.295	.027
(13) Occupational Prestige	−.189	.189	.246	.148	.259	−.042	.082	.198
(14) Monthly Income	.060	.124	.129	.130	.248	.020	.082	.128
(15) Social Status in Vietnam	−.121	.170	.211	.174	.236	.010	.151	.174
(16) Sex (0-Male, 1-Female)	.049	−.131	−.110	−.136	−.033	−.025	−.109	−.043
(17) Age	.220	−.019	−.055	−.024	−.008	−.056	−.037	−.188
(18) Marital Status (0-Not Married, 1-Married)	.307	.070	.042	.040	.001	.022	−.016	−.100
(19) English Usage	−.121	.243	.400	.089	.261	−.018	.088	.297
(20) Education	−.200	.211	.335	.169	.304	.059	.050	.255
	(1)	(2)	(3)	(4)	(5)	(6)	(7)	(8)
Means:	5.121	2.248	1.410	4.490	1.073	.617	3.969	1.395
Standard Deviations:	2.757	1.205	.942	4.412	1.714	.331	1.820	1.522

.036											
−.114	.399										
.008	.354	.598									
.017	.043	.078	.093								
.130	.028	.058	.145	.300							
−.017	−.022	.015	.080	.216	.244						
−.049	−.022	−.082	−.046	.069	−.023	.023					
.083	−.028	−.227	−.136	−.133	−.017	.086	−.016				
.156	−.020	−.126	−.055	−.057	.068	.084	−.059	.375			
−.013	.015	.142	.146	.464	.284	.339	−.053	−.264	−.092		
.041	−.006	.114	.152	.509	.303	.376	−.076	−.166	−.102	.712	
(9)	(10)	(11)	(12)	(13)	(14)	(15)	(16)	(17)	(18)	(19)	(20)
.611	26.809	26.972	27.758	21.989	1220.	2.053	.243	42.316	.660	7.117	4.491
.309	2.712	2.735	2.502	15.685	516.22	.636	.429	11.395	.474	2.831	2.500

Table 3.3   Regression of Social Contact, Earlier Reference Group Assimilation, and
             Control Variables upon Later Reference Group Assimilation (n = 349)

Social Contact	b	Beta
Number of Members in Household — Year 1	−.011	−.012
Number of Close Vietnamese Friends in U.S. — Year 1	−.237	−.114*
Number of Close American Friends in U.S. — Year 1	.108	.041
Number of Close Vietnamese Friends in U.S. — Year 2	.013	.023
Number of Close American Friends in U.S. — Year 2	−.124	−.085
Other Vietnamese at Work — Year 2 (0 = No, 1 = Yes)	−.441	−.058
Number of Close Vietnamese Friends in U.S. — Year 3	−.242	−.176***
Number of Close American Friends in U.S. — Year 3	.084	.051
Other Vietnamese at Work — Year 3 (0 = No, 1 = Yes)	.819	.101*
Earlier Reference Group Assimilation		
Year 1	.135	.147***
Year 2	.434	.475***
Control Variables:		
Occupational Prestige	−.002	−.001
Monthly Income	.005	.099*
Social Status in Vietnam	.312	.079
Sex (0 = Male, 1 = Female)	−.137	−.023
Age	−.006	−.028
Marital Status (0 = Not Married, 1 = Married)	.038	.007
English Usage	.005	.006
Education	.055	.055

*denotes $p < .05$
**denotes $p < .01$
***denotes $p < .001$

Intercept = 23.944
Adjusted Multiple R^2 = .400

between having other Vietnamese at work and reference group assimilation. The relationship between having other Vietnamese at work in year two and reference group assimilation in year three is negative but not significant. Current fellow employees of the same ethnic group are apparently more important for reference group assimilation than are former fellow ethnic employees.

The significant relationship between monthly income and reference group assimilation gives support to the economic success-assimilation hypothesis. There is no association between occupational prestige and reference group assimilation after controls nor are any of the other control variables significant.

Conclusions

Refugees and immigrants can maintain as much of their traditional values, beliefs, norms, and behavior as is possible or they may try to become part of the new society. A crucial aspect in this normative orientation is the reference group they hold. The refugees could have anything between an extremely traditional Vietnamese reference group and an extremely assimilated American reference group. Our primary research question here has been the degree of differential stability and change in that reference group orientation.

Overall, the data indicate considerable stability in reference group orientation. This is reflected in the positive association between the scales for all three years. There was, however, a slow change toward a more Americanized reference group and away from traditional Vietnamese beliefs and values. While the group as a whole was thus undergoing assimilation, certain individuals were changing faster. Refugees with more close Vietnamese friends were less assimilated in terms of reference group orientation than were other refugees. Number of American friends was not significantly related to reference group assimilation. Having other Vietnamese at work was positively related to reference group assimilation in year three.

While the refugees as a whole were becoming increasingly assimilated, the process was slow. Vietnamese refugees with a greater number of Vietnamese friends quite probably had a membership reference group. Friends could discuss American culture, but probably a great deal of their interaction involved acting and reinforcing Vietnamese behavior and norms. Speaking Vietnamese, celebrating "Tet" together, and other such activities could reinforce traditional Vietnamese culture. Selection as well as socialization could also play a role. Traditional Vietnamese may seek more traditional Vietnamese friends. More assimilated Vietnamese refugees perhaps seek fewer traditional Vietnamese friends, more assimilated Vietnamese friends, or more American friends. While the relationship between number of American friends and reference group assimilation is not significant, it is possibly due to the potential effect being outweighed by the greater number of Vietnamese friends.

The positive association between having fellow ethnic workers and reference group assimilation in year three stands in contrast to the negative association between number of Vietnamese friends and slower assimilation. One can pick one's friends but rarely one's fellow employees. A more traditional Vietnamese can select and be reinforced by Vietnamese friends. At work, he or she may encounter fellow refugees, ranging from traditional to assimilated. Year by year fellow employees become more assimilated. The refugee is exposed to a greater range of ethnic dress, speech, attitudes and beliefs as models for personal change. The slowly increasing Americanization of refugees in general can partially offset the traditionalism of friends. While the *Gemeinschaft*-like traditionalism of a large number of friends can be a membership reference group reinforcing traditional values, the *Gesellschaft*-type of work relationships encountering an array of assimilation styles can be a reference group favoring assimilation. Therefore, primary and secondary refugee groups and groupings can provide both stability and change in reference group orientations.

Finally, there was a positive association between income and assimilation, probably also due to selection and socialization. The more assimilated Vietnamese refugee is more likely to be financially rewarded. The well-paid employee is more likely to be reinforced by more Americanized attitudes and behavior and, therefore, more likely to repeat this type of assimilation in the future.

Survey Research and Southeast Asian Refugees

Sample survey research constitutes a large part of all research performed in the social sciences. Each year more than thirty million households and one hundred million interviews are conducted in the United States (Rossi, Wright, and Anderson 1983). While surveys are extremely popular, they are not without problems. Samples may not adequately represent the population of interest. Bias in samples can come from various sources including out-of-date or impossible-to-obtain lists. Nonresponses from people refusing to answer some or all of the questions can affect the results. The "not-at-homes" also add to sampling problems (ibid.). Sampling problems can be extremely vexing when studying Southeast Asians because of their primary and secondary migration.

The Achilles heel of survey research is measurement (i.e., asking questions). Whether the survey involves an interview or a mailed questionnaire, surveys rely upon the validity of the respondent's reports of demographic characteristics, attitudes, beliefs, values and behavior (Selltiz, Wrightman, and Cook, 1976:291–329). Respondents in many cases do not give accurate self-reports. Respondents may lie, not understand the question, exhibit poor memory, or truly not know their cognitive or emotional state. For whatever reason, self-reports are rarely, if ever, totally accurate. Other problems include the difficulty of asking sensitive questions and the potential for interviewer bias (Nachimias and Nachimias 1981:181–208). The possibility of artificial and superficial replies makes it difficult to fully analyze complex social processes in a natural setting (Dillman 1978; Babbie 1983). Finally, the researcher may have a considerable gap between his or her conceptualization and eventual operational measurement of an issue (Blalock 1979, 1982). Asking Southeast Asians questions also usually involves the problem of translation. There is often a cultural and linguistic gap between the researcher and the respondent.

Survey research, while not perfect, has many strengths. Sample surveys are good for descriptive studies of large populations. A large amount of standardized data can be collected in a relatively short period of time (Dillman 1978; Babbie 1983). Due to lack of temporality, causation can be difficult to establish with cross-sectional surveys, but with longitudinal surveys such as panel studies, the establishment of social causation is more feasible (Simon and Burnstein 1985).

Measuring change among Southeast Asian refugees as they encounter American culture is relevant to both practical program and policy matters as well as to more general studies of race and ethnic relations. The United States is primarily a nation of immigrants, but few of these immigrants were systematically studied when they arrived in America. To a large extent, the study of Southeast Asian immigrants represents an opportunity to investigate the dynamics of adaptation and define the problems of a new immigrant or refugee group. The refugees' problems with achieving economic self-sufficiency can lend a new perspective to the general study of the relationship between race and social stratification. As the refugees encounter prejudice and discrimination, their experiences inform the scholarly study of majority-minority relationship. The refugees' experience with psychological distress can lend a different perspective to the mental health literature.

The differential amount of assimilation exhibited by the refugees casts a light upon the more general study of assimilation of ethnic and racial groups. Why do some refugees assimilate and some do not? The answers to such questions help to empirically inform the theoretical discussion of assimilation versus pluralism. Besides being an important topic in itself, the study of Southeast Asian refugees can be seen as a sample of the more general population of social interaction in general, and race and ethnic relations in particular. Due to the differences both among the refugees themselves, and between different refugee and immigrant groups, generalizations must be made cautiously. However, the social processes and interactional experiences are similar enough to allow some generalization, and the survey research on Southeast Asian refugees can contribute extensively to a better understanding of race and ethnic relations.

Appendix:
Questionnaire Items Relating to Reference Group Assimilation

1. Where would you like to be buried when you die?
2. Do you want to change your name to an American name?
3. At night, when you are sleeping where do your dreams take place?
4. Do you celebrate your relatives' birthdays?
5. Would you like to become an American citizen?
6. Many of the Vietnamese customs and traditions are no longer adequate for the problems of the modern world. In contrast, the American way of life is more modern, more scientific, and more progressive.
7. The American way of life may be good enough for others but not for me.

8. The schools in America should provide both Vietnamese and English instruction for Vietnamese students.
9. The Vietnamese may adapt themselves to American society in order to earn a living, but they must stay together as a group to preserve their own culture.
10. It is the eldest son's duty to provide financial aid for his aged parents.
11. In general, Vietnamese boys are more attractive looking than American boys.
12. In general, Vietnamese girls are more attractive looking than American girls.
13. A woman's place is in the home.
14. A wife's job is as important as her husband's job.
15. I feel that Vietnamese in America should celebrate "Tet" and celebrate it as traditionally as possible.
16. The way of life in the United States is close to ideal.
17. It is a shame for a Vietnamese child not to be able to speak Vietnamese.
18. Do you think of yourself as American?
19. When in need of financial aid it is best to rely mainly on relatives.
20. After living in the U.S.A., I would feel out of place in Asia.
21. It would be more comfortable to live in a neighborhood which has at least some other Vietnamese than in one which has none.
22. It is foolish for parents to be very informal and act as friends with their children.
23. Those Vietnamese who are Americanized usually do not adopt the good things in the American culture.
24. Vietnamese who enter into new and unfamiliar places without any expectations of discrimination from Caucasians are naive and/or unsophisticated.
25. Many Caucasians are not prejudiced.
26. It is easy for me to act natural (be myself) when I am with a group of Caucasians.
27. I am proud to be a Vietnamese.
28. Vietnamese should stick together in order to keep company with each other and to be assured of mutual assistance in case of emergency.
29. If the Vietnamese in America had certain parts of towns or cities where they lived together, I would then prefer to live there most of all.
30. It is desirable for Vietnamese boys and girls to marry with Americans.
31. Vietnamese people have a refinement and depth of feeling that is rarely found among others.
32. I feel more favorable toward Asians than to members of any other racial group.
33. If I were a religious person, I would prefer to worship in an all-Vietnamese religious group.

4

Vietnamese in America: The Adaptation of the 1975–1979 Arrivals

Bruce B. Dunning

By the end of 1979, nearly a quarter of a million Vietnamese refugees had been resettled in the United States. Such an influx of refugees from a society so markedly different from that of America raised numerous questions about how the refugees were faring in their new country of residence, as well as about the efficacy of policies and programs intended to facilitate the refugees' transition to life in the United States and to protect the interests of the American public. At the same time, the presence of this large group of immigrants, most of whom were known, listed, and presumably locatable, offered a unique opportunity for social scientists to study the processes by which immigrants from one culture adapt to and are assimilated by a new culture and society.

The widespread general interest in Southeast Asian refugees masked at least two overlapping but often disparate agendas for research. On one hand, those concerned with policies and programs tended to accept rapid assimilation of refugees as necessary and to ask how quickly it was proceeding as well as how it could best be facilitated by institutional intervention. In this context, questions for research were most often pragmatic and specific: for example, what are the causes, extent, expected duration, and legitimacy of welfare dependence; how quickly, to what extent, and by what means have refugees been integrated into the American labor force; what are the refugees' citizenship intentions; what are the effects of existing policies and programs on the achievement of economic and social independence by refugees?

On the other hand, those interested in studying the processes of assimilation tended toward a broader focus in which assimilation was seen not so much as a goal to be promoted by intervention as it was as a natural process to be observed and understood; the emphasis was not so much on what was happening with the refugees as on how whatever was happening had come about. In a search for models that could explain processes of assimilation, almost all aspects of the refugees' lives, both before and after arrival in the United States, were important. Among the topics relevant in this approach were (including both the Vietnamese and American situations): parental background, family and household structure, marital history, offspring, locations of birth and subsequent residence, educational history, occupational history, predominant activities over time, religious profession and affiliation, social participation, cultural orientations, attitudes about life, perceptions of social and economic status, and expectations about the future.

In 1979, the Social Security Administration awarded a grant to the Bureau of Social Science Research, Inc. (BSSR) for a study of Vietnamese refugees, which, as it evolved, came to incorporate both of these agendas.[1] The study's objectives, as stated retroactively in the final report, were to:

- assess the extent of social, psychological and economic adaptation to life in the U.S. by Vietnamese refugees;
- identify correlates of different levels of adaptation;
- trace the processes through which Vietnamese refugees sought to accommodate themselves to exigencies of their new lives.

To achieve these objectives, a remarkably large and eclectic set of data was collected. In the end, time and funding limitations prevented a thorough analysis of so complex a data set, and integration of the findings into coherent models of adaptive behavior. The product of the study became a largely descriptive inventory of the data, based for the most part on crosstabular analyses of a few variables at a time, and a few, exploratory, multivariate nominal analyses.

Although the full potential of the data was never realized, the data remain in existence.[2] It is with this in mind that this chapter is largely descriptive, unlike several other chapters in this volume that report the results of rigorous analyses applied to specific issues and research questions. Following a rather detailed discussion of the methods used, which readers who are not technically inclined may wish to skip, the scope and content of the data are demonstrated by descriptions of representative data and findings from the study. The author's critical appraisal of the study closes the chapter.

Methods

The study population included all adults (18–79 years of age) who were Vietnamese nationals before coming to the United States during the years 1975 through 1979, and who were living in January 1980 in one of three areas: Los Angeles and Orange Counties, California; Houston and Galveston, Texas; and New Orleans, Louisiana.

To facilitate sampling, the three study sites were defined operationally by three-digit ZIP code areas selected to conform as closely as practicable to political boundaries in California and to boundaries of the relevant Standard Metropolitan Statistical Areas in Texas and Louisiana.

A tape listing of alien registrations submitted to the U.S. Immigration and Naturalization Service (INS) in January 1980 was still available during the period in which the sample was being constructed. Despite an INS estimate that the list undercounted the Indochinese population by 15–20%, we felt that its use would provide distinct operational advantages over the assembly of lists from networking or local records, and would provide at least as good coverage as those alternative methods. Accordingly, we obtained from INS a tape that listed all residents of reported Vietnamese nationality in California, Texas, and Louisiana. We then extracted from the INS tape all cases that fitted the population parameters. The result was a tape that listed information (name, address, sex, year of birth, nationality, and year of entry) for 28,755 persons. We drew from this sampling frame a random, probability sample stratified on study site and year of entry.[3]

While the study design called for completion of 600 interviews from the three sites, 555 useable responses were obtained in the end.[4] These responses represented 83% of all sample members and 54% of all cases in the sample for whom searches were started.

The very broad scope of the study's objectives dictated development of an interview instrument that was unusually extensive even after a large number of proposed items were eliminated. Among the exclusions were a number of items related to an ambitious plan for objective testing of English-speaking capability. A majority of the 220 substantive items retained provided structured response sets.

Several requirements, which arose during the design of the instrument, made it necessary to use special techniques for recording data. First, we wanted insofar as possible to identify changes in the refugees' feelings about themselves and their lives as they moved from Vietnam to America. Such changes, in self-assessments of social status, economic status, and sense of general well-being, would not only be of interest in themselves, but might provide typologies of subjective states that would yield variables predicting adaptation-related outcomes. For this purpose, we used some scaled items twice, once for Vietnam and once for America. Care had to be taken to place these items in the instrument so as to minimize order or proximity bias.

Secondly, we wanted to be able to establish patterns of behavior over time with respect to the refugees' principal activities in America (e.g., looking for work, working, going to school, housekeeping, doing nothing in particular, etc.), their receipt or nonreceipt of income support, and their places of residence. Items were developed to obtain these data from respondents on a month-by-month basis, and "grids" or charts were included in the instrument to permit quick recording of responses. When entered into appropriate computer data files, these data permitted not only synchronic

analyses of refugee behavior at selected points in time, but also establishment of patterns of behavior over time.[5]

We were also very much interested in data on the refugees' household
and family situations both in Vietnam and in America. We wanted to
examine the refugees' household structures for both situations and also to
be able to link the last household in which a respondent had lived in
Vietnam with his or her current household in the United States. Tables were
used to record the identity of each household member in each of the two
locations as well as some demographic and recent biographical information
about each member. Again, use of appropriate computer data filing techniques permitted linking of Vietnamese and American households as well as
tracking of individual members of those households. Additionally, tables
were used for recording information on the respondents' children from
current marriages, most recent marriages for those no longer married at
time of interview, and for any previous marriages of those currently married.[6]

Whenever a survey instrument is translated from English into another
language for use in the foreign language, independent back-translation into
English is desirable. Unfortunately, time limitations precluded back translation during the development of this instrument. Alternatively, following
translation into Vietnamese by a highly-skilled translator, the Vietnamese
version was reviewed and compared with the English version by a panel of
three English-fluent scholars who were themselves immigrants from Vietnam. The instrument was then pretested on Vietnamese refugees in Arling-
ton, Virginia by three English-speaking, Vietnamese interviewers, and a
Vietnamese-speaking, American observer.

Actual interviewing commenced in late December 1980. English-speaking, Vietnamese interviewers were recruited and trained, under on-site
supervision of BSSR representatives, by subcontractors located in the three
study areas. Interviews were conducted in Vietnamese, usually in the
respondents' homes, and lasted a little over two hours on the average.
Supervisor verification of 10% of the interviews was required. Coding of
responses, when required, as well as manual editing were carried out in
Washington by BSSR staff personnel. Additionally, a wild-code check, a
consistency check, and a structured file SORTFIELD analysis were conducted by computer in the OSIRIS IV System. Subsequent data processing
and analysis were also carried out by the BSSR staff.

Inevitably—and properly—a number of questions can be raised about the
results of any survey research. Was some sort of self-selectivity operating
among those who agreed to be respondents so that the results were biased
by differences in the characteristics of respondents and nonrespondents or,
in this case, sample members who could not be located? Did the respondents truly represent the characteristics of the population being studied?

How valid and reliable was the information provided by respondents? Can the results obtained be assumed to hold for the entire country?

As for most surveys conducted in real-world conditions, these questions can only be answered partially. We do not know if the exclusion of Vietnamese refugees who were not listed by INS biased results because of differences in their characteristics from those of our respondents. We were, however, able to compare respondents, nonrespondents, and unlocatables on two variables: sex and age. There were somewhat fewer men among nonrespondents than among respondents, but the overall distribution on sex did not reach statistical significance at the 5% level (Chi Square). Nonrespondents tended to be slightly younger, and unlocatables were noticeably younger (by about 4 years at the median) than respondents. The age distribution of the three groups was statistically significant at the 5% level (Chi Square). This difference could have affected some outcomes: for example, exclusion of the younger unlocatables may have increased the observed proportion of people in the labor force rather than in school. We do not believe, however, that such differences were sufficient to vitiate the major findings of the study.

We were also able to compare respondents' sexes and ages with those of the listed, Vietnamese populations of the three study sites. Taking all three study sites together (all data reported in this chapter are aggregated across the three sites) the sex distribution of the respondents was identical with that of the Vietnamese population, while the age distributions were quite similar. On these measures, at least, our respondents were representative of the Vietnamese population of the study sites.

But, did our respondents really tell us the way it was? Virtually every survey researcher faces this problem and, ultimately, has to have faith in his or her respondents. We had a few built-in reliability checks which suggested that most of the respondents were being as truthful and accurate as they could. In a few cases in which responses were patently inconsistent with other evidence, the doubtful data were rejected. There was one area in which widespread inconsistency led us to doubt seriously the accuracy of the data. This area involved the *amounts* and *sources* of income support received. In a large number of cases, measures of income support simply did not add up. We did not believe that this resulted from either reticence or deception on the part of respondents, but attributed the problem instead to the inadequacy of the questions and to the fact that many of the respondents simply did not know how much they received, much less from whom they received it. The data were somewhat better with respect to income other than income support. Workers did know their hourly wages with what seemed to be reasonable accuracy, and internal checks suggested that data on the respondents' *personal* and *total household* incomes from all sources were reasonably reliable. In the end, we retained those income measures and eliminated all others as well as all analyses of data on amounts and sources of income support received.[7]

The study thus collected a wide range of data from a sample of Vietnamese refugees in three local areas of the United States, and used it to assess their experiences and current situations in American life. It would, however, be risky to assume that our findings apply equally to Vietnamese refugees in all parts of the country. The population for this study comprised only a small proportion (about 12%) of all Vietnamese immigrants in the United States at the time. Given differences in local attitudes, states of the economy, labor market structures, and so on, it is reasonable to assume that there were differences in the experiences of refugees in other areas. Nonetheless, a description of what was found will not only suggest further uses for the data obtained, but will yield useful qualitative, if not wholly accurate quantitative, insights into what many Vietnamese refugees faced when they arrived in the United States during the first five years of major Vietnamese immigration into this country. The following sections of this chapter delineate representative examples of what we found out from these Vietnamese refugees.

Respondents' Backgrounds in Vietnam

Almost all of the refugees, 56% of whom were men, had been born in Vietnam, two-thirds in South Vietnam. Three-quarters claimed Vietnamese ethnicity, and virtually all of the rest said that they were Vietnamese of Chinese ethnic origin (referred to hereafter as Sino-Vietnamese).

When viewed against the largely rural, agrarian identity of Vietnam,[8] the backgrounds of these refugees were disproportionately urban and middle-class. Over half (55%) were born in urban areas of Vietnam (28% in Saigon, 7% in Hanoi, 20% in other "designated cities" in the North or South). About two-thirds of their fathers, although only a quarter of their mothers, had completed nine or more years of education. A majority (60%) of the fathers had been employed in professional, technical, and managerial occupations or clerical and sales occupations, while the mothers were predominantly housewives (43%) or were reported as having had no occupations (24%).[9] While two-thirds of the refugees identified their parents as having been at the midpoint of the Vietnamese social hierarchy, almost an additional quarter reported that their parents had been of higher than middle social status.[10]

Allowing for influences of a wartime situation, the characteristics of the refugees themselves reflected those of their parents. Almost three-quarters (71%) had lived in a city just before leaving Vietnam, over half of them in Saigon. A majority last lived in Vietnam in two-generation, nuclear households, albeit somewhat larger (median = 6.5 members) than such households are likely to be in the United States. Like their fathers, the refugees tended not to be farmers or fishermen. If not in military or paramilitary service (28%), the men had been employed in Vietnam in professional/technical/managerial occupations (16%) and clerical/sales occupations (11%). A quarter of the men reported having had no occupation in Vietnam; most of these were probably students there.

Unlike the women of the preceding generation, women among the refugees had frequently worked in Vietnam in occupations other than housewifery. While 44% still reported having been housewives or as having had no occupation, half had worked in Vietnam in white-collar occupations.

Over half (59%) of the refugees classed themselves as having been at the midpoint of the social scale in Vietnam and an additional 22% put themselves above that point. They weren't quite as sanguine about their former economic statuses in Vietnam: 44% said they had been "about average" and 42% put themselves below that level.

Of every ten refugees, five were Buddhists in Vietnam, three were Catholics, two professed other persuasions, and one claimed no religious adherence. Most (70%) felt that religion had been important to them.

Leaving Vietnam to come to the U.S. was not the first experience of having to flee from one's home for many of the refugees. About a third (30%) had previously been refugees from North to South Vietnam or internal refugees within South Vietnam. When they arrived in the United States, the respondents were relatively young (the median age was about 30 years), with 20% under 21 years of age and only 9% over 50. Half of them had

Table 4.1   Respondents' Main Occupations in Vietnam, by Sex

| | Sex | | |
Occupational groups	Men	Women	Both
Professional, technical and managerial	16	23	19
Clerical and sales	11	27	19
Military and paramilitary	28	—	14
Industrial (processing, machine trades, structural, and miscellaneous, including laborers)	7	3	6
Agriculture and fishing	7	1	4
Service	4	1	3
Housewife	—	7	3
No occupation	26	37	31
Total	99[a]	99[a]	99[a]
(N)	(308)	(244)	(552)
(DK/NA)	(1)	(2)	(3)

[a] Does not total 100 percent because of rounding error.

completed at least ten years of education before arriving. The women, however, were somewhat less educated (median = 8.9 years) than the men (median = 11.2 years) and older refugees, especially those over 50, tended to have much less education.

Very few of the refugees (2%) felt that they could speak English "very well" when they arrived, and only an additional 16% thought that they spoke English "fairly well." Again, English-speaking ability at these levels was less prevalent among women than among men, rare among Sino-Vietnamese, and virtually nonexistent among refugees over 50 years of age.

At the time of the study, much was being made of differences in the modal characteristics of the successive entry cohorts. For example, the 1975 cohort was widely presumed to benefit from inclusion of "elites" who accompanied the American air evacuation of Saigon in the Spring of 1975. Consequently, a key aspect of the original study design was stratification of the sample by year of entry in order to insure ability both to examine the effects on adaptation of different cohort characteristics and to investigate the effects of time in the United States on economic success. As it turned out, the differences between the cohorts were not as dramatic as expected.

Insofar as distinctive profiles can be discerned among the yearly arrival groups, the 1975 cohort did fare well on characteristics that might have been expected to facilitate adaptation to life in America. The 1975 group was relatively young, predominantly Vietnamese, and included a substantial proportion of adherents to Catholicism, the principal Western religion in Vietnam. It was the best educated of any year's group, with a relatively high proportion speaking useable English, and ranking itself the highest of any group on the Vietnamese social and economic scales. But differences between the 1975 and succeeding cohorts were modest for most characteristics and, in any event, it is doubtful if those differences can be attributed principally to selective inclusion in the American airlift.[11]

The 1976 cohort is of particular interest because, although small, it seems to have been the most successful economically of any of the five cohorts. It was similar to the 1975 cohort in some respects: education, English ability, and former social and economic status. But it included the highest proportion of men of any of the year groups, a substantial proportion of Sino-Vietnamese and a fairly high proportion of Buddhists. Eight of ten of its members had last lived in Vietnam in a city and a substantial proportion of its members (44%, data not shown in Table 4.2) had been white-collar workers, including a number of former merchants. This cohort may have drawn heavily on the Sino-Vietnamese population of the Cholon area of greater Saigon.

The 1977 and 1978 cohorts were somewhat more mixed in their characteristics. But it was the 1979 cohort that differed most from those that preceded it. Predominantly Sino-Vietnamese, with the only noticeable proportion of Chinese-born (8%, data not shown in Table 4.2), this cohort was almost two-

Table 4.2 Summary of Characteristics of Yearly Arrival Cohorts

Cohort characteristic	1975		1976		1977		1978		1979	
	Rank	Datum	Rank	Datum	Rank	Datum	Rank	Datum	Rank	Datum
Sex (% male)	3	52	1	69	2	63	3	52	4	47
Age (median years)	2	28.6	4	30.8	1	27.7	3	29.5	5	31.5
Ethnicity (% Vietnamese)	1	90	3	70	2	76	2	76	4	40
Urban place of birth (%)	3	46	4	45	3	46	2	63	1	65
Urban last household in VN (%)	4	71	1	82	5	68	3	73	2	74
Religion (% Catholic/% Buddhist)[a]	1	42/44	3	34/51	2	40/49	4	27/44	5	10/65
Education (median years completed)	1	10.5	2	10.2	3	10.0	3	10.0	4	9.2
Self-assessed English-speaking capability (% speaking English "very well" or "fairly well")	2	25	1	27	4	11	3	12	5	5
Self-assessed social status in Vietnam (mean score)[b]	1	2.82	2	2.85	4	3.16	3	3.09	5	3.23
Self-assessed economic status in Vietnam (% "well to do" or "much better off than others")	1	45	2	43	5	32	3	40	4	37

[a]Ranked on percent Catholic
[b]Mean score on 5-point scale with 1 = top of Vietnamese social hierarchy and 5 = bottom of Vietnamese social hierarchy

thirds Buddhist, and it was highly urbanized both by virtue of place of birth and by location of last residence in Vietnam. Its educational level was the lowest of any of the arrival cohorts, effective English-speaking ability was rare, and its members had rated themselves low on the Vietnamese social and economic scales.

To the extent that people can be described by aggregating and counting them, these were the Vietnamese refugees who came to the United States during the first five years of major Vietnamese emigration to America. More importantly, perhaps, is how they fared after they arrived. This is the subject of the succeeding sections of this chapter.

Economic Activity in America

It was clearly in the interest of the American people, of governmental institutions at all levels, and of the refugees themselves, that the refugees integrate rapidly into the American economic system. How they did this and how well they succeeded is the subject of this section.

Throughout the course of analysis, certain relationships between refugee characteristics and outcome variables repeated themselves in similar ways. A good deal of repetitious detail can be eliminated from the ensuing discussions by stating these relationships at the outset as "general findings."

1. *Both education completed in Vietnam and the ability to speak at least some English were associated with "desirable" outcomes (being in the labor force, working, higher hourly wages, etc.) on almost every measure of economic success.* For example, both prior education and English-speaking ability increased the likelihood that a refugee would be in the labor force for a substantial proportion of his or her time in the United States. As shown in Table 4.3, the likelihood of never having been in the labor force since arriving in the United States decreased steadily as level of education increased (from 56% for those with no educational certificate or only a Primary Certificate to 14% for those with more than a BACC II). Conversely, the chance of having been always in the labor force increased with each step in the Vietnamese educational process. Of course, education before arriving in the United States was interrelated with English-speaking ability, and both were differentially associated with such other characteristics as sex, age, and ethnicity. Still, we estimated that the proportion of time spent in the American labor force increased by 3 percentage points for each additional year of education completed in Vietnam, independently of the effects of other background characteristics. Later research has also stressed the importance of prior education *vis à vis* labor force participation; Bach (1984) reported the same 3 percentage point increase in labor force participation per year of prior education, and, in her recent review of research on adaptation and integration of refugees in the United States, Forbes (1985:9–

Table 4.3   Proportion of Time in the American Labor Force by Academic Degree or Certificate Held in Vietnam [a] (in weighted percentages)

Percent of time spent in the labor force	Degree or Certificate					
	None	Primary	BEPSI	BACC I/ BACC II	Higher	All
0	56	56	34	21	14	37
1–50	13	9	14	13	11	12
51–99	25	27	36	44	36	34
100	7	8	17	21	39	17
Total	101[b]	100	101[b]	99[b]	100	100
(N)	(68)	(115)	(127)	(157)	(48)	(515)[c]
(DK/NA)	(2)	(—)	(1)	(1)	(1)	(5)

[a] A Primary Certificate required completion of 5 years. The BEPSI, the first cycle of Secondary School, required 4 additional years. A BACC I was awarded on completion of the second cycle of Secondary School (3 years). The BACC II was awarded on the basis of national competitive examinations. Applies to the former South Vietnam.
[b] Totals more or less than 100 because of rounding error.
[c] Excludes respondents with no education and those for whom level of degree or certificate was unknown.

10) cites education in country of origin as "among the most important predictors of labor force participation after controlling for other factors."

While inability to speak English was not a bar to labor force participation, refugees who spoke better English remained in the labor force longer. In Table 4.4, 42% of those who spoke little or no English were in the labor force for more than half the time since arriving in this country. But almost two-thirds (63%) of those who spoke English "fairly well" were labor force

Table 4.4   Proportion of Time in the American Labor Force by Self-assessed English-speaking Capability (in weighted percentages)

Percent of time spent in the labor force	Speaks English				
	Very well	Fairly well	Not very well	Hardly or not at all	All
0	—	21	22	52	36
1–50	—	16	17	7	12
51–99	65	30	48	28	36
100	35	33	14	14	17
Total	100	100	101[a]	101[a]	101[a]
(N)	(11)	(76)	(168)	(278)	(550)
DK/NA	(—)	(—)	(4)	(1)	(5)

[a] Totals more than 100 because of rounding error.

participants for more than half the time, and the proportion rose to 100% among the few who spoke English "very well." Strand (this volume) also points to English-speaking ability as an important factor affecting labor force participation. But Forbes (1985:10) notes, after citing a similar finding, that the question of language effects on economic behavior is complex, and that the influence of language on "employment" has been shown to be less clearly defined than that of education.

2. *On most measures, women were less likely than men to be out-of-home participants in the economic system and when they were such participants, they tended to achieve lower levels of success (e.g., lower wage levels).* If "homemakers" were considered part of the American labor force, the women among our refugees would have been labor force participants as frequently—in fact, slightly more frequently—as the men. Nonetheless, our data indicated that the Vietnamese women who were in the labor force fared less well than the men in many cases.

3. *In general, the youngest refugees (18–20 years old) and elderly refugees (over 50) were less likely than others to be engaged or successful in economic activities. The same was often true for people of Sino-Vietnamese origin.* Economic inactivity of the youngest group was accounted for by the fact that 77% of them were in school. But again, the interdependence of age and ethnicity with other factors, including Vietnamese social and cultural factors, has to be taken into account. While advancing age did have its own effect on inhibiting economic activity, related factors may have been more important. Coming from a society in which modernization and the end of colonial status were relatively recent, elderly Vietnamese refugees tended to be considerably less educated, and to have been less exposed to English than their younger counterparts. Still, whatever the proximate "cause," it was the elderly who were disadvantaged. It is necessary to stress this point of interdependence of factors even more forcefully with respect to Sino-Vietnamese refugees. This does not mean that it was their ethnicity, *per se,* which was responsible for their disadvantage in this country. It is likely that a degree of segregation as well as the roles which the Sino-Vietnamese tend to play in Vietnamese society (as small merchants for many) accounted for lower levels of education and English speaking ability, which, in turn, disadvantaged them initially in this country.

4. *Economic activity tended to be somewhat lower for each succeeding entry cohort—except for the 1976 cohort which was, for still unexplained reasons, slightly more successful than the 1975 cohort in many areas.* The positive effect of time on the economic integration of Southeast Asian refugees has been documented in a number of studies; see, for example: Strand (this volume) and Whitmore, Trautmann and Caplan (this volume). With these general findings in mind, we can shift our emphasis to how the economic integration of Vietnamese refugees proceeded.

Occupations and Income

On the assumption that labor force participation was a key to economic integration (as it turned out to be), one of the first analytical efforts of the study was determination of the principal activities of refugees during the months following their arrival. In December 1980, the month just completed when most of the respondents were interviewed, slightly over half (54%) of the refugees were in the labor force, either working or looking for work. These included six out of ten men and four out of ten women. An additional quarter of the women identified themselves as homemakers. Disregarding the women who were homemakers, most of the labor force nonparticipants were in school, vocational training, or English-language training. Only 10% of the refugees were out of the labor force because of some sort of disability or predilection. Very similar distributions of activities were found in January and May 1980 when those two months were examined synchronically.

However, labor-force participation rates in single months say nothing about participation over time. Month-by-month records of the refugees'

Table 4.5　Respondents' Principal Activities in December, 1980, by Sex
(in weighted percentages)

| | Sex | | |
Principal activity	Men	Women	Both
Looking for work	2	*	1
Working[a]	62	42	53
Subtotal in labor force	64	42	54
Going to school (academic)	12	12	12
In vocational training[b]	8	2	5
ESL training	5	5	5
Homemaking[c]	2	27	14
Home sick, disabled, or hospitalized	4	7	5
Doing nothing in particular	4	5	5
Subtotal not in labor force	35	58	46
Total	99[d]	100	100
(N)	(308)	(243)	(551)
(DK/NA)	(1)	(3)	(4)

*Less than 0.5 percent.
[a] Includes *paid* OJT or apprenticeship.
[b] Includes vocational training school and nonpaid OJT or apprenticeship.
[c] Housekeeping, staying at home caring for children, or other family members.
[d] Total less than 100 because of rounding error.

principal activities, previously described in the "Methods" section of this chapter, permitted an examination of patterns of behavior over time. Some 37% of the refugees (a quarter of the men and half of the women) had never been in the labor force since arriving in the United States. But 41% (54% of the men, 20% of the women) had been in the labor force for at least three-quarters of the months since arrival.

Participation in the labor force almost always meant having a job and working. Unemployment (that is: in the labor force, but looking for work rather than working) was very low in December 1980: 2.9% among the men and 0.3% among the women. As in the case of labor-force participation rates, unemployment rates in January and May 1980 were similar to those for December 1980. It should be noted that unemployment rates such as these were remarkably low compared to those found by other investigators. For example, in San Diego, California in July 1981 Strand found very high unemployment (Strand, this volume).[12]

Refugees usually got their first jobs in the United States through some sort of personal contact or on their own initiative. About half of those who had worked at some time were sent to their first employers by a sponsor, friend, or relative; an additional third answered newspaper advertisements, or simply walked in to the employer's office or workplace. Direct employment by a sponsor, friend, or relative was rare, as was employment obtained through official or voluntary agencies.

More than half (62%) of the employers were companies or corporations; only a fifth were businesses run by individuals or families. Most of the employers were described as white Americans and over half of the places of employment were staffed predominantly by white Americans.

First-job occupations among men most frequently involved service occupations, followed by the assembly, repair or installation of electrical and electronic equipment, and then by professional, technical, and managerial work. Women were frequently engaged in bench work (often in the fabrication of textile goods), followed by professional, technical and managerial jobs (most often in educational or administrative work), and then clerical work. However, these occupational category titles probably exaggerate the importance of many of these jobs since the average wages received in them were quite low: $3.66 an hour for the men, and $2.97 among the women.

People who had held more than one job since arriving in the United States found their currently held or most recent jobs (referred to hereafter as "current jobs," whichever the case) in much the same ways as their first jobs, except that slightly more found them on their own initiative, slightly fewer used personal contacts, and a few more used official and voluntary agencies. Employers continued to be predominantly white-managed companies or corporations staffed largely by white Americans. In the aggregate, these current jobs were distributed among the broad occupational categories in much the same way as were the first jobs, except for modest movement

Table 4.6 Occupations: First Jobs in the United States (in weighted percentages)

Occupational group[a]	First jobs		
	Men	Women	Both
Professional, technical, and managerial	14	18	16
Clerical	9	18	13
Sales	3	8	5
Service	21	9	16
Agriculture and fishery	5	2	4
Processing operations	4	5	4
Machine-trade occupations	11	1	7
Benchwork occupations	11	23	16
Structural work occupations	17	14	16
Miscellaneous occupations	4	2	3
Total	99[b]	100	100
(N)	(218)	(120)	(338)
(DK/NA)	(13)	(1)	(14)

[a] One-digit occupational categories from the *Dictionary of Occupational Titles.*
[b] Total is less than 100 because of rounding error.

out of service occupations into machine trade and structural work occupations. Individually, though, there was a great deal of change with almost two-thirds of the workers changing from one occupational group to another. The variety of the most frequently occurring current job occupations is shown in finer-grained detail in Table 4.7.

These current jobs were noticeably more remunerative than the refugees' first jobs. The average hourly pay rate for men increased to $5.40 (from $3.66), while that for women rose to $4.09 (from $2.97). These average pay rates reflect the progress of 85% of the workers who received, on the average, $2.91 more in their latest jobs than in their first jobs. But about one out of ten workers lost ground, averaging $1.28 an hour less in their later jobs.

Income and income support data proved difficult to get, at least with acceptable degrees of confidence. Nonetheless, sufficient data were collected to estimate that at the time of interview, median monthly *personal* incomes, including both earned and unearned income, amounted to $618. Whitmore, Trautmann and Caplan (this volume) point out the importance of the "multiple wage-earner strategy" among Southeast Asian refugees and, hence, of looking at the household as an economic unit. Among our respondents, too, median household incomes increased systematically with size of household (data not shown), and the personal incomes of our respondents (only 4% of whom lived alone) constituted only half of their respective household incomes ($1,386 at the median). Extrapolating median,

Table 4.7   Most Frequent Occupations: Current or Most Recent Jobs in the U.S.
            (in weighted percentages)

Occupations[a]	Percent
Electrical assembly, installing and repair (structural work) [b]	15
Computing and account recording (clerical)	10
Metal machining (machine trades)	7
Fabrication and repair of textiles, leather and related products (benchwork)	6
Architecture, engineering and surveying (professional, technical and managerial)	5
Managers and officials, n.e.c. (professional, technical and managerial)	5
Welders, cutters and related occupations (structural work)	4
Food and beverage preparation and service (services)	4
Packaging and materials handling (miscellaneous)	3
Education (professional, technical and managerial)	3
Percent of all current or most recent jobs accounted for	62

[a] Two-digit categories from the *Dictionary of Occupational Titles.*
[b] Terms in parentheses are the DOT one-digit categories into which the cited occupational groups fall.

monthly, household incomes to an annual basis, we estimated that the median, annual, household income of Vietnamese refugees was about $16,600. At this level of income, Vietnamese households were considerably less affluent than white households in metropolitan areas of the country, but better off than either black or Hispanic households.

Among these refugees, roughly 45% were receiving or benefiting from cash income support in any given month. Yet, only about one-quarter of the refugees had benefited from income support during their entire stay in the United States and one third had never received or benefited directly from such support. At the median, refugees received, or someone on whom they were dependent received, income support during one quarter of the months they had been in the United States.

At the time of study, a nagging question was whether or not refugees were leaving welfare rolls once they obtained work. For the most part, they did. In December 1980, only one of ten working refugees was benefiting from income support, while among the nonworking, eight of ten were receiving such support. We estimated that, independent of the other factors considered, each percentage point increase in the proportion of time in this country spent in the labor force (which usually meant working) accounted for an average 0.6% decrease in the proportion of time here during which a refugee benefited from income support. In a similar vein, Whitmore, Trautmann and Caplan (this volume) demonstrate that as the earned income of a *household* increased, the *household's* reliance on income support decreased.

Education and Training

Obtaining employment in America ranked high among the serious concerns of Vietnamese refugees; an element in this concern was developing the skills necessary to compete in the American labor market. But, as Whitmore, Trautmann, and Caplan (this volume) show, pragmatic motives were buttressed by cultural values that favored a strong drive toward achievement. Given the importance that the refugees ascribed to improvement of their salable, personal resources, whether for pragmatic or cultural reasons, it isn't surprising that substantial numbers of refugees took advantage of American educational and training opportunities following their arrival in the United States.

Roughly a quarter of the refugees had obtained academic education after arriving in the United States. In December 1980, 12% of the adult refugees were in school. Over half of these students were 18–20 years old and most of the rest were 30 years of age or less. Still, every age group was represented except for those over 60 years of age. This participation in the American educational system may have stemmed more from desires to continue education—or the confidence necessary to do so—than from the availability of previously unavailable opportunities since, up to the Vietnamese graduate level, the more education a person had received in Vietnam, the more likely that person was to enter the American educational system. An apparent corollary of this is that those who were educationally disadvantaged when they arrived, were likely to remain so. But if this disadvantage operated for some of the refugees themselves, it didn't extend to their children whose educational achievements have been remarkably high (Whitmore, Trautmann, and Caplan, this volume). It is likely that a good many of the older refugees were willing to defer improvement of their own situations in favor of their children; 97% of our respondents either "agreed" or "agreed strongly" with the statement: "Vietnamese in America must concentrate on their children getting ahead, even if they do not do very well as a result."

As in the case of academic education, roughly a quarter of the refugees obtained some sort of vocational training following arrival in the United States. Such training covered a wide variety of occupations representing every broad occupational field. But, probably reflecting local industrial bases and available programs, installation and repair of electrical and electronic products engaged nearly half of the women and slightly more than half of the men who received vocational training. Training in metal machining was in second place among the men, clerical work among the women. Again, prior education—having completed at least eight years of school in Vietnam—and the ability to speak at least some English markedly increased the chances of receiving vocational training. But whatever the educational backgrounds of the trainees, 90% of those who were out of training by the time of interview had completed their programs.

The refugees clearly recognized ability to speak English as essential both for making a living and for getting along in everyday life: 78% felt that speaking English was absolutely essential for getting a job and working, and 85% mentioned language as a "serious problem" with which refugees have to grapple early in their stay in this country. By the time they were interviewed, 70% had received English-language training. By their estimates, the duration of this training was substantial: 350 hours on the average, almost nine, full, working weeks. These English students were virtually unanimous in saying that such training had been useful. Comparisons of self-assessed English capabilities at time of arrival (retroactively) with those at time of interview bore this out in a good many cases. Among those who received training, almost half (47%) felt that their English had improved while less than a quarter (22%) of the non-trainees indicated improvement (see Table 4.8). Still, the other side of the coin should be noted: half of the trainees' self-assessments indicated that their English hadn't improved.

Problems, Services, and Service Usage

Many of the early programs intended to assist Vietnamese refugees in adapting to their new lives were designed on the basis of what Americans assumed would be the problems that the refugees would encounter. Therefore, we were interested from a programmatic standpoint in discovering what aspects of their new lives the refugees felt had been most troublesome. We also felt that knowing what problems the refugees perceived as serious and how they went about dealing with these problems were important in understanding the dynamics of social and cultural adaptation.

Table 4.8   Changes in Self-assessed English-speaking Capabilities Between Arrival and Time of Interview (in weighted percentages)

	Percent of respondents	
Change	Received training	Didn't receive training
Improved English Ability	47	22
No Change	51	72
Regression in English Ability	2	6
Total	100	100
(N)	(361)	(175)
(DK/NA)	(12)	(5)[a]

[a]There were 2 DK/NA on receipt of training.

Respondents were thus asked what problems they considered serious for refugees arriving in the United States—when they first arrived and over the longer run. The problems most often perceived as serious were the same for both periods: maintaining ethnic identity, finding employment, learning English, and sociocultural adjustment (understanding and getting used to American customs.) But the actual frequency and the order of frequency with which these subjects were mentioned were quite different for the early and longer run lists (see Table 4.9). The refugees were unanimous in feeling that maintenance of cultural identity was a serious problem early on, but were much less concerned with that over the longer run. Learning English was the second most-frequently-mentioned problem, both as an early problem and over time, but was much less frequently mentioned as a long-term problem. Sociocultural adjustment moved up on the long-term list although, again, was less frequently mentioned than it had been as an early problem. Perhaps reflecting a more pragmatic approach to life in America as the result of early experiences, it was getting a job that moved into first place as a long-term problem.

Many of the services provided for refugees were, as mentioned earlier, intended to assist them with the problems they were expected to face. But such services can be effective only if refugees are aware of them and use them. In an attempt to assess awareness of, need for, and receipt of services, respondents were asked about six types of services often provided to refugees.[13] Table 4.10 shows the proportions of refugees aware of, needing, and receiving each of these services. But awareness and need are not independent of each other: awareness of service availability may not come

Table 4.9　Perceptions of Serious Problems Most Frequently Encountered on First Arriving in the U.S. and Over the Longer Run (in weighted percentages)[a]

Rank	Early problems	Percent of respondents	Longer-run problems	Percent of respondents
1	Maintaining ethnic identity	100	Employment	48
2	English language	85	English language	23
3	Employment	33	Sociocultural adjustment	17
4	Sociocultural adjustment	23	Maintaining ethnic identity	9
5	Transportation	18	Housing	6
			Financial	6
			Education, self or children	6
			Discrimination, prejudice	6
6	Housing	14		
	(Others 5% or less each)		(Others less than 5% each)	

[a] Multiple responses permitted

Table 4.10 Awareness of, Need for, and Receipt of Six Types of Service
(in weighted percentages) [a]

Services	Percent of refugees perceiving service as available [b]	Percent of refugees needing service [c]	Percent of refugees needing services who received them [c]
Government	83	76	95
Job	62	53	62
Housing	57	48	87
Reunification	56	56	54
Education	55	46	84
Day-care	30	12	40

[a] Types of services are defined in note 13.
[b] DK/NAs, not shown, are included in the percentaging base on the assumption that "don't know" or "no answer" amounts to nonawareness of availability.
[c] DK/NAs included in percentaging base.

until a need is felt, *or* awareness of availability may generate perceived need. Whichever the case, with the exception of day care—which wasn't needed by many—majorities of those who needed each type of service received that service. Almost all of the refugees expressed satisfaction with the services they received (data not shown in Table 4.10). Relatively rare expressions of dissatisfaction occurred with respect to job services (11%) and housing services (7%).

Conventional wisdom at the time of the study suggested that Vietnamese refugees would seek to solve many of their problems within their own ethnic groups in the manner often ascribed to earlier groups of Asian immigrants in this country. A test of this assumption was of considerable interest because of the insights it might yield on the extent to which the refugees would reject American, institutional sources of help in favor of reliance on familial and personal relationships within the Vietnamese community. Therefore, the refugees were asked to whom they would turn for help in each of five, anecdotally described, problematic situations. [14]

As it turned out, they said they would seek help from family members or the Vietnamese community in a good many cases, but this was by no means universal; only in the case of a financial problem was this the modal choice. Family conflict was seen as a situation which most would handle themselves or within the Vietnamese community, with only one in five likely to seek professional or institutional help. Self or community reliance was also important in the mental health situation, but, in this situation, almost half would seek professional or institutional help. In the event of a medical problem involving their own sickness, about two-thirds said they would seek professional help—although no distinction was drawn between practitioners of Western medicine and practitioners of traditional, Asian medicine. Per-

Table 4.11 Sources of Help in Problem Situations (in weighted percentages)

Indicated source of help	Financial	Family conflict	Mental health	Medical	Juvenile delinquency
Self	3	43	25	3	15
Family, friend or Vietnamese community	78	38	30	28	9
Professional/institutional	15	19	45	69	76
No one	4	—	—	—	—
Total	100	100	100	100	100
(N)	(425)	(386)	(407)	(514)	(371)
(DK/NA)	(97)	(136)	(115)	(8)	(151)[a]
Modal source:	Friend-47	Self-43	Doctor/hosp.-33	Doctor/hosp.-61	School-71

[a] Excludes 33 cases DK/NA on a control variable for the crosstabulation from which these data were taken.

haps most surprising was the very large proportion (76%) who said they would turn to professional or institutional sources of help, usually the school authorities, if their child was in trouble. However, the magnitude of this response may have been an artifact of the item that mentioned "having trouble in school."

Homes and Families

Many observers have pointed to the centrality of the family and household in Southeast Asian societies. Whitmore, Trautmann, and Caplan (this volume) emphasize the contribution that economic cooperation of household members has played in the achievement of economic well-being among Southeast Asian refugees, as well as the importance of family values to the achievement of academic success among children. But what happened to Vietnamese families and households as a result of immigration to the United States?

While the move to America seems not to have occasioned cataclysmic changes in the structure of Vietnamese households, noticeable changes did occur, and it seemed likely that many families were under considerable stress. The proportion of one-generation and two-generation, nonnuclear households increased at the expense of two-generation, nuclear, and three-generation households. The increase in one-generation households (from 7% in Vietnam to 22% of all households in the United States) was the most noticeable aspect of this shift. Concomitantly, two-generation, nuclear households declined from 59% to 47% while three-generation households dropped from 18% to 11%. In the United States, one-generation households were particularly prevalent among younger people and married couples. Vietnamese refugee households here were smaller than those lived in before leaving Vietnam (median = 4.5 members in the U.S., 6.5 members in Vietnam). While the presence of unrelated household members was almost nonexistent in Vietnam, occurring in only one percent of the households, one out of ten multiple-member households in the United States included one or more unrelated members. Still, kinship or marriage relationships remained the central feature of Vietnamese household organization. Excluding single-member households (6% of all households in which respondents lived at time of interview), there were no households consisting entirely of unrelated members; in 92% of the households, more than half of the members were related.

Yet it is clear that the emigration of Vietnamese refugees to the United States resulted in considerable family disruption. Some 41% of the members of the refugees' last households in Vietnam didn't leave Vietnam with the refugees; of those who stayed behind, seven out of ten were still in Vietnam at the time of the interviews. Not surprisingly, very old people were often left behind—more than four out of five elders over 70 years of age stayed behind. However, two of every ten former household members under 21 years of age were also still in Vietnam.

Despite the pressures imposed on Vietnamese refugee families, stable marriages were the rule. Among the majority (61%) of our respondents who had been married at one time or another, almost nine out of ten (87%) were married and living with their spouses when interviewed. When separation had occurred, it was usually involuntary (7% of all marriages) or the result of the death of a spouse (5%). Three-quarters of these marriages had taken place in Vietnam and almost all the rest after arrival in the United States. There were very few interethnic marriages; even the Vietnamese-Sino-Vietnamese line was seldom crossed.

About half of the currently married couples had three or fewer children. While the ages of offspring from current marriages varied from one year to 51 years, half were 11 years of age or less. About 80% of all the children were living with their parents; among those not living with their parents at the time of interview, a third were living in the same area as their parents, a third were living somewhere else in the United States and one-quarter were still in Vietnam.

Becoming Vietnamese-Americans: Continuity, Change and Ambiguity

What has been described so far suggests that substantial numbers of the Vietnamese refugees moved quickly toward integration into the American economic system, either by working or by preparing themselves for work by involvement in American educational and training systems. Programs and services intended to help the refugees had been useful for many. While the circumstances surrounding emigration to the United States had obviously placed families under stress, kinship remained central to household organization, and stability of marriages remained the rule.

But acceptance of and by a new society involves much more than relative success in earning the resources necessary to survive independently. To what extent immigrants participate in the social and cultural life of their new milieu or, conversely, isolate themselves within their ethnic group and cling to their own customs and values, are important indicators of adaptation. Further, it is necessary to look at how immigrants themselves feel about their new lives, at their internal states of mind. When we undertook this study, we wanted to discover as much as was practicable about the refugees' lives outside the workplace as well as about how they felt about themselves in their new lives. In that attempt, we used a number of structured-response questions about noneconomic aspects of the refugees' lives, and a number of Likert-like scales aimed at tapping their perceptions of their social and economic well-being, as well as overall quality of life. What follows is a selective summary of how the refugees responded.

If the necessity of earning a living or learning new skills threw many of the Vietnamese refugees quickly into predominantly American settings, their private lives retained a strong Vietnamese flavor. Although availability and affordability usually dictate where anyone obtains housing, two-thirds of the refugees said that they would prefer to live in substantially Vietnamese neighborhoods, and over half of them actually did so. They also found their best friends almost entirely within their own ethnic groups, even observing the distinction between Vietnamese and Sino-Vietnamese most of the time. Participation in social organizations—clubs, associations or other nonwork groups—was rare. When it occurred, it occurred within the ethnic group by almost a two-to-one margin.

Religion remained important for two-thirds of the refugees, and there was little change in their professed religious affiliations. Only about one in twenty changed his or her religious preference after leaving Vietnam; 45% professed adherence to Buddhism here while 39% identified themselves as Christians (Catholic in nine of ten cases).

Presumably, participation in religious activities with Americans could have been a resocializing influence. This seems not to have been the case, at least by the time of the study. Notwithstanding the growth in Vietnamese Buddhist Associations in a number of localities, Buddhist pagodas and temples were not widely available in the United States. It wasn't surprising, therefore, that most of the Buddhist refugees rarely, if ever, worshipped at a pagoda or temple. Moreover, when Buddhist refugees did visit a pagoda or temple, it was almost always a predominantly Vietnamese place of worship. Christian churches would seem to have afforded a better opportunity for resocialization of refugees given their ubiquity and the wide range of social activities customarily supported by American churches in conjunction with their religious functions. However, even though the Christian refugees were very likely to attend services at least once a week (87% of the Catholics said they did so), over half of the congregations with whom the refugees worshipped were entirely or mostly Vietnamese in composition, and an additional quarter were about half Vietnamese.

Despite their recognition that the ability to speak and understand English was of crucial importance in America, and the fact that four out of ten felt that they were able to use English at least "fairly well" in their everyday lives, the refugees continued to speak their primary languages in their homes. Virtually all of the Vietnamese usually spoke Vietnamese at home; three-quarters of the Sino-Vietnamese refugees spoke Chinese at home, with most of the rest speaking Vietnamese.

However much the refugees sought or didn't seek to Americanize their private lives, three-quarters (77%) recognized the probable permanence of their residence here by saying that they intended to apply for U.S. citizenship. Only 5% said they did not intend to do so; these were most likely to be elderly, undereducated, non-English-speaking persons. Among the 1975 arrivals who were just beginning to become eligible for citizenship, a quarter had applied by the time they were interviewed.

Despite the fact that most of the refugees apparently recognized their residence here as permanent, with or without citizenship, and were moving rather quickly toward making their own way in American life, there was a pervasive sense among them that they had lost a great deal in their migration. Over half (58%) placed themselves lower on the social scale in America than had been the case in Vietnam. Even greater numbers felt that they had lost economically with 71% responding that they were "poor" or "living in poverty" relative to non-Vietnamese Americans (only 14% had placed themselves in those categories with respect to their economic status before leaving Vietnam). That a tendency to exaggerate disadvantage was at work here is indicated by the fact that over half (57%) felt themselves to be similarly disadvantaged with respect to other Vietnamese refugees. It can also be argued that, objectively, given differences in standards of living, the Vietnamese refugees were better off in this country than in Vietnam. But, perceived economic status is culturally relative. A refugee can be living a better material life here than he or she had in Vietnam, but still feel deprived relative to the norms of the society.

In an attempt to get at the refugees' overall, nonspecific evaluations of the quality of their lives, we asked them to place themselves on a ten-point "Ladder of Life" scale with 1 being "the happiest sort of life you think you could achieve" and 10 being "the unhappiest sort of life." Six of ten refugees found themselves below the middle of the scale with respect to their lives in America. More importantly, two-thirds placed themselves lower on the scale of life in America than they did when evaluating themselves on a similar scale regarding their lives in Vietnam: only 13% felt that their lives in America were better than their lives had been in Vietnam.

Despite this malaise about their current lives, most of the refugees expected their lives to improve markedly within five years. They felt this way about occupational advancement, about income, and about the overall quality of their lives. If there was a dim note in these expectations, it was that many of the expectations seemed so optimistic as to be unrealistic.

Obviously, not all Vietnamese refugees are the same, nor are all of the refugees put into one or another of our categories of responses to our questions. We were dealing with 555 individuals, each of whom came to the United States with his or her own biological and demographic characteristics, his or her own life experiences, his or her own attitudes and aspirations. That differences in individual characteristics as well as differences in the intensities with which native cultural values are held will affect response to immersion in a new culture has been recognized for a long time. Roberts and Starr (this volume) review the literature on differential cultural orientations and reference group theory in laying the groundwork for their rigorous studies of Southeast Asian refugees within the framework of reference group theory. Khoa and Van Deusen (1981) hypothesized that Vietnamese refugees could be characterized by one or another of three patterns of response to the necessity for coping with a new cultural environment: an "Old-Line Pattern," characterized by a deeply-rooted loyalty to traditional beliefs and a "Defensively Conservative" reaction to factors in American life threatening to their own values, an "Assimilative Pattern" characterized by an eagerness to integrate into American life and precipitous rejection of the old culture, and a "Bicultural Pattern" in which attempts to preserve traditional values and beliefs are accompanied by acquisition of new values and practices needed in a successful life in the new society.

We attempted to identify such patterns among our respondents by using a nine-item battery of "agree-disagree" statements including several borrowed from Starr's earlier work.[15] The analysis of the responses failed to yield clearly definable clusters of cultural orientation. However, the responses were useful in highlighting, impressionistically, a marked ambivalence in the attitudes of many refugees. For a good many, a strong desire to retain aspects of Vietnamese culture and refusal to admit any superiority of American culture coexisted with views that the American way of life was more modern, scientific, and progressive, and that many Vietnamese customs and traditions were no longer appropriate. This stressful, simultaneous attraction to contradictory values differs significantly from the rational, selective rejection of old values and acceptance of new values implied by Khoa's and Van Deusen's "Bicultural Pattern."

While this finding of ambiguity in the attitudes of Vietnamese refugees toward two different cultures lacked robustness and methodological rigor, it suggests a powerful dilemma faced by the refugees. At the time of the study, none of the respondents had been in this country for more than five years. The departures of many from their homeland had been traumatic. Unquestionably, many of the refugees knew little of what to expect in America. By the same token, the influx of so many Vietnamese refugees, for whom the U.S. government and many American people felt a special measure of responsibility, created confusion on the American side, confusion about what to expect from these people, and what to do for them.

Presumably, some of the confusion and ambiguity has resolved itself since 1980. As we saw it at the time of the study, however, the Vietnamese refugees were moving rapidly toward adaptation to and integration in the American economic system, but social and psychological adaptation were proceeding at a much slower pace. The final report expressed fear that too much reliance on economic success as a measure could lead to false conclusions about the adaptation of Vietnamese refugees to life in America. Furthermore, the report suggested that until the malaise detected in the findings was removed, until refugees no longer saw themselves as deprived, disadvantaged, and suffering because they had had to leave Vietnam for America, until they saw themselves as Americans of Vietnamese descent rather than as Vietnamese living in America, they could not be considered fully adapted. The dilemma for the Vietnamese refugees, as it has been for other immigrants, was and is that when such a level of adaptation is achieved, they or their descendants will no longer be Vietnamese. They will have lost all but superficial manifestations of their ethnic identity and their rich cultural heritage.

Some Personal Comments on the Study

In retrospect, it is clear that the BSSR study of Vietnamese refugees attempted too much. Pressures to accommodate divergent objectives, which were defined only in general terms, resulted in a "shotgun" approach in which data were collected on every conceivable topic that could be accommodated within the limits of practicality. Given more rigorous attention to the development of analytical plans, harder-nosed and more competent technical management at BSSR, and more time and money, effective use might still have been made of such a rich data set. As it was, analysis became an extensive fishing expedition at a superficial level, with few criteria to suggest what was important and what was not, and only the vaguest of conceptual models to guide integration of findings into some coherent model of the adaptation process. The result was a final product that described a great deal, but answered few questions and left adequate analysis for an indeterminate future. In this sense, this chapter has reflected the characteristics of its source. One lesson from this study is, of course, that if social science research is to be effective and useable, both clients and purveyors of research must decide at the outset what they are attempting to do and how they are going to go about doing it.

Yet, both its timing and, ironically, the factors that led to the study's principal faults underlie the study's principal and, in some cases, unique values.

First, this study was probably the most extensive investigation undertaken with respect to the refugees who arrived during the first five years of major Vietnamese immigration into this country. The data therefore constitute an important baseline regarding the periods of initial adjustment to American society by members of a new, major group of immigrants.

Second, the data cover most of a period in which significant gaps occurred in the collection of Southeast Asian refugee data: the period between termination of U.S. resettlement camps in 1975 and early 1981 when the U.S. Office of Refugee Resettlement assumed responsibility for the creation of records according to comprehensive specifications (Gordon, this volume).

Finally, the data cover a wide range of topics: labor force behavior, employment, education and training, language capability, household structure, marriages and offspring, geographic mobility, religious preferences and participation, social participation, cultural orientations, attitudes, and self-assessments. Data of such scope, pertaining to a single set of respondents, are seldom found in more highly focused and rigorously designed studies. Some of these topics are seldom covered at all. Further, I believe that this data set is one of the few in existence that permits linking important variables in the respondents' backgrounds in Vietnam with similar variables pertaining to their experiences in America.

If this study was seriously flawed, as I think it was, perhaps some of the onus is removed by its legacy of a rich, still-existing data set.

Notes

1. Drs. Darrel Montero and Anthony Pfannkuche initiated the study. The Social Security Administration awarded a grant to the Bureau of Social Science Research, Inc. (BSSR), Washington, D.C. for conduct of the study with Dr. Montero as nonresident Study Director. He continued in that function until the last five months of the Study. Dr. Anthony Pfannkuche codirected the study during its initial planning stage. The author of this chapter supervised BSSR's central-office and field work, directed the final stage of the study, and prepared, with the assistance of Joshua Greenbaum, the final report.

   Study results were reported in, *A Systematic Survey of the Social, Psychological and Economic Adaptation of Vietnamese Refugees Representing Five Entry Cohorts, 1975–1979,* Washington, D.C.: Bureau of Social Science Research, Inc., 1982, and summarized in *Survey of the Social, Psychological and Economic*

Adaptation of Vietnamese Refugees in the U.S., 1975–1979, AFDC and Related Income Maintenance Series, U.S. Social Security Administration, Washington, D.C.: 1982. (Both of the publications were reproduced from a draft without adequate editing and verification. They contain numerous typographical and computational errors. Data from these publications should be checked for consistency before use. I recommend that those interested in extensive use of the data obtain access to the original tape data files. See following notes.)

The author is solely responsible for the contents of this chapter.

2. The Bureau of Social Science Research, Inc. is no longer in existence. Along with other BSSR archives, the data files and all supporting documentation from this study are now held by The McKeldin Library of The University of Maryland. Persons wishing to obtain access to materials from this study, including tape data files and technical documentation, should contact: Collection Management Office, The McKeldin Library, The University of Maryland, College Park, MD.

3. The file of eligible names was sorted by location and year of entry, providing 15 strata, one for each study site and year of entry into the U.S. For each stratum, the needed number of names was selected using a random number generator in the Michigan Interactive Data Analysis System (MIDAS). Cases were assigned in the order drawn to one of three samples for each stratum until that stratum was filled. The sample segments were a small pretest sample, a primary sample of the size necessary to fulfill completed interview requirements, and a replacement sample from which shortages in the primary sample due to nonlocation could be filled. Ultimately, the frequency of unlocatables required the drawing of a second replacement sample. This second replacement sample was drawn in the way just described after removal of the primary sample from the sampling frame.

   This stratified sampling procedure required that data be weighted subsequently to return response values to proportionality with the populations of the study sites.

4. Table 4.12 summarizes the sample design and the actually attained sample.

5. All responses to all items were archived on tape in a Basic Data File using the OSIRIS IV program in MIDAS. Additionally, the OSIRIS IV hierarchical file capability was used to construct hierarchical tape files (i.e., separate subfiles within each respondent's basic file) for the "grids" described in the text. Thus, in the case of Monthly Activities, each respondent's coded responses constitute

Table 4.12 Designed and Obtained Samples (in unweighted frequencies)

Year of entry	Los Angeles and Orange Counties		Houston and Galveston Area		New Orleans Area		All	
	Design	Useable completed interviews	Design	Useable completed interviews	Design	Useable completed interviews	Design	Useable completed interviews
1975	60	69	30	29	30	31	120	129
1976	60	57	30	25	30	15	120	97
1977	60	56	30	25	30	27	120	108
1978	60	57	30	28	30	31	120	116
1979	60	57	30	28	30	20	120	105
All	300	296	150	135	150	124	600	555

a separate subfile linked to the Monthly Activity variable address in the respondent's individual file. As an example of the flexibility provided by this procedure, each respondent's subfile can be examined starting from calendar month and year of entry or, in order to place all respondents on the same scale of elapsed time, starting from "first" month in country. For other applications, data for specified calendar months or specified sequential months can be called out for any specified segment of respondents.

Hierarchical files were produced for the following grids: Monthly Activities, Monthly Income Support, Monthly Place of Residence.

Since the OSIRIS IV program was not available to many social scientists at the time of the study, the OSIRIS IV Basic Data File was also converted to a Statistical Program for the Social Sciences (SPSS) flat file.

6. Hierarchical files were also produced for the following data-recording tables in the interview instrument: VN Household Structure (last household in Vietnam), U.S. Household Structure (at time of interview); Offspring Tables: Current Marriage (at time of interview), Most Recent Marriage (respondents married once but no longer married at time of interview), Terminated Prior Marriage (respondents married more than once).

Hierarchical files of Household Structure, for example, permit linking of each member of a respondent's last household in Vietnam with presence or absence from the respondent's household in the U.S. at time of interview.

7. We also rejected in their entirety and counted as nonresponses 27 completed interviews because of incompleteness, irreconcilably inconsistent data, erroneous nationality, or undue influence by a third person present during the interview. We had anticipated that, given the close group ties and family interdependence characteristic of Vietnamese society as well as the insecurity felt by many refugees, we could expect strong pressure to allow third parties to be present during interviews. Interviewers were instructed to make every effort to interview respondents alone but not to risk losing the interview if the respondent insisted on the presence of another person. Our expectation was correct—214 interviews had to be conducted with a person or persons present other than the respondent and interviewer. In such cases, interviewers were required to describe the circumstances as well as their assessment of whether or not the respondent's answers were influenced by another person. All cases of reported influence were examined by a senior BSSR analyst who made a decision as to whether or not to accept the interview. Of the 27 interviews rejected for all reasons, 19 were rejected because of influence.

8. Smith (1967:65) reported that 87.2% of the labor force in South Vietnam in 1964 was engaged in agriculture or fishing.

9. In order to compare occupations in Vietnam with occupations in America, we coded both sets according to a coding scheme derived from the *Dictionary of Occupational Titles* (DOT) (U.S. Employment Service, 1977). But the occupational structure of Vietnam is not the same as that of the United States; neither are occupational definitions identical. Consequently, we had to "force" some Vietnamese occupations into American categories. For example, when we think of a sales person in America, we tend to think of a person employed in a fairly large store, of a teacher as one who usually teaches in a fairly large school, of someone engaged in manufacturing farm implements as a person employed in a factory and utilizing a fairly complex technology. This may have been the case in Vietnam also. But in Vietnam, there was a better chance that the person reported as having been in sales or as having been a businesswoman was actually a market or street vendor with a few baskets of locally produced fruits or

vegetables; that the teacher had taught in a small, village school, and that the farm implement manufacturer had fabricated simple implements in a small workshop. Still, the Vietnamese occupational distributions we observed demonstrated a remarkably diversity and a degree of "middle-classness" relative to Vietnamese society.

10. Trczinski (1981) reported that use of Likert-like scales yielded little variance among Vietnamese respondents when used for subjects such as self-assessed, English-language competence. We used a number of such scales: for social and economic status as well as for English-speaking capability. On both 5-point, numerical, social scales with two points defined verbally (1 = "upper class," 5 = "lower class") and 5-point, verbally-defined, economic scales (1 = "living in poverty," 2 = "poor but able to get along," 3 = "about average," 4 = "rather well-to-do," 5 = "much better off than others"), we encountered fairly heavy clustering at the midpoint, but still useable variance. Further, when we compared response distributions on items in the context of life in Vietnam to those of identical items in the context of life in the U.S., we observed marked shifts from the midpoint to above or below the midpoint. This led us to believe that midpoint clustering was not simply an artifact of Likert-like item structure. For self-assessed, English-speaking capability, we found considerable variance on several measures.

11. Insofar as the 1975 cohort was overrepresented in categories presumed to be advantageous, it was usually so only to a modest degree. This group was, in fact, quite diverse. Its members were represented in every category on each of the background and demographic characteristics we recorded. The characteristic in which this cohort was most homogeneous and in which it differed most from the other cohorts was its Vietnamese ethnicity (90% compared to 76% for the next two ethnically most homogeneous cohorts: 1977 and 1978).

Actually, the American air evacuation in April, 1975 contributed only modestly to formation of the 1975 arrival cohort. If all of our respondents who said they left Vietnam by air during the first six months of 1975 arrived in the United States that same year and were, therefore, included in the 1975 entry cohort, they would have constituted only 21% of that cohort. In point of fact, about three-quarters of the refugees who left Vietnam in 1975 (73% of our respondents who left that year) left by boat.

12. Detailed comparative analyses of the data would be required to explain the magnitude of this difference. Although Houston was enjoying a boom when we were interviewing and economic conditions were also good in Orange and Los Angeles Counties, it seems unlikely that conditions in San Diego were sufficiently worse than our study sites only six months later to account for such a difference. Another possibility is that Strand's sample was somewhat older than ours since he focused on heads of household who, in Southeast Asian cultures, are most often the oldest members of their households. While not all of Strand's respondents were heads of household, he reports that 89% of his male respondents and 50% of his female respondents (females accounted for only 16% of his sample) were the oldest members of their households. Among our respondents, only 45% were heads of household and, presumably, the oldest members of the household in most cases. Some weight is given to this age hypothesis by the fact that roughly 11% of our respondents who were over 50 years of age were unemployed in December, 1980. This figure is much closer to Strand's datum than our overall unemployment rate.

13. The following explanations of what was meant by each of the types of services were read to respondents:

Government Services: Help in getting government services like welfare, immigration, and citizenship assistance, and so on.

Job Services: Help in finding and getting a job in the United States.

Housing Services: Help in getting a place to live.

Education Services: Help with respect to your children's education—information about schools, how to get your children enrolled in school, and so on.

Reunification Services: Help in getting reunified with members of your family.

Day-care Services: Help in getting someone or someplace to care for very young or very old people in your household while you and other adults are away.

14. Anecdotal situations were presented to respondents as follows:

Financial: You need $500 quickly to make a payment on which you have fallen behind.

Family Conflict: A family you are close to is having frequent conflicts and even fights and you think help is needed to keep the family from breaking up.

Mental Health: A good friend of yours is very depressed and you think you must get help for him.

Medical: You are sick and need medical help.

Juvenile Delinquency: Your child is having trouble in school and running around with others you think might get your child in trouble.

15. Of the nine items in our battery, one reproduced one of Starr's items, five were adaptations of his items, and three were our own items. I remain deeply indebted to him for his encouragement at the time this study was being designed as well as for his permission to use his items.

5

Personal, Social, and Economic Adaptation: 1975–1979 Arrivals in Illinois

Young Yun Kim

Between 1975 when the first group of refugees was evacuated from Vietnam and 1979 when the present study began, approximately 254,000 Southeast Asians had been resettled within the United States. Of this number, the largest concentrations were in California (33%) and in Texas (10%). Pennsylvania, Washington, West Virginia, Louisiana, Virginia, and Illinois each had 3% to 4.5% of the total population.[1]

From the beginning, the Indochinese resettlement program had been a joint effort of the private and public sectors. The private, voluntary agencies had undertaken almost all of the initial sponsorship and resettlement of refugees in this country. Through their religious congregations and the support of their benefactors, virtually all of the 254,000 refugees in the United States had been resettled with American individuals, families, or groups throughout the country. The federal government had, at the same time, provided full support for the state and local government agencies that had provided for the welfare and special social service needs of the refugees.

During the initial five years of resettlement, federal and local government had begun to investigate the resettlement and adaptation situations of the refugees by providing research grants. The states of California and Texas (the two states with the largest concentration of refugees) had previously conducted extensive studies of their respective refugee populations.[2] In November 1978, the author and Perry N. Nicassio, under contract to Travelers Aid Society of Metropolitan Chicago Incorporating Immigrants' Service League, began a comprehensive assessment of Southeast Asian refugees in the State of Illinois. The project had been made possible by funding from the Illinois Department of Public Aid and the Governor's Information Center for Asian Assistance (under PL95–549).

Research Design

The research project was initiated with the primary goal of providing an empirical basis for reviewing the adequacy of social and educational services rendered to the Southeast Asian refugee population throughout Illinois and for planning future service programs. In order to reach this goal, we investigated both the current resettlement and adaptation of the refugees and the current state of the Illinois service programs. By examining both the refugees and the service agencies, we hoped to obtain a comprehensive picture of Southeast Asian refugees, their adaptation problems, and the services offered to assist their adaptation.

We began the project by surveying 34 governmental, educational, and social service agencies throughout the state that were providing direct or indirect services to the refugee population. The survey of the agencies took place between December 1978 and February 1979 through personal interviews, telephone interviews, and mailed questionnaires. This survey was designed to serve a number of important functions for both service providers and the large population for whom such services had been developed. The principal objectives of the survey were: (1) to construct a comprehensive profile of existing service programs, (2) to identify problems and obstacles experienced by the agencies in delivering and coordinating services to the refugees, (3) to identify personal, social, and economic needs of the refugees as perceived by the agencies, (4) to describe the underlying philosophies and future prospects of service delivery of the agencies, and (5) to provide an empirical basis for establishing content domains for questionnaires that would be developed to assess the needs of the refugee population directly.

Upon completion of the survey of the agencies, we conducted a survey of the refugees themselves during May through September 1979. The main objectives of the refugee survey were: (1) to provide a basic demographic profile of the refugees, (2) to assess their personal, social, and economic adaptation status, (3) to analyze their awareness, utilization, and evaluation of existing services, and (4) to identify the specific adaptation problems that they were experiencing at the time of the study.

In this survey, all identifiable refugee family households in Illinois were approached. Because many of the refugees maintained an extended family system sharing common resources, a family household was defined in this study as the collective residential unit consisting of one or more members of an immediate or extended family. Within a household, one adult, preferably the head of the household, was requested to participate in the survey. When there was more than one family identified in the same residence, the head of each of them was included.

Due to the highly mobile nature of the refugee population within the state, the inflow and outflow due to secondary migration between states, and the rapid increase in refugee arrivals from Southeast Asia, considerable time and effort was devoted to compiling a comprehensive, accurate list of the names and addresses of as many Indochinese refugees as possible. The lists were provided primarily by four voluntary agencies and six educational and public assistance institutions. After eliminating any duplication of names and addresses, a total of 3370 households was located, of which 248 were Cambodians, 352 were Hmong, 250 were Lao, and 2,520 were Vietnamese.

The survey comprised three phases: *Phase 1* (May–June, 1979), a mail questionnaire survey was sent to all refugee households throughout the state; *Phase 2* (May–July, 1979), a survey was administered to refugees attending English classes in 13 Illinois community colleges and other educational institutions; and *Phase 3* (July–September, 1979), throughout the state, refugees were interviewed in their homes. The adoption of this three-phase research strategy permitted access to a larger, more diverse, and more representative group of refugees than would have been achieved through any single method of data collection. Varying the mode of data collection also provided an internal check on the reliability and validity of the findings obtained in any one phase. The data collection process further provided sufficient flexibility to measure diverse aspects of the refugees' lives, ranging from standard socio-demographic indicators to psychological and social indicators. In addition, the research strategy made the overall data collection process economically feasible, effective, and efficient without being limited to any one method (and thus ensuring responses from nonliterate as well as literate refugees).

A standard questionnaire was used in the three phases of the survey. Each questionnaire was translated into three languages: Cambodian, Laotian, and Vietnamese. A "back-translation" method (Werner and Campbell 1970) was used to minimize any discrepancies in meaning between the original English version and the translated versions. The questionnaire consisted of two parts, each addressing different thematic issues. The first part of the questionnaire dealt with the refugees' demographic characteristics (including economic indicators), service utilization and evaluation, and major service needs and problems of adjustment in the United States. The second part contained questions about the respondents' personal (psychological) and social interaction. In the mail questionnaire survey (Phase 1), only the first part of the questionnaire was used, to maximize the return rate and accuracy of response. In Phase 2 and Phase 3, both parts of the questionnaire were used.

All in all, 1,777 of the 3,370 questionnaires used in the three phases of the survey were completed for a return rate of 52.7%. Almost three quarters (73.9%) of the 1,593 nonresponses were due to a change of address. The actual return rate among those who did receive a questionnaire through the mail or who were contacted in person was 81%. Among the 1,777 questionnaires completed and returned, 968 were from Phase 1, 349 were from Phase 2, and 460 were from Phase 3.

Reflecting the comprehensive nature of the present research design, findings from this research were presented in five volumes: (1) *Introduction, Summary and Recommendations,* (2) *Methods and Procedures,* (3) *Population Characteristics and Service Needs of Indochinese Refugees,* (4) *Psychological, Social, and Cultural Adjustment of Indochinese Refugees,* and (5) *Agencies and Organizations Serving Indochinese Refugees.* Due to the limited space of this chapter, however, only the findings from the survey of refugees will be reported in the following sections.[3]

Population Profile

From a map of the refugees' locations in Illinois, highly concentrated residential distribution patterns were observed. Approximately half (53%) of the total refugee households were located in Cook County. Other counties with more than 100 refugee households were: DuPage (6.4%), Peoria (5.8%), and Kane (5.0%). The majority of the households were concentrated primarily within urban areas. Slightly less than half (44%) of the total households were located in Chicago. About one fourth (26%) were in the suburban areas around Chicago, with 13% in other cities and towns throughout the state. Only 17% were in rural areas. A higher concentration of new arrivals was observed within Chicago, while the earlier arrivals were more widely distributed outside the city.

An average household size was estimated to be 4.2 among all refugees. (This relatively small household size reflects the study's definitional emphasis on family links rather than simple co-residence.) Of the four ethnic groups, the Hmong households reported the largest average household size (5.5), and the Cambodian households reported the smallest (3.6). The Lao and the Vietnamese reported an average size of 4.4 and 4.0 respectively. As a whole, the refugee population was a relatively young population. More than half (55%) were under 21, and 40% were between the ages of 21 and 50. Only 5% were older than 50 years. Of the four ethnic groups, the Hmong reported the largest proportion of children under 11 (40%) and of adults over 50 (6%). On the other hand, the Cambodians reported the smallest proportion of children under 11 (27%) and young persons between the ages of 11 and 20 (15%). Nearly 9 out of 10 (88%) refugee households reported at least one missing family member, dead or separated escaping from their home country. The Hmong and the Lao reported a higher proportion of households with missing family members than did the Cambodians and the Vietnamese.

Among the heads of refugee households, 7% did not have any formal education. The proportion of refugees with no formal education was the highest among the Hmong (26%), with the second highest among the Cambodians (13%). The Vietnamese and the Lao reported more extensive educational backgrounds with only 1.5% each without any formal education. The educational levels of the early arrivals, who had come to the United States more than three years prior to the survey, were generally better educated than the later arrivals. Although less than 4% of the earlier arrivals had no formal education, 7% to 19% of the subsequent arrivals reported no formal education. Similarly, more than 15% of the earlier arrivals were college graduates, compared with less than 9% of the later arrivals.

In addition to the above-summarized general population characteristics, an in-depth description of the refugee population was made based on the data collected from the 809 respondents who participated in Phase 2 and Phase 3. (As noted, the questions concerning psychological and social adaptation were not included in the general survey of Phase 1.) Of the 809 respondents, 43% were Vietnamese, 23% were Lao, 20% were Hmong, and 14% were Cambodian. This ethnic composition closely corresponds to that in Phase 1 of the survey. More than half (56%) of the 809 respondents had been living in the United States less than one year at the time of the survey. The remaining 44% included respondents who had been living in the United States from one to five years.

The adaptation patterns of respondents were assessed in three dimensions—personal, social, and economic. Personal adaptation referred to the perceptual, attitudinal, and behavioral attributes of refugees. Social adaptation referred to their participation in American society through interpersonal, organizational, and mass communication processes. Economic adaptation referred to the financial and occupational status that refugees had acquired in the United States. Key findings regarding these three dimensions are highlighted in the following sections.

Personal Adaptation

Certain elements of the refugees' perceptions, attitudes, and behavior provide insight into the personal dimension of their adaptation. This personal dimension has been the primary research focus of the majority of immigrant studies in psychology and psychiatry (e.g., Chance 1965; Graves 1967). In the present study, the personal adaptation of the refugees was assessed through four indicators considered to be the most significant aspects of individual adaptation to a new cultural environment: acculturation motivation, images of self/others, alienation, and English competence (cf. Kim 1979, 1982, in press).

Psychologists have generally distinguished between motivation and action—between the desire to achieve and actual achievement (cf. McClelland 1965). Motivations are conceived as psychological dispositions to strive for certain goals. They energize human behavior when the situation arouses the expectancy that the performance of an act is instrumental to the attainment of a goal. Accordingly, acculturation motivation was defined in this study as the degree of eagerness to learn about, participate in, and be oriented toward the American sociocultural system.

As shown in Table 5.1, a majority (67%) of the respondents indicated that it was very important to learn about and understand the American people's behavioral and thought patterns, and to learn about current political, economic, and social situations and issues in American society (73%). On the other hand, a relatively smaller proportion (50%) of the respondents felt it was very important to make friends with American people. The results suggested that the refugees, on the whole, were strongly motivated to learn about the American cultural and social system, but were less strongly inclined to actually socialize with American people.

The second indicator of the refugees' personal adaptation was their image of Self in relation to the image of others around them. Here, the refugees' image of Self/Others was considered a cumulative result of dynamic interaction between them and the new sociocultural environment. Their perception of Self in relation to Americans and to refugees was measured using an eight-item Likert scale for eight personality attributes selected and pre-tested for their effectiveness in contrasting the refugees and the American people. The eight items were: "tense," "patient," "withdrawn," "selfish," "happy," "poor," "confident," and "humble."

The respondents' ratings of Self, Americans, and other Refugees (see Table 5.2) showed a tendency for refugees to evaluate themselves significantly more negatively than they evaluated either Americans or other refugees on such personality attributes as "tense," "withdrawn," "happy," "poor," and "confident." On the other hand, the Americans were rated more negatively than Self and other refugees on such characteristics as "patient," "selfish," and "arrogant." Refugees tended to give "don't know"

Table 5.1   Responses to Acculturation Motivation Items

	Very important	Somewhat important	A little important	Not important	Total (N)
Understanding the ways that American people behave and think	67%	26%	5%	2%	100% (767)
Making friends with American people	50%	34%	9%	7%	100% (764)
Learning about events and issues of American society	73%	21%	5%	1%	100% (766)

Table 5.2   Responses to Items on Self, Refugees, and Americans

		Very	Moderately	Slightly	Not at all	Don't know	Total	(N)
Tense	S	15%	20%	28%	23%	14%	100%	(765)
	R	11	24	30	15	20	100	(752)
	A	9	16	17	17	41	100	(758)
Impatient	S	2	12	39	41	6	100	(763)
	R	1	10	38	36	15	100	(765)
	A	8	10	24	15	35	100	(751)
Withdrawn	S	12	22	31	28	7	100	(762)
	R	9	24	31	17	19	100	(757)
	A	4	10	12	35	39	100	(746)
Selfish	S	5	16	24	45	10	100	(770)
	R	6	22	32	20	20	100	(752)
	A	18	21	11	13	37	100	(752)
Confident	S	7	39	34	13	7	100	(763)
	R	23	22	34	15	6	100	(759)
	A	46	29	19	4	2	100	(775)
Arrogant	S	5	17	36	26	22	100	(761)
	R	2	16	34	26	22	100	(749)
	A	19	16	15	11	39	100	(745)
Happy	S	6	18	37	23	16	100	(766)
	R	13	18	32	23	14	100	(765)
	A	28	48	18	5	1	100	(753)
Poor	S	44	34	14	5	3	100	(770)
	R	28	35	14	7	16	100	(761)
	A	1	11	19	37	32	100	(750)

Note: S = Self, R = Refugees, A = Americans

answers concerning Americans more often than concerning Self and other refugees.

Based on the above-reported images of Self/Others, the degree of incongruity between the images was examined by the relative distance between the images of Self and of others. The image incongruity between Self and Americans was greater than the image incongruity between Self and other refugees. Specifically, the average incongruity score for Self/Americans was 11.1, for Self/other refugees, 6.3, and for Americans/other refugees, 9.3.

Another psychological state in relation to the American sociocultural environment was assessed by a 10-item Likert-type Alienation scale. The ten items were developed for this study based on their relevance and significance to the refugees' adaptation. The first set of the ten items,— social isolation—measured feelings of loneliness and rejection, as well as difficulties in making American friends. The second set—cultural estrangement—consisted of items measuring feelings of awkwardness about living in the United States, and difficulties in understanding the American way of life. The third set—powerlessness—measured the extent to which the respondent felt in control of life in the United States.

Results, summarized in Table 5.3, indicate that a considerable feeling of alienation existed among the refugees. The overall response patterns to the Alienation Scale appear to reflect the difficulties that the refugees were experiencing, their doubts about the attitudes of Americans toward them, and their concern about their future in the United States. About half (54%) of the respondents agreed, moderately or strongly, with the statement, "I feel awkward and out-of-place in America," and 62% to "It is difficult for me to understand the American way of life." Also, a majority disagreed with such statements as "The future looks very bright to me in America," "As an individual, I can contribute something to American society," and "I feel that the Americans that I know like me."

A final key aspect of personal adjustment is English competence. The importance of knowledge and skill in English is self-evident, and has been

Table 5.3   Responses to Alienation Items

	Strongly agree	Agree	Disagree	Strongly disagree	Don't know	Total	(N)
"I feel awkward and out of place in America."	25%	29%	23%	12%	11%	100%	(766)
"It is easy for me to make American friends."	23%	31%	24%	22%	0%	100%	(687)
"The future looks very bright for me in America."	11%	15%	41%	22%	11%	100%	(768)
"Many things my parents taught me in my home country are not useful in America."	9%	10%	27%	46%	8%	100%	(765)
"As an individual, I can contribute something to American society."	5%	14%	44%	30%	7%	100%	(766)
"It is difficult for me to understand the American way of life."	26%	36%	18%	9%	11%	100%	(775)
"I feel like I belong in American society."	29%	29%	30%	12%	0%	100%	(675)
"There is little I can do to improve my life in this country."	13%	21%	42%	17%	6%	100%	(751)
"I feel that the Americans that I know like me."	9%	23%	42%	15%	11%	100%	(757)
I feel all alone in America."	25%	38%	22%	8%	7%	100%	(749)

repeatedly shown to play a pivotal role in any cross-cultural adaptation
situation. In this study, respondents' English knowledge and skill was
assessed by a three-item English Competence Scale. The three items dealt
with: (1) the degree of difficulty respondents had in understanding Americans, (2) the degree of difficulty for Americans in understanding the respondents when they spoke in English, and (3) the frequency of hesitation in
talking to Americans. It was assumed that the respondents' evaluation of
their English competence was closely linked to their actual command of the
language.

Results in Table 5.4 show an overall lack of English competence. About
70% of the respondents reported that they comprehended less than half of
the English spoken during a conversation. About the same percentage of
respondents felt that Americans understood their English less than half of
the time. Almost all (92%) indicated that they frequently hesitated to speak
to Americans because of their inability to express themselves in English.

Social Adaptation

Patterns of refugees' social adaptation were assessed by the degree to which
they participated in the communication processes of the American society.
Below, findings on the refugees' participation in interpersonal communication processes via interpersonal relationships and in mass communication
processes are reported.

Interpersonal relationship patterns reflect social adaptation. Two individuals who develop an intimate friendship with each another necessarily
share a high degree of shared social orientation (cf. Lazarsfeld and Merton
1964; Pearce and Stamm 1972). Refugees' interpersonal relationship development with Americans on various levels of intimacy was, therefore, considered a vital aspect of their sociocultural participation in the United States.
Conversely, their interpersonal ties with individuals in their own ethnic
community were considered to reflect their ethnicity and lack of cross-

Table 5.4   Responses to English Competency Items

	None	A little	Half	Most	Almost complete	Total	(N)
Listening comprehension	23%	47%	13%	15%	2%	100%	(791)
Speaking ability	25%	44%	15%	14%	2%	100%	(788)
Self-confidence	57%	35%	13%	15%	—	100%	(755)

cultural adaptation (cf. Berry 1980; Kim 1979, 1982, in press; Taft 1957). In this study, these interpersonal relationship patterns of the respondents were examined on three levels: (1) those of casual acquaintances they knew well enough to talk with when they happened to meet them, (2) those of casual friends or colleagues who were close enough to be invited to each other's home, and (3) those of intimate or close friends with whom they could discuss private and personal problems.

Results show that, on all three levels of interpersonal relationships, there was a consistent pattern of affiliation predominantly within the ethnic community. Interaction between respondents and individuals outside the ethnic community was minimal, particularly on the two more intimate levels of interpersonal relationships (casual friends and intimate friends). The median number of acquaintances was 25 within the respondents' own ethnic group, 10 among other Southeast Asian refugees, 10 among White Americans, 4 among Black Americans, and 5 among other foreign immigrants. The distribution was different for the levels of casual friends and intimate friends. The median numbers of casual and intimate friends within the respondents' own ethnic community were 10 and 4 respectively, but 0 for all other categories (see Table 5.5).

In addition to interpersonal interaction, use of mass media enables the refugees to participate in the social processes of the American society. Explicitly and implicitly, mass media messages convey American sociocultural patterns to new immigrants and refugees. The influence of television, radio, newspapers, and other forms of mass communication (such as movies, magazines, and books) plays a crucial role in learning the host culture and achieving social integration. Mass media enable immigrants and refugees to extend the scope of their social participation beyond the particular milieu in which they carry out daily activities (cf. Nagata 1969; Kim 1979, in press, for a review of literature).

The present assessment of the respondents' use of American mass media included: (1) exposure to television programs, (2) listening to radio programs, and (3) newspaper readership. The results showed that the refugees, on average, used the American mass media only minimally. They reported

Table 5.5   Median Numbers of Acquaintances and Friends (N = 753)

	Acquaintances	Casual friends	Intimate friends
Own ethnic group	25	10	4
Other Indochinese	10	0	0
White Americans	10	0	0
Black Americans	4	0	0
Other foreign immigrants	5	0	0

that they watched television between 30 and 60 minutes daily, listened to radio programs less than 30 minutes daily, and read English language newspapers once or twice a week.

Economic Adaptation

Economic adaptation patterns of the refugees were assessed in terms of their occupational status, monthly income, dependency on public aid, car ownership, and telephone ownership. Because findings on all of these indicators were highly consistent, only the findings on income level and occupational status will be reported below.

The respondents' occupational status was assessed by classifying their occupations into six levels: (1) unemployed (or full-time student without income), (2) unskilled laborer (e.g., farmer or factory worker), (3) skilled laborer (e.g., technician, office clerk, military personnel), (4) semiprofessional or white-collar worker (e.g., government worker, social worker, nurse), (5) lower-level professionals (e.g., pharmacist, teacher, business person), and (6) higher-level professionals (e.g., professor, lawyer, medical doctor).[4]

In Table 5.6, results showed that approximately one third of the respondents were unemployed at the time of the survey. The remaining respondents were employed either full-time (61.9%) or part-time (6.7%). About half of the employed respondents (52.4%) were working as laborers, and there was a significant number of the respondents (10.9%) attending school. Other categories were office workers (4.4%) and technicians (3.5%). The generally low occupational statuses of the refugees reflected a substantial downward change from their former statuses in their home countries.

The respondents' income level was assessed by their gross monthly income per household. More than half (54.3%) of the respondents reported their income as less than $700 per month; one-fourth (26.6%) earned less than $400 per month. Only 13.7% reported more than $1300 per month as their family income. The percentages with incomes below the $700 figure varied with ethnicity; for Vietnamese it was 46.8%, for Lao 52.2%, for Hmong 69.7%, and for Cambodians 72.3%. Such differences reflect a broader consistent pattern among the four refugee groups in their personal and social, as well as economic adaptation, as demonstrated in Table 5.7. Consistently, the Lao and the Vietnamese refugees show a more positive situation than the Cambodian and the Hmong refugees.

The Interrelatedness of Adaptation Dimensions

The personal, social, and economic dimensions of adaptation reported so far should be viewed as interactive and interdependent rather than separate

Table 5.6 Previous and Current Occupation (N = 1473)

	Previous occupation in home country	Current occupation
Unemployed	3.8%	31.4%
Student	14.0%	10.9%
Farmer	5.1%	.6%
Laborer	10.0%	36.0%
Technician	1.4%	3.5%
Office worker	3.9%	4.4%
Military	34.4%	1.0%
Government	6.7%	.6%
Social worker	1.4%	1.6%
Business	4.6%	.7%
Nurse	1.4%	1.6%
Pharmacist	4.6%	.7%
Teacher	.8%	.3%
Professor	3.1%	.5%
Lawyer	.7%	.2%
Medical doctor	1.0%	.5%
Clergyman	.3%	.1%
Other	7.3%	7.0%

Note: Figures here reflect both full-time and part-time occupations.

and independent of one another. Adaptation experiences in a new cultural environment involve virtually all aspects of life. A refugee faces the host environment in its totality, just as a native-born child discovers it and learns its elements and their interrelatedness throughout the socialization process. This all-inclusive nature of the adaptation process required that the investigation accommodate the multidimensionality and interrelatedness of the dimensions by integrating the typically sociological interests (economic and social adaptation) and the typically psychological interests (i.e., the personal dimension).

In this multidimensional, interactive approach, each refugee was viewed as an open system interacting with the host environment. Each refugee was further viewed as possessing the ability to adapt (i.e., to react to the new cultural environment in a way that is favorable in some sense to the continued operation of his or her existence). Further, in the systems perspective, each aspect of a refugee's life activities in the new society is viewed as functionally interrelated with all other aspects. The invisible psychological processes are linked with the more visible social activities, including the way refugees relate to other individuals (and thus find their

Table 5.7   Ethnic Groups' Differences in Adaptation

Indicators	Cambodian	Hmong	Lao	Vietnamese
Personal				
Self-image	20.9	22.9	25.3	24.3
Alienation	26.5	27.4	24.0	22.0
English competence	6.9	5.0	7.6	6.8
Social				
American acquaintances	6.0	6.0	10.0	10.0
Newspaper readership	1.4	1.4	2.2	1.9
Economic				
Unemployment rate	48.8	46.2	29.9	23.7
Income under $700	72.3	69.7	52.2	46.8

Note: Self-image, alienation, English competence, and newspaper readership are indicated in mean (X) scores. American acquaintances are indicated in median numbers. Unemployment rate and income level are indicated in percentages (%).

"place" in the American society), as well as the way they make their livelihood.

Findings from the study clearly indicated the interrelatedness of the three dimensions of adaptation. First, the trends in the refugees' personal, social, and economic adaptation show great similarity and suggest that the dimensions "move together" over time. Second, the interactive nature of the adaptation dimensions is further suggested by correlational analyses that provide statistically significant associations between indicators of the three adaptation dimensions. Findings regarding each of these two points are reported below.

Developmental trends were inferred from cross-sectional comparisons of the adaptation patterns of refugees with different lengths of residence in the United States. Results from these analyses suggested that the refugees' personal adaptation tended to improve during the first five years. An acculturation motivation score (computed by combining the three acculturation motivation items into a composite score) was consistently strong for three years and then began to trail off as the refugees overcame their initial uncertainty and instability (see Table 5.8). The self-image also tended to improve slightly over the five years (data not shown). Conversely, the perceived incongruity between self and Americans was greater during the first year (11.8) than during the subsequent years. Among the fifth-year residents, the self/American incongruity score was reduced to 9.3, suggesting the refugees' gradual psychological adaptation to the United States. Also, a general decrease was seen in the refugees' feelings of alienation. The

Table 5.8   Trends in Acculturation Motivation, Perceived Incongruity, and Alienation

Length of residence	Motivation score[a]	Incongruity score[b]	Alienation score[c]
0–1 year	10.7	11.8	24.4
1–2 years	10.7	11.1	24.7
2–3 years	10.7	11.4	25.9
3–4 years	10.3	9.4	22.4
4–5 years	8.7	9.3	20.7

Notes: [a]Minimum Motivation score = 12; maximum Motivation score = 3.
[b]Minimum incongruity score = 0; maximum incongruity score = 30.
[c]Minimum Alienation score = 10; maximum Alienation score = 40.

Table 5.9   Trends in English Competence, American Relationships, and Use of Mass Media

Length of residence	English competence score[a]	% American relationships			Use of mass media[b]
		Acquaintances	Casual friends	Intimate friends	
0–1 year	5.6	20%	0%	0%	7.9
1–2 years	6.8	22%	15%	20%	10.3
2–3 years	6.8	17%	9%	13%	10.6
3–4 years	9.3	17%	17%	29%	12.1
4–5 years	8.9	50%	20%	25%	12.0

[a]Minimum English competence score = 3; maximum English competence score = 12.
[b]Minimum score for mass media use = 4; maximum score for mass media use = 19.

alienation scores of first-year (24.4) and second-year (24.7) residents increased slightly to 25.9 among third-year residents, but subsequently declined to 22.4 among fourth-year and 20.7 among fifth-year residents.

A similar improvement was observed in English knowledge and skill. The average English Competence score was 5.6 among first-year residents, but 9.3 and 8.9 among fourth- and fifth-year residents. Trends in the refugees' social adaptation showed a similar improvement in both interpersonal and mass communication indicators. For all lengths of residency, the refugees' interpersonal interactions were primarily within their respective ethnic community. However, the ratio of relationships with Americans increased for the longer residents. On the casual friendship level, for example, the percentage of American friends increased from 0 among the first-year residents to 20 among the fifth-year residents. On the intimate friendship level, the percentage changed from 0 to 25. Similarly, the refugees' use of American mass media showed a consistent increase. The composite score for mass media use increased from 7.9 for first-year to 12.0 for fifth-year residents, indicating improvement in their adaptation in general, and in their English competence in particular.

A similar trend was also seen in economic indicators as presented in Table 5.10. A modest improvement was indicated in occupational status for the initial three years of residence, with occupational status greatly enhanced among the fourth-year residents (4.4) and fifth-year residents (4.6). The difference in the respondents' occupational status was particularly substantial between the third- and the fourth-year residents. Similarly, the income level of the respondents showed a steady improvement. The majority (85.0%) of the first-year refugees reported less than $700 as their monthly household income. The proportion of households with less than $700 income, however, declined to 65.1% among second-year residents, and was further reduced to 22.6% among fifth-year residents. At the same time, an overall increase was seen in the proportion of households with more than $1600 per month. Only 2.4% of the total first-year residents reported an income level beyond $1600 per month, compared with 17.2% of the fifth-year residents (data not shown in Table 5.10).

Given the limitations of basing temporal trends on survey data from one point in time, relational analyses were also conducted by computing the first-order Pearson correlation r's between the three dimensions. As indicated in Table 5.11, nearly all correlations between indicators of the personal, social, and economic dimensions were statistically significant. The refugee's self-image, acculturation motivation, and English competence were positively associated with greater interpersonal involvement, mass media use, higher occupational status, and higher income. Also, the perceived discrepancy between themselves and Americans and feelings of alienation were negatively associated with all other social and economic indicators of adaption.

All in all, the results of the trend analyses and the relational analyses suggested that the refugees' personal, social, and economic situations were

---

Table 5.10 Trends in Occupational Status and Household Income

Length of residence	Occupational status[a]	% Refugee households with less than $700 monthly income
0–1 year	2.4	85.0
1–2 years	2.3	65.1
2–3 years	2.8	57.1
3–4 years	4.4	32.1
4–5 years	4.6	22.6

[a]Minimum score of occupational status = 1; maximum score for occupational status = 6.

Table 5.11 Zero-order Correlation Coefficients between Indicators of Adjustment

	Self-image	S-A[a]	Alienation	Accult. motivation	English	American acquaint.	Media use	Occup. status	Income
Self-image	1.00	-.47**	-.37**	.00	.18**	.18**	.18**	.02	.20**
S-A		1.00	.35**	.03	-.30**	-.11*	-.20**	-.08*	-.26**
Alienation			1.00	-.19**	-.37**	-.16**	-.22**	-.11**	-.35**
Acculturation motivation				1.00	.10**	.08*	.00	.08*	.19**
English					1.00	.33**	.48**	.18**	.46**
American acquaintances						1.00	.13**	.13**	.24**
Media use							1.00	.08*	.22**
Occupational status								1.00	.39**
Income									1.00

[a]Perceived discrepancy between Self and Americans.
*Significant at $p < .01$.
**Significant at $p < .001$.

depressed, but were steadily improving over time. The results further indicated that these three dimensions tended to move together in the direction of greater adaptation. The refugees' more positive perceptual, attitudinal, and behavioral orientation accompanied an improved social participation and an improved economic status in American society.

Summary and Conclusions

To briefly reiterate the key findings presented here, this study of 1975–1979 arrivals in Illinois showed highly clustered ethnic residential patterns in urban centers, particularly among new arrivals. The refugee population as a whole was found to be a relatively young group, with more than half under the age of 21. Almost nine out of ten family households were suffering from being separated from, or having lost, at least one family member. The Cambodians and the Hmong were particularly disadvantaged because of their more limited educations. About one in every eight Cambodians and one in every four Hmong had never been formally educated.

Reflecting these conditions and the hardships of encountering the new sociocultural challenges of American society, the refugees as a whole expressed a low self-image (in relation to their image of Americans) and the perception of a large gap between themselves and Americans at large. They were also experiencing a great deal of alienation and a lack of confidence in their ability to understand and use English. These generally depressed psychological orientations, however, were countered by their high acculturation motivation, and their willingness to learn about and adapt to life in the United States.

Socially, the majority of the refugees interacted predominantly with their fellow refugees, particularly on the more intimate levels of relationship, although some limited communication activities occurred with Southeast Asian refugees outside their own ethnic group and with other foreign immigrants. In addition, the refugees did not utilize various American mass media extensively. Newspaper readership was more restricted than the use of television and radio, probably due to the relatively greater language barrier involved in reading newspapers.

Given these personal and social adaptation patterns, it is not surprising to observe the rather limited economic circumstances of the refugees, particularly of the Cambodians and the Hmong. Approximately one-third of the refugees were unemployed and more than half reported a less-than-$700 monthly household income. In the case of both the Cambodians and the Hmong, the unemployment rate was almost 50%, and about 70% reported a monthly income of less than $700.

These descriptive findings show a strong interrelatedness among the three dimensions of adaptation. The trend analyses reinforce this observation by showing close parallels in the developmental patterns of the refugees in all three dimensions. Over the initial five years of residence in the United States, the refugees' overall levels of acculturation motivation, image of self/ others, feeling of alienation, and English competence showed an almost identical trend of gradual improvement. Similarly, their levels of participation in interpersonal and mass communication processes of the American society increased consistently, as did their occupational status and income.

The apparent interrelatedness of the refugees' adaptation experiences in the three dimensions is further supported by the significant statistical associations between indicators of the different dimensions. The greater the refugees' acculturation motivation, self-image, and English competence, the greater their interpersonal and mass communication participation in the American society, and the greater their income and occupational status. Also, the less the refugees' perceived psychological distance between themselves and Americans, and the less extensive their feelings of alienation, the greater their social and economic adaptation.

These findings support the theoretical reasoning that the process of refugee (and immigrant) adaptation involves the total life experience, in which each individual experience sooner or later affects all other aspects of adaptation. Successful adaptation thus means successful adaptation in all three dimensions: a successfully adapted refugee has attained a healthy psychological orientation, an active social participation, and a satisfactory occupation and income. The adaptation process, as such, is multidimensional and interactive, and, by implication, cannot be fully understood when one focuses on only one of the adaptation dimensions without understanding the other interrelated dimensions as well. The psychological, sociological, and other disciplinary approaches to individuals' adaptation must therefore be integrated, so that these approaches as a whole may enable us to offer comprehensive descriptions and explanations of the adaptation process— what happens to individuals as they strive to carry out their life activities in an unfamiliar sociocultural milieu.

At the same time, such interrelatedness allows us to infer many aspects of individuals' adaptive experiences by knowing about only one aspect. We can, for example, predict with reasonable confidence that a refugee who is illiterate and has had no formal education is likely to be less capable of learning the language of the host society, and is more likely to have a low self-image in relation to the host nationals, to have a great sense of alienation, have difficulty in developing close relationships with the host nationals, be unable to use the host mass media, and remain in poverty and in a low status job for a long period. In contrast, a refugee who is highly educated is likely to show a greater facility in adapting to the host environment personally, socially, and economically.

Along the same line of reasoning, service agencies and organizations that focus on any one or more of the critical elements of adaptation—personal, social, and economic—ultimately contribute to all other aspects of adaptation. Job training, for instance, is directly aimed at enhancing the refugees' employability. Once the refugees succeed in securing employment, they are also likely to succeed in improving their internal, psychological orientation, and their language skill, as well as their participation in American society. Conversely, serious impairment in any one of the adaptation dimensions leads to impairment of all other elements. A serious problem in a refugee's self-image or the inability to obtain a stable income, for instance, is likely to negatively influence all other personal, social, and economic aspects of life.

In the end, it is largely the refugees themselves who determine their adaptation. It is a matter of their conscious (or unconscious) decisions that contribute to the extent to which they will accomplish their own life goals in the United States. If they hope to become functional members of American society, they must work toward improving the individual aspect(s) of their personal, social, and economic conditions, and, ultimately, toward creating an integrated adaptation of all these dimensions. They must do so with as much determination and dedication as they can muster. The history of the United States is filled with stories of successful immigrants and refugees who have willingly and courageously overcome the many challenges of the new environment. The Southeast Asian refugees, in particular, have demonstrated an ample amount of this willingness and resilience. With active learning and participation, they promise an enormous success in pursuit of an "American dream" of their own.

Notes

1. The figures on the number of Southeast Asian refugees in the United States were based on the information reported in APWA (1979).
2. Research reports in other states available at the time of the present study were Aames et al. 1977, and Sedanko and Tutchings 1978.
3. Readers interested in obtaining copies of this five-volume report should contact the Illinois Department of Public Aid, Office for Employment and Social Services, Refugee Resettlement Program, 624 South Michigan Avenue, Chicago, Illinois 60605, or the author.
4. The categorization of occupational status was based on the scheme employed by the Bureau of the Census (cf. U.S. Bureau of the Census 1979:43).

6

The Indochinese Refugee Experience: The Case of San Diego

Paul J. Strand

This chapter describes the results of a study of Indochinese refugees who resettled in San Diego, California between April 1975 and June 1981. The study, conducted in July 1981, was designed to document the background, experience, current status, and resettlement needs of these refugees. The study grew out of a joint effort between the Social Science Research Laboratory at San Diego State University and ACCESS, a San Diego area private service provider contracted by the State of California to provide services to Indochinese refugees. The effort resulted in modest funding from the Regional Employment and Training Consortium for a needs assessment survey of San Diego area Indochinese refugees. The in-person interviews provided information on demographics, household composition, labor force participation, level of English communication skills, awareness and utilization of resettlement services, health status and health service utilization, and acculturation. The objective in obtaining this information was to identify existing resettlement barriers, anticipated resettlement needs, and the current resettlement status of this population.

San Diego is an excellent venue for studying the resettlement of Indochinese refugees. Of the approximately 500,000 Indochinese refugees who resettled in the United States between April 1975 and June 1981, approximately 200,000 resettled in California and an estimated 30,000 resettled in San Diego. San Diego has not only been a major resettlement location for Indochinese refugees, its refugee population includes sizable communities from each of the four major ethnic groups.

Since the findings from this survey have already been presented in descriptive report and in academic monograph format, the following discussion presents sequential and very general overviews of the inevitable sampling problems faced in survey work on refugees, the basic design of the survey, and the general findings, with particular emphasis on differences by ethnicity and year of arrival. Concluding remarks will address the problems experienced with subsequent utilization of the data.

Sampling

The primary obstacle in identifying the San Diego Indochinese refugee population was the absence of a complete, reliable, current, and accessible population list. Recognizing this constraint, three criteria were used to evaluate alternative population lists. First, the list had to be current in order to include usable addresses for early arrivals, recent arrivals, and secondary migrants. Second, the list could not systematically exclude certain groups of refugees (e.g., employed refugees, early arrivals). Third, the list had to be accessible. Some lists are protected by the Privacy Act and could not be released. A variety of sampling strategies was considered in light of these criteria. Among them were Immigration and Naturalization Services (INS) alien registration files, English-as-a-Second Language (ESL) class rosters, Indochinese Mutual Assistance Association (IMAA) membership rosters, private service provider participant lists, Indochinese Orientation and Employment Program (IOEP) participant lists, Voluntary Resettlement Agency (VOLAG) user lists, and the local telephone directory.

The Indochinese Orientation and Employment Program (IOEP) was operated by the San Diego County Welfare department. It consisted primarily of job counselling and job placement services. Refugees who applied for public assistance were required to enroll in IOEP as a condition of receiving the assistance. Although participation in IOEP (current and past) was believed to be quite high, the use of these files as a population list would systematically undersample refugees who were self-sufficient. Self-sufficient refugees would not be included in closed IOEP files. And, though they may be included in closed 10EP files, these files would not likely include current addresses or telephone numbers. Furthermore, closed files were likely to include refugees who were no longer living in the San Diego area.

As refugees were eligible to receive a number of services from private service providers, private service provider user lists were also considered as a possible population list from which to draw a sample. However, these lists were rejected. They would undersample refugees who were not currently receiving services. In addition, private service provider lists were subject to duplication as refugees could receive services simultaneously from a number of different providers.

Indochinese Mutual Assistance Associations were organizations composed of, and managed by, refugees. Many refugees joined these organizations to exchange experiences and obtain resettlement information from members of their own ethnic community. Each major ethnic group had at least one IMAA organization. The Vietnamese community included a number of them. However, the extent to which IMAA membership lists were complete was assumed to vary considerably from one ethnic group to another. The Vietnamese lists were assumed to be the least complete. Because the Vietnamese represent a large proportion of San Diego's Indochinese refugee community, and because it was impossible to determine the differences between IMAA members and nonmembers, a decision was made not to use the IMAA lists.

User lists from the Voluntary Resettlement Agencies (VOLAGS) were considered but were found to be dated and did not contain secondary migrants. These agencies were responsible for the initial resettlement of refugees. After initial resettlement, refugees were directed to other agencies to obtain further assistance and services. Since early arrivals may have relocated since their last VOLAG contact, and since secondary migrants would not have contacted a local VOLAG, the use of VOLAG lists would have resulted in an undersampling of early arrivals and secondary migrants. This was the primary reason for rejecting VOLAG files as a primary population list.

Current and past English-as-a-Second Language (ESL) class rosters were considered a potential population list because the classes were widely attended by Indochinese refugees. In addition, ESL class rosters were assumed to include representative samples of secondary migrants and recent arrivals. Although the addresses of early arrivals (from past ESL rosters) were not expected to be current if ESL classes were no longer being attended, this was not the primary reason for rejecting this as a population list. An extensive review of ESL class rosters indicated that the procedure for storing participant information had changed in 1978. Prior to 1978, re-enrollment would appear as a multiple entry in the list. This practice would make it very difficult to ensure that each refugee had an equal probability of being included in a sample. Furthermore, the rosters often included persons who were not Indochinese refugees.

The telephone directory was considered (and ultimately selected) as a population list. The major problem posed by use of the directory was completeness. If refugees did not generally have access to a telephone, a population list generated from the telephone directory would not be representative of the entire population. If they did have access, the telephone directory could be assured to be current, as it is revised every year. It could also be assumed to be nonexclusive of secondary migrants or early arrivals because migration and arrival status were not criteria for obtaining a telephone.

The issue of access was investigated by reviewing service provider lists. These lists contained data on telephone access. The review indicated that approximately 90% of the refugees on these lists were able to specify a current telephone number. Recent arrivals were given special attention in this regard because they were assumed to be the least likely to have access to a telephone. In this case, representatives from local VOLAG offices indicated that most recent arrivals had telephones because telephones were considered necessary for communication. Indeed, installation deposits for telephones were often subsidized by VOLAG agencies.

The only remaining problem with the use of the telephone directory was the inclusion of the most recent arrivals in the list. The most recent telephone directory available at the time of the study (June 1981) was published in January 1981 and included new listings through October 1980. Arrivals between November 1980 and June 1981 could not possibly be included in the telephone directory. This problem was resolved by obtaining from each area VOLAG the numbers of refugees that had resettled between December 1980 and June 1981. This number was then figured as a proportion of the estimated number of refugees presently living in San Diego (20,000). By these calculations, approximately 10% of the San Diego refugee population had arrived since November 1980. The same proportion was included in the final sample of 800 by randomly selecting 80 respondents from VOLAG lists of refugees who had been resettled between November 1980 and June 1981. Thus, the final sample included 720 respondents drawn from the telephone directory and 80 respondents drawn from VOLAG lists of refugees resettled since November 1980. The only refugees excluded by this technique were secondary refugees who had no telephone or an unlisted telephone number. Given the alternatives, this approach was determined to be the least biased.

The process of extracting names, addresses, and telephone numbers of refugees from the telephone directory was simplified by the fact that their names were easily identifiable according to the ethnic group to which they belong (Vietnamese, Lao, Lao-Hmong, Cambodian). Accordingly, those who were hired to translate the survey instruments were also instructed to review every entry in the telephone directory and record each entry from the ethnic group for which they were translating. The results of each review were rechecked on a random basis for completeness. The resulting lists were maintained as separate ethnic group files.

The total number of refugee names, addresses, and telephone numbers obtained by this process is given for each ethnic group in Table 6.1. It was assumed that each entry would represent one household and at least one family unit (more than one family unit would be represented in cases where different families shared the same household and telephone).

The VOLAG list for recent arrivals differed from the telephone list in that it contained individuals rather than households. As stated above, the two

Table 6.1   Ethnic Distribution of Refugees from the Telephone Directory

	Vietnamese	Lao	Hmong	Cambodian	All groups
Percent	63.7	13.5	9.8	13.0	100.0
Total N	1,091	231	168	222	1,712

lists were merged by assuming that there were 20,000 refugees in San Diego. The VOLAG lists from November 1980 to June 1981 contained 2,062 entries or approximately 10% of the entire population. Thus, 10% of the 800 respondents were selected from the VOLAG list. The ethnic distribution from the VOLAG list is given in Table 6.2. (Note that the percentage of Vietnamese had dropped considerably among the more recent arrivals.) Entries were drawn at random from both lists to obtain a final sample of 800.

The results of the sampling procedure, the composition of the final sample, and response, are given in Table 6.3. The Vietnamese had the lowest completion rate and were the most likely to have disconnected numbers. They were also the most likely to have moved. The completion rates for the other groups were extremely high.

Table 6.2 Ethnic Distribution of Refugees Identified from Voluntary Agency Lists (VOLAG)

	Vietnamese	Lao/Hmong	Cambodian	All groups
Percent	40.8	37.2	21.9	100.0
Total N	842	768	452	2,062

Table 6.3 Sampling Procedure Results

	Vietnamese	Lao	Hmong	Cambodian	All groups
Attempted	644	203	114	144	1,105
Completed	430	160	100	110	800
Completed: telephone list	397	140	90	93	720
Completed: VOLAG	33	20	10	17	80
Refusals	55	2	2	3	62
Disconnects	59	4	1	7	71
Moved	47	24	3	7	81
Unable to connect*	53	13	8	17	91
Completion rate: percent attempted	65.7%	78.8%	87.7%	76.4%	72.3%
percent completed	87.2%	98.7%	98.0%	97.3%	92.3%

*After four attempts to make telephone contact

Research Design

This study was based on personal interviews with 800 heads of refugee households. The interviews were to be conducted in the primary language of the respondent by an interviewer who shared the respondent's ethnic identity. A number of atypical interviewing problems were anticipated in this study and were addressed in the development of the questionnaire that was used in the interviews. For example, it was assumed that respondents would be relunctant to answer some of the more important questions given their uncertain residency status and lack of exposure to U.S. political and judicial customs. It was also assumed that the cultural background of refugee families would interfere with the identification of respondents who would be most capable of providing useful information on the economic self-support aspect of the resettlement experience. Many of the design procedures described below were intended to solve these and other problems.

In order to minimize the risk of including items that would be offensive to respondents or excluding items relevant to refugee needs, an Advisory Committee was established to review early drafts of the questionnaire. This committee was composed of representatives from San Diego Community College District's ESL program, local Indochinese Mutual Assistance Associations, Voluntary Resettlement Agencies, the County Welfare Department's Indochinese Orientation and Employment Program (IOEP), the state's Employment Development Department, and local private service providers. Community leaders from each of the four major ethnic groups were included on the committee in one or another of these capacities. The committee held five monthly meetings to review the drafts of the questionnaire and recommend five major revisions. Their recommendations were reflected in the final draft of the questionnaire.

The final draft of the English language version of the questionnaire was translated into Lao, Cambodian, and Vietnamese by experienced translators. These translations were then reviewed by a second team of translators. When a disagreement in translation occurred, a third translator was included and the item was discussed until a consensus was reached on item syntax and semantics. Finally, the interviewers were asked to review both the English and the primary language versions of the questionnaire to determine whether or not the versions conveyed the same information. If disagreement appeared at this stage, a discussion of the item was reopened until a consensus once again was established.

The questionnaire was designed to be administered to one member of each selected household. It was decided that the most appropriate person to interview would be the person who was primarily responsible for the support of the household. However, this person may not always be considered by members of the household to be the head of household, particularly in cases where the oldest male in the household is handicapped or unemployed. In order to avoid giving offense in a situation where cultural norms require deference to head of household, the interviewers were instructed to make initial contact with the culturally designated head of household. If the head of household was not the member most responsible for support, the interviewer then identified another household member to be interviewed.

In addition to providing extensive information on the household member designated to be responsible for the household's economic self-support, the questionnaire provided some information on all other household members. This information was not extensive, but included employment status, demographics, and awareness and utilization of resettlement services. It was assumed that this information would provide a valuable insight into employment barriers related to sex, age, and family structure.

The procedure outlined above generated a result that closely reflected the objective of interviewing the person most responsible for the support of the household. Of the respondents 84.4% were male and 15.6% were female. Of the male respondents 88.6% were the oldest male member of the household; 97.6% of the households with male respondents contained no older male who was currently employed. Half (50.4%) of the female respondents were the oldest member of the household, while 86.4% of the households with female respondents contained no older employed member.

Overview of Survey Findings

The survey thus provides information, mostly on household heads, about the Southeast Asian refugee population in one specific locality at a key point in the history of this influx, well into the so-called second wave of resettlement, but before the effects of the recession became extreme. This section provides an overview of the findings regarding the nature of the population, their language competence and employment situation, and the problems they perceived—the data for which appear in more detail in the accompanying series of tables.

Table 6.4 describes the relationship between ethnicity and year of arrival among those interviewed. The Vietnamese were more likely than members of other ethnic groups to be early arrivals; Lao and Cambodians were predominantly later arrivals. The mean household size for each group is given in Table 6.5. The Vietnamese have the smallest households and the Hmong have the largest. The size of Hmong households is due to larger nuclear families as well as larger numbers of extended family members. As Table 6.6 indicates, San Diego was the initial resettlement location for 75% of the respondents, with another 8% being secondary migrants from other places in California. The remaining 17% were thus initially resettled outside California—the figure was much higher for the Vietnamese than the other groups.

Table 6.4   Number of Households by Ethnicity and Year of Arrival

	Vietnamese	Lao	Hmong	Cambodian	All groups
1975	28.8%	1.9%	0.0%	4.5%	16.5%
1976	0.2%	3.8%	19.0%	9.1%	4.5%
1977	2.3%	0.6%	1.0%	0.0%	1.5%
1978	10.0%	11.9%	19.0%	8.2%	11.3%
1979	28.6%	29.4%	27.0%	39.0%	30.0%
1980	22.1%	35.6%	34.0%	26.4%	26.9%
1981	7.9%	16.9%	0.0%	12.7%	9.4%
Total N	430	160	100	110	800

Table 6.5   Mean Household Size by Ethnicity and Household Type

	Vietnamese	Lao	Hmong	Cambodian	All groups
Nuclear family	4.10	4.83	5.32	4.51	4.46
Extended family	0.90	1.73	2.71	0.83	1.29
Nonfamily	0.27	0.24	0.03	0.48	0.26
Mean household	5.28	6.81	8.07	5.84	6.02
Total N	2246	1053	810	649	4758

Table 6.6   Initial Resettlement Location by Ethnicity

	Vietnamese	Lao	Hmong	Cambodian	All groups
San Diego	70.5%	76.3%	86.0%	82.7%	75.3%
California other than San Diego	8.1%	9.4%	4.0%	8.2%	7.9%
States other than California	21.4%	14.3%	10.0%	9.1%	16.8%
Total N	430	160	100	110	800

The issue of English language communication skills is addressed in Table 6.7. Approximately half of the refugees indicated they were capable of completing an English language job application. The Vietnamese respondents were the most likely to be literate, and the Cambodians the least likely. Some of the differences in literacy are most certainly related to length of residence, as literacy levels increased from 24% among the more recent arrivals to 87% among the early arrivals (see Table 6.8).

Labor force participation and employment rates among this population do

Table 6.7   Ability to Fill Out Job Application or Write Letter in English by Ethnicity

	Vietnamese	Lao	Hmong	Cambodian	All groups
Able	57.0%	48.1%	41.0%	32.7%	49.9%
Not able	42.6%	50.6%	59.0%	67.3%	49.6%
No answer	0.5%	1.3%	0.0%	0.0%	0.5%
Total N	430	160	100	110	800

Table 6.8   Ability to Fill Out Job Application or Write Letter in English by Year of Arrival

	1975	1976	1977	1978	1979	1980	1981	Overall
Able	87.1%	94.4%	75.0%	47.8%	42.5%	36.3%	24.0%	49.9%
Not able	12.1%	5.6%	25.0%	52.2%	56.7%	63.3%	76.0%	49.6%
No answer	0.8%	0.0%	0.0%	0.0%	0.8%	0.5%	0.0%	0.5%
Total N	132	36	12	90	240	215	75	800

Table 6.9   Employment Status by Year of Arrival

	1975	1976	1977	1978	1979	1980	1981	Overall
Employed	81.1%	77.8%	66.7%	47.8%	35.0%	15.3%	1.3%	38.0%
Unemployed, seeking employment	6.1%	11.1%	25.0%	20.0%	27.1%	27.9%	5.3%	20.3%
Unemployed, not seeking	12.1%	5.6%	8.3%	30.0%	34.5%	53.0%	92.0%	39.0%
Don't know/ no answer	0.8%	5.6%	0.0%	2.2%	3.3%	3.7%	1.3%	2.8%
Total N	132	36	12	90	240	215	75	800

not differ from those reported in other studies. Table 6.9 presents data on these rates by year of arrival. Among the more recent arrivals, unemployment was high and participation in the labor force was low, while among the earlier arrivals, the opposite was true. Ethnic differences in employment are given in Table 6.10. The differences in these figures are almost certainly related in part to length of residence. Nevertheless, the Cambodians seem to have a different pattern than the other three groups. Specifically, employment for them appears to be more difficult to obtain. The overall impression from the data is that the refugees are adapting very well in a relatively short period of time. However, the experience of the recent arrivals may not be

Table 6.10 Employment Status by Ethnicity

	Vietnamese	Lao	Hmong	Cambodian	All groups
Employed	43.0%	35.0%	42.0%	19.1%	38.0%
Unemployed, seeking employment	16.3%	22.5%	23.0%	30.0%	20.3%
Unemployed, not seeking	40.0%	41.3%	33.0%	37.3%	39.0%
Don't know/ no answer	0.7%	1.3%	2.0%	13.6%	2.8%
Total N	430	160	100	110	800

Table 6.11 Reason for Not Seeking Employment by Year of Arrival

	1975	1976	1977	1978	1979	1980	1981	All groups
None	5.9%	0.0%	100.0%	3.4%	9.9%	6.6%	12.9%	8.7%
Illness	35.3%	0.0%	0.0%	24.1%	12.1%	3.3%	2.9%	9.0%
Child care	11.8%	25.0%	0.0%	27.6%	11.0%	1.6%	4.3%	7.8%
Do not speak English	5.9%	0.0%	0.0%	20.7%	39.6%	57.4%	40.0%	42.2%
Other	41.2%	25.0%	0.0%	17.2%	13.2%	19.7%	12.9%	17.4%
Don't know/ no answer	0.0%	50.0%	0.0%	6.9%	14.3%	11.5%	27.1%	15.0%
Total N applicable	17	4	1	29	91	122	70	334

the same as that of the early arrivals. In general, the more recent arrivals did not have the same skills as the earlier ones and so could not be expected to obtain employment as easily.

The initial importance of English language ability to labor force participation—a common theme in the wider research—is suggested by the data presented in Tables 6.11 and 6.12. These tables describe responses to the question "Is there any reason why you are not looking for a job?" Among the more recent arrivals, English language ability was cited for about half of the decisions not to seek employment. Among the earlier arrivals, health status and childcare were of greater importance. As Table 6.12 indicates, the Hmong felt especially limited by English language literacy problems. More than three-quarters of them cited poor English as the reason for not seeking employment.

To gain a better understanding of what refugees themselves perceived to be their most serious problems in resettlement, respondents were asked to

Table 6.12 Reason for Not Seeking Employment by Ethnicity

	Vietnamese	Lao	Hmong	Cambodian	All groups
None	2.3%	23.5%	2.9%	14.3%	8.7%
Illness	12.6%	0.0%	5.7%	10.7%	9.0%
Child care	13.7%	0.0%	2.9%	1.8%	7.8%
English	40.0%	20.6%	77.1%	53.6%	42.2%
Other	29.1%	0.0%	8.6%	7.1%	17.4%
Don't know/ no answer	2.3%	55.9%	2.9%	12.5%	15.0%
Total N applicable	175	68	35	56	334

rank the seriousness of ten potential resettlement problems. Table 6.13 presents the overall means and rankings for each ethnic group. The most serious problems noted were personal adjustment problems: English language skills, separation from families, and war memories. These types of problems are predictable for migrants who are forced to leave their homeland during a war. Nevertheless, the ranking of problems is not uniform for all the ethnic groups. For example, the violence and destruction of war

Table 6.13 Perceived Problems in Adaptation

	Vietnamese		Lao		Cambodian		Hmong	
	Mean	Rank	Mean	Rank	Mean	Rank	Mean	Rank
Not enough money	1.377	1	1.579	4	2.700	9	1.020	1
Separation from family	1.432	2	1.706	5	1.091	2	1.270	6
War memories	1.509	3	1.974	10	1.064	1	1.515	10
English language	2.123	4	1.866	1	1.355	3	1.060	4
Lack of help getting a job	1.564	5	1.520	3	2.037	6	1.060	4
Lack of job skill	1.908	6	1.345	2	1.891	5	1.040	2
Lack of child care services	2.015	7	1.973	9	2.879	10	1.394	7
Transportation problems	2.080	8	1.809	6	2.560	8	1.470	8
Difficulty understanding American life	2.123	9	1.866	7	2.355	7	1.091	9
Difficulty with American agencies	2.162	10	1.879	8	1.752	4	1.182	5

appeared to have left a relatively stronger mark on many Cambodian and Vietnamese refugees, and the Hmong and Vietnamese seemed more likely than the Lao and Cambodians to view money problems as a primary concern.

Ethnic differences in adaptation are also indicated in the data presented in Tables 6.14 and 6.15. These tables indicate the sources refugees used to obtain information on employment and living at the time of interviews and when they first arrived in the United States. In terms of locating a job, none of the Hmong relied on their own efforts, and two in five didn't know where to go to get information on jobs. The Vietnamese and Lao were considerably more self-reliant. In terms of learning about living in San Diego, a somewhat similar pattern emerged. Although self-reliance was higher among the Hmong, nearly half of them did not know where they would go to get assistance. The other groups initially depended most heavily on friends and relatives and were, at the time the survey was conducted, more likely to rely on their own efforts. These data are presented in Table 6.15.

Two extensive multivariate analyses of these data have also been conducted, and are reported elsewhere (Strand 1984, Strand and Jones 1985). One focused on health services utilization, and the other on employment. The results of these analyses are consistent with the impressions given in this descriptive status summary. Specifically, both analyses indicated major ethnic differences in utilization and employment status. In a several-variable model of health services utilization, the best predictor of physician contact was ethnicity. The Hmong were significantly less likely than other refugees to have visited a physician, despite the fact that they generally perceived their health status to be worse. Ethnicity was also a major variable in the employment model, although some of its initial effect was explained by such other variables as length of residence and English language communication skills. The importance of English was also evident in the employment model, but failed to play a major role in explaining health services utilization.

Conclusions

These data provide an image of San Diego's Indochinese refugee population as it existed in 1981. The image is complex. There are both major shared problems and major differences. English language communication skills are a major shared problem, but do not affect all groups to the same extent. The data also indicate a pattern of assimilation and economic self-sufficiency that is encouraging. Communication skills, labor force participation and employment do appear to increase with length of residence. However, differences between recent and early arrivals imply a need for caution in predicting a continuation of that same pattern. There is no doubt that recent arrivals do not come with the same preparation as did their predecessors. The different

Table 6.14 Assistance in Locating Jobs by Ethnicity

	Vietnamese		Lao		Hmong		Cambodian		All groups	
	Past	Present	Past	Present	Past	Present	Past	Present	Past	Present
Government agencies	6.0%	1.9%	10.0%	6.3%	12.0%	4.0%	2.7%	3.6%	7.1%	3.3%
Private agencies	16.3%	4.2%	24.4%	5.0%	33.0%	21.0%	21.8%	14.5%	20.8%	7.9%
Relatives, friends	11.6%	7.4%	12.5%	7.5%	11.0%	19.0%	20.0%	20.0%	12.9%	10.6%
Self	28.1%	54.9%	18.8%	21.3%	2.0%	0.0%	0.9%	2.7%	19.3%	34.1%
Don't know/no one	24.0%	19.5%	12.5%	13.8%	26.0%	42.0%	20.0%	19.1%	21.4%	21.1%
Others	14.0%	12.1%	21.8%	46.1%	16.0%	14.0%	34.6%	40.1%	18.5%	23.0%
No answer	9.3%	10.5%	18.8%	44.4%	12.0%	14.0%	22.7%	29.1%	13.4%	20.3%
Total N	430	430	160	160	100	100	110	110	800	800

Table 6.15 Assistance in Learning about Living in San Diego by Ethnicity

	Vietnamese		Lao		Hmong		Cambodian		All groups	
	Past	Present	Past	Present	Past	Present	Past	Present	Past	Present
Government agencies	0.5%	0.5%	1.3%	1.3%	0.0%	0.0%	1.8%	1.8%	0.8%	0.8%
Private agencies	17.4%	1.9%	28.1%	8.1%	14.0%	9.0%	28.2%	16.4%	20.6%	6.0%
Relatives, friends	43.7%	21.4%	63.1%	51.3%	15.0%	20.0%	36.4%	27.3%	43.0%	28.0%
Self	27.2%	64.0%	50.0%	3.8%	23.0%	17.0%	20.0%	30.9%	21.3%	41.5%
Don't know/no one	0.5%	0.7%	0.0%	3.1%	40.0%	45.0%	0.9%	0.9%	5.4%	6.8%
Others	10.7%	11.5%	0.0%	32.4%	8.0%	9.0%	12.7%	22.7%	8.9%	16.9%
No answer	0.0%	0.0%	0.0%	30.0%	3.0%	7.0%	1.8%	13.6%	0.6%	8.8%
Total N	430	430	160	160	100	100	110	110	800	800

perspectives that emerge among the various ethnic groups also suggest that resettlement programs need to be sensitive to ethnicity; what works for one group may not be effective for another.

A number of barriers were encountered in the utilization of these data by San Diego's resettlement program. Some were organizational and others were substantive. First, there is little evidence that the findings were disseminated to either policy makers or those involved in the implementation of refugee policy on a local level. Why? The report was massive and largely descriptive and was not well organized to serve those who are already overcommitted. In addition, the study was not tied to specific policies or policy outcomes, so it was not directly and immediately relevant to most refugee policy makers and administrators. The study covered, on a general level, a wide range of issues. The nature of the coverage would likely be of more interest to scholars of immigration and forced migration than to resettlement administrators. Such problems might have been avoided by having greater participation of policy makers and administrators at the development stage and by a more streamlined presentation of results.

On a substantive level, the study did not reveal any specific, major policy elements to which economic self-sufficiency or successful adaptation could be attributed. The data on job placement and job training utilization exhibited no relationships with employment status. Refugees who used the services were employed at about the same level as those who did not use them. Awareness was related to employment—those without jobs were more aware of services than those with jobs. But the relationships were not strong. There is simply no major, clear finding on program effectiveness or ineffectiveness that comes out of this study.

The study does, however, reveal several facts that, although assumed to be true by most people involved in refugee resettlement, could not be known with the precision that the study allows. First, English is a major problem. But, its importance diminishes with time. The program focus on ESL training receives major support from this study though the specific design of such programs is not addressed. Second, refugees are obtaining employment in a relatively short period of time. They are apparently using whatever resources they need to make themselves employable. Third, there are major differences between the refugee groups. The Hmong are extremely vulnerable and uncomfortable with their present situation. The Vietnamese are more adaptive. These are perhaps the not-too-surprising results that the study provided.

In sum, utilization of these data is limited by weak program identification and weak program effects. It is also limited by the tedious presentation of a large amount of data, a presentation that may be responsible for limited dissemination and use. If there is a lesson to be learned from this effort, it would be the need to establish a closer relationship among researchers and administrators, a more detailed specification of objectives, and a more critical appraisal of design relative to those objectives. These would most certainly enhance the potential uses of the data for those most directly involved in resettlement.

7

The Socio-Cultural Basis for the Economic and Educational Success of Southeast Asian Refugees (1978–1982 Arrivals)

John K. Whitmore, Marcella Trautmann, and Nathan Caplan

The Institute for Social Research (ISR) of the University of Michigan conducted two surveys among Vietnamese, Chinese, and Lao refugees from Southeast Asia who lived in five sites: Boston, Chicago, Houston, Seattle, and Orange County, California.[1] The first of these two surveys was contracted by the Office of Refugee Resettlement (ORR) of the Department of Health and Human Services for an examination of the economic self-sufficiency among Southeast Asian refugees who had arrived from October 1, 1978 to November 1, 1982, and took place in the summer and fall of 1982. This survey included interviews with 1,384 adults, aged 16 years and older, in an equal number of households that contained a total of 4,160 adults and 2,615 children (under 16 years of age). Of the respondents, 50% were Vietnamese, 30% were Lao, and 20% were Chinese.

Using these 1,384 households as the source, we derived the second survey, funded by a grant from the Spencer Foundation of Chicago, to examine the scholastic achievement of the Southeast Asian refugee children, and reinterviewed 200 households. The interviews took place in the summer and fall of 1984 with one adult from each household (not necessarily the same respondent as before, since we wanted to interview a parent of the child). Later, we mailed questionnaires to children eleven years and older in the interviewed households. Of the households, 48% were Vietnamese, 27% were Lao, and 25% were Chinese.

Our work has created a large data base on the major segment of the second wave of Southeast Asian refugees. Dunning, Roberts and Starr, and Strand in this volume cover from the first wave of 1975 into the early second wave (1979, 1980, or 1981). Only in 1985 did ORR's survey look at a period similar to ours (see Gordon in this volume). Our work examined Vietnamese,

Chinese, and Lao, while the others focus either on the Vietnamese (with the Chinese mixed in) or include the other refugee groups as well (particularly the Khmer and the Hmong). The second-wave refugees are much more diverse ethnically, socially, religiously, and educationally, than the first wave.

Where others have examined the day-to-day problems many of the refugees have had, we have chosen to concentrate on the general pattern of refugee achievement. Overall, we have found these refugees to be making their way successfully in our society—the adults in the world of work, the children in the schools. Why this is so leads to examinations of the cultural and social systems and values brought by the refugees from their homeland to these shores. The maintenance of these systems in this country, we would argue, has enabled the refugee to "get ahead" in our world. The chapter necessarily begins, however, with the complexities of data collection.

Data Collection

To examine the economic self-sufficiency and scholastic standing of the refugees, we recruited local interviewers in the five sites and sent them into the refugee communities. The interviews for both surveys were undertaken in the respondent's native language (Vietnamese, Chinese, or Lao) by a native speaker of the language. The questionnaires had been translated into each language with much input from the interviewers as part of their training. For the first survey, the interviews averaged around 1 hour 45 minutes and supplied data on the following topics: *household information,* background information on each household member; *employment,* jobs and employment facts and history on each person in the labor force; *nonemployment,* data on all household members not in the labor force; *income,* data on income from all sources other than employment; *expenses,* data on household needs and strategies to become self-sufficient; *English ability,* fluency level and participation in English classes; *use of program services,* types and degree of involvement in assistance services; *health,* health problems and care; and, *attitudes and behavior,* perceptions of problems faced in resettlement. Economic self-sufficiency was gauged on the refugees' reported income.

The second set of interviews averaged 1½ hours on these subjects: *cultural values,* assessment of the relative importance of a set of values and goal items; *neighbors' perception,* perceived characteristics of nonrefugee neighbors and other Americans; *locus of control,* degree of perceived control over events that affect one's future, particularly with regard to educational achievements; *family roles and parenting,* role-sharing, decision-making and division of labor among family members; *background demographics,* more explicit data on SES-related items than was obtained in the first interview; and, *economic update,* changes in economic status and workforce participation. For this second survey we also obtained parental permission to see school transcripts. This allowed us to determine objectively the scholastic achievement of the refugee students.[2]

A key aspect of our data collection is the manner in which we drew our sample from the refugee community in each of our five sites. Some detail on the sampling is in order to illustrate the representative nature of the data for these refugee communities.

Our method of sampling differs from that of the other studies in that it used a dual frame. Where other studies began their sample by drawing on official records or other documentation (including telephone books), we also went into neighborhoods to seek out refugees. We tried to stay away from "convenience" or "availability" sampling to obtain as random a sample as possible. This dual sample frame included: (1) lists comprised of data from government agencies, voluntary agencies (Volags), mutual assistance organizations, and support service organizations; and (2) area probability frames. Lists of refugees maintained for administrative purposes offered certain initial advantages. They could provide respondent addresses and additional information, such as date of arrival and ethnicity, which could be used to organize the sample.

In each of the five sites, an effort was made to determine what administrative lists existed, their completeness, their currency and their availability. After obtaining the lists, we estimated (1) the proportion of the site universe covered by the names on all the lists, (2) the proportion of the site universe covered by the names on each individual list, and (3) the extent of overlap among lists. Such information provided the basis for developing procedures to select respondents from each list. After the sampling procedures were instituted and interviewing began, the information from the lists was continually updated to improve the accuracy of our probability estimates and the area probability frames for each site.

To make certain that there were enough people who used refugee service programs in the sample, we initially oversampled service provider lists and weighted these subsamples when aggregating the data. Often there were statistical and practical problems associated with using the lists. Each list provided only partial coverage of the study population. Furthermore, the addresses and other information provided on the lists might not be current, and concerns about confidentiality either prevented the staff from getting access to lists or required that the agency contact the eligible respondents to find out if they would be willing to be included in the sample.

Having encountered such difficulties, it became necessary to resort to area probability sampling earlier and more heavily than originally expected. The area frame is a consistent, well structured tool for developing probability samples of general household populations. However, it is costly and time consuming. It requires the use of household enumeration and screening methods. With the aid of disproportionate sampling methods, the efficiency of the household screening can be improved, but it still remains a relatively costly and time-consuming procedure. If conducted properly, the area frame approach provides the best coverage of the survey population and permits more generalizable findings and safer inferences. In studies like the present one, where lists for a variety of reasons had their limits, the area probability approach is the only supplemental sampling procedure that should be relied upon to increase scientific integrity. Thus at each site, when the limits of available lists were reached, or if conditions precluded the practical use of lists, the staff shifted to area probability sampling.

Theoretically, area probability methods offer complete coverage by identifying areas where persons with certain similiar characteristics can be linked (usually through their area of primary residence). Most probability samples are stratified multi-stage cluster samples. The samples are stratified into distinct groups and each group is sampled independently to improve the precision of the estimates. The design ensures that each of the groups is presented in the sample in the proper proportion.

In our first survey, those proportions were determined on the basis of the degree and type of success achieved by sampling from lists by site. The multi-stage cluster nature of the sample refers to the successive sampling and subsampling of area units in order to group sample persons close together. Such stratification was used in the study to locate areas within each site containing high-, medium-, and low-level densities of eligible persons. The team used local informants and telephone books to develop this information and relied on community leaders to spread the word about the nature and value of the survey. We then chose square block segments and sampled therein.

There is variation from site to site in the percentages of respondents drawn from the List Frame and the Area Probability Sample. In the original survey, two sites had higher percentages of respondents drawn from list frames (mainly from local affiliates of voluntary agencies): Boston had 65% and Seattle 60%. In Houston and Chicago, the percentages were almost equal and in one site, Orange County, a higher percentage of respondents (65%) came from an area probability sample. No site had its respondents drawn totally from either list frame or area probability sample.

The procedures used for listing households and for determining eligible respondents were worked out with the individual agencies. The actual enumerations and screenings were conducted by the interviewers under the supervision of field coordinators and university-based staff. The problem of determining how many and which persons should be interviewed by area probability procedures was based on the success of the list sampling frame at each site. We believe that relying more heavily upon the area probability sampling and reducing dependency upon available lists for selection helped reduce error. Any departure that increases the amount of area frame over list frame is generally a positive step in achieving optimal allocation to dual frame designs. Out of necessity, we had to take that step in order to locate eligible respondents. We then applied the relevant statistical analysis to determine the differences between weighted and unweighted results for our assorted sources. Because the results were virtually the same, we chose to conduct the analyses of the study using unweighted procedures.

The result was the 1,384 interviews, approximately 300 each from four of the sites with only Houston falling short. For the second survey, we took the 781 households with at least one school-age child for the academic year 1983–1984, and then chose the 200 households by random probability procedures.

How representative is the sample of the refugee communities of the Vietnamese, Lao, and Sino-Vietnamese in the United States? This is difficult to say. The site selection procedure focused on counties having high concentrations of Southeast Asian refugees, and the five sites are all urban or suburban areas. The sample appears to be fairly representative of the Vietnamese, Lao, and Sino-Vietnamese who live in large American cities and their surburban areas. The results of this survey may not carry over to refugees living in medium and small towns or in rural areas. Nevertheless, the data base reveals a great amount of commonality among the refugees across all five sites and, therefore, suggests greater generalizability than was originally foreseen.

Refugee Achievement

The magnitude of the difficulties these refugees faced in seeking to settle and survive in this country may be inferred from a statistical description of some of their characteristics. About one in four adults (26%) had completed a high school education, and one in two (52%) had primary school or less education. Only about one in a hundred spoke English fluently upon arrival in the United States; two out of three arrived with no knowledge of the language. The data show, however, that *in general* both adults and children of the three refugee groups were performing well. The adults, while not in good situations, were moving rapidly toward economic self-sufficiency; the children showed great ability in whatever schools they attended. Here we wish to present, in a very general fashion, the findings of both the self-sufficiency and the scholastic achievement studies.

First, it is necessary to stress that the household (that is, all the individuals living in a single dwelling unit) has served as the focus for both studies. Our definition of economic self-sufficiency had two aspects: whether or not anyone in the household was receiving public assistance; and how the total income of the household (including both assistance and earned income) compared to the official poverty level (about $800 per month for a family of four). As it turned out, these aspects tended to be interrelated with regard to the economic self-sufficiency of the refugee-household unit. For the scholastic achievement study, the household forms the backdrop for the analysis of how well the children are doing in school. The large data set allows us to look at a number of potentially significant variables relating to the household, and we have examined many of them in our attempts to determine the major predictor variables.

The conclusions for the self-sufficiency study emphasized three elements: labor force participation, income source, and economic status (Caplan et al. 1985a). Even though the unemployment rate was 42% among adults and the job status of those working was not high, optimism about the refugees and their future is possible for two reasons. First, this survey took place during the worst economic recession in the United States since the Great Depression, and yet the refugees were making remarkable progress toward economic self-sufficiency. Second, length of time in the country (Table 7.1) shows a sharp drop in unemployment from those here four months or less to those here over three years.

In this volume, Gordon and Strand both indicate that the incidence of employment improves the longer adult refugees live here. Yet, Gordon rightfully cites the analysis of Robert Bach that mere "time in the country" for a refugee adult is not a sufficient variable for a complete explanation of that person's situation. Our work and that of Dunning and of Strand in this volume point to the ability to speak some English and to a pre-arrival education as significant variables affecting employment. In addition, it is essential to look at the household as a whole, not at the pattern of a number of individuals. The manner by which refugee households progress in the United States is by increasing the number of their occupants who are

Table 7.1   Unemployment Rate by Time in the United States

Months in the U.S.	Unemployment rate
4	86%
8	77%
12	75%
16	58%
20	61%
24	52%
28	41%
32	40%
36	35%
40	36%
44	19%
44+	30%

working and bringing in earned income—that is, by a multiple-job strategy. When seen from this standpoint, a very different and far more encouraging picture emerges. Table 7.2 shows changes in the percentage of households with no job, one job, or two or more jobs over four-month intervals. The steady, almost monotonic increase in the percentage of households with two or more jobs is a most significant feature. It is the number of jobs per household, rather than the character of the individual jobs themselves, that makes the major difference in understanding the degree of economic self-sufficiency gained by the refugees. That is, the crucial issue is the support, willingness, cooperation, and diligence of a variety of household members to seek out and hold any kind of job in order to achieve economic independence and to improve the economic standing of the household.

Similarly, there is a major change over time in the percentage of households receiving public cash assistance (transfer income) and/or bringing in earnings. As more household members enter the labor force, there is a greater chance for self-sufficiency. At the same time, there is an equally steady move from transfer to earned income, with or without an in-between phase. Table 7.3 shows the steady change, particularly in the first two years, for the three income groups. Households totally on transfer income dropped from almost 80% in the first four months to about 30% after three years. Those on earned income alone rose fairly steadily from 3% in the first four months to about 50% after three years. The percentage of households with combined income (both transfer and earned) rose from almost 20% in the first four months to double that from 16 to 32 months, before falling off to about 30% thereafter.

Of the households sampled, 50% fell below the federal poverty level (about $800 per month for a family of four), and 8% had incomes at 50% or

Table 7.2   Jobs per Household by Time in the United States

Months in the U.S.	No job	1 job	2 or more jobs
4	82%	14%	4%
8	78%	20%	2%
12	66%	21%	13%
16	61%	26%	13%
20	52%	29%	19%
24	37%	34%	29%
28	36%	35%	29%
32	32%	39%	29%
36	31%	37%	32%
40	25%	31%	44%
44	24%	34%	42%
44+	22%	31%	47%

Table 7.3   Income Source by Time in the United States

Months in the U.S.	Percent of Households		
	Transfer income	Combined income	Earned income
4	79%	18%	3%
8	76%	19%	5%
12	66%	24%	10%
16	61%	29%	10%
20	49%	37%	14%
24	35%	40%	25%
28	27%	39%	34%
32	31%	37%	32%
36	36%	27%	37%
40	15%	32%	53%
44	26%	26%	48%

less of the poverty level. The majority of households on transfer income fell below the poverty line, and those with earned income alone had earnings well above the poverty line. Specifically 64% of the transfer group, 28% of the combined group, and 12% of the earned group were under the poverty line. There is also change through time, as seen in Table 7.4 Here we see that of households in the United States "four months or less," income was only 46% of government-defined poverty (about $800); households here for three years had incomes close to 1½ times the poverty level, and households here for four years had income almost twice the poverty level.

Table 7.4   Percent of Poverty Standard Met by Time in the United States

Months in the U.S.	Percent of needs met
4	46
8	96
12	101
16	112
20	118
24	118
28	140
32	135
36	143
40	128
44	178
44+	197

Gordon, in this volume, correctly recognizes the great importance for the household's economic self-sufficiency of the changing composition of that household. Table 7.5 shows the relationship between household composition and percent of households below the poverty line. Note that households with a greater number of adult members tended to be less frequently under the poverty line, while the nuclear-family type of household was more often under the poverty level.

Of utmost importance for getting ahead economically is thus the multiple-wage-earner strategy illustrated in Table 7.2. When one person gets a job, the household's ability to meet basic needs over the poverty-level standard is improved. But the big change in living standards occurs when a *second* person from the household finds gainful employment. This is particularly important (and difficult) for the nuclear family. Thus, dramatic changes in economic status occur when additional family members take jobs rather than from changes in wages through the job advancement of a single individual in the household. Of the households with no jobs, 17% were above the poverty level, compared to 68% of those with one job and 93% of those with at least two jobs. This sharp advance in the percentage of households above the poverty level means simply that more working adults per household improves the standard of living.

A picture of more rapid success comes from the scholastic achievement of the refugee children (Caplan et al. 1985b). If there are questions regarding the future of the refugees in America, the striking success of the Southeast Asian children in their realm of achievement, schoolwork, should set the questions to rest. Intrigued by scattered, but increasingly frequent success stories of refugee children, we interviewed our subsample to determine the accuracy of the popular belief that these children were doing well. Five hundred and twenty nine children (248 Vietnamese, 132 Chinese, and 149 Lao) were studied. We were able to obtain the grades of 355 of these students, ranging from kindergarten to twelfth grade for the spring 1984

Table 7.5 Household Composition by Poverty Level

Household composition	Percent living below poverty line
Unrelated singles	9%
Extended family and single(s)	20%
Multiple family and single(s)	27%
Nuclear family and single(s)	29%
Single, living alone	29%
Multiple family	40%
Extended family	43%
Nuclear family	61%

term. Table 7.6 shows the range of Grade Point Average (GPA) for these students.

Of the students, 27% had an overall GPA in the A range. Exactly 10% had a perfect 4.0, or straight-A, average. Another 52% had overall GPAs in the B range; 17% were in the C range; and only 4% had GPAs of D or less. The refugee student performance was even more impressive for mathematics: 44% received a 4.0 GPA in math, while another 3% earned either a 3.7 or 3.8. Another 32% had a grade of B; 15% C; and 6% below C. The mean overall GPA is 3.05, the mean math grade is 3.18, and the mean science grade is 2.90.

Of the 97 refugee students for whom the California Achievement Test (CAT) scores were obtained, 29% placed in the top 30% nationally, 45% placed from the fortieth percentile to the sixty-ninth, and 25% fell below the fortieth percentile. Overall, the refugee students did better on the CAT than did all students nationally, with fewer in the lower 40%, more in the middle 30%, and almost the same in the top 30%. In general, the refugee students did better in mathematics than in reading and language, though spelling was an area in which many excelled. Thus while 61% of the refugee students placed in the top 30% nationally in mathematics, they were slightly below the national average in reading and language.

These impressive results on standardized tests showed no significant variation among the different school systems. It is important to note that many of these students attained high academic marks in schools that are in low-income or inner-city areas. That is, they succeeded in schools generally considered to be less fortunate with respect to economic and related resources and, at the same time, associated with less motivated and more disruptive student bodies. Had the refugee students done well only on GPA, there would be reason to discount their achievements. That they did very well when compared nationally on the CAT would argue that their scholastic achievements are impressive by both local *and* national standards.

The scholastic achievement of these children is high, regardless of factors such as the quality of their schools, the number of children in their families,

Table 7.6   Grade Point Averages: Overall and Mathematics

	Percent of students	
Grade	Overall GPA	Math GPA
A (3.6–4.0)	27.0	46.7
B (2.6–3.5)	52.1	32.3
C (1.6–2.5)	17.2	14.7
D (1.5 or below)	3.7	6.3
Total	100.0	100.0

the income level of their households, or other factors that usually effect differences among people or achievement among children. In addition, this extraordinary level of scholastic achievement is true for the group as a whole and is not merely the result of a few exceptional children raising the overall mean. We can expect these refugee students to do even better in the future. As literacy improves, it is reasonable to expect that grades will improve in all courses, and accordingly, the overall GPA will also rise.

Social and Cultural Values

The chief reason for the success of these children in particular and of the refugees in general appears to be the compatibility of their cultural values— cohesive family structure, achievement orientation, and the ability and willingness to adopt new coping strategies—with the requirements and opportunities for success in the United States.

To account for the achievement, hundreds of variables drawn from the data base, from both the economic self-sufficiency study and the education study, were used to build an explanatory model. While the explanatory power of the model is limited by several factors, we offer the following interpretations of the achievements of this group, because the model represents the best conceptual framework for giving meaning to the data.

In interviews for the second survey, the refugee families rated the importance of each of a list of cultural values. The single item viewed as highly important by virtually every household was "Educational Achievement" (99%). It was followed closely by "A Cooperative and Harmonious Family" (97%), and "Responsibility About Carrying Out Obligations" (97%). Next in perceived importance was a set of family-centered values: "Respect for Family Members"; "Respect for Elders"; "A Cohesive Family"; "Family Loyalty"; and "A Family Guided by Morality and Ethics." Between 88 and 94% rated these values extremely or very important. Of the family-related values in the list of twenty-five items, the above six were viewed as being among the most important by about 90% of the respondents. Other items in the value hierarchy viewed as important emphasize commitment, the work ethic, and impulse control: "Restraint and Discipline"; "A Belief in the Value of Hard Work"; and "Willingness to Sacrifice the Present for the Future."

When asked which three value items were considered most important, the refugees responded: "Educational Achievement"; "A Cohesive Family"; and "A Belief in the Value of Hard Work." These items were cited by over 95% of the respondents. When asked to indicate the goals and preferences they view as most important for their nonrefugee, non-Southeast Asian neighbors, the two cited most often were "Seeking Fun and Excitement" and "Desire for Material Possessions"—that is, the very two items cited *least* often as important by the refugee respondents when designating their own value preferences.

The technique used to analyze the data on values, a multivariate analysis, took into account simultaneously the effects of several potentially important variables, allowing us to develop a more comprehensive and realistic understanding of the determinants of GPA. In doing the multivariate analysis, the value item best able to account for, or "explain," differences in GPA among many households was the degree of importance respondents placed on the statement, "Finding a Place for the Family in the Community and in Relation to the Past." Variation in the response to this value statement explained 13% of the variance on GPA. It is the lengthiest, and perhaps the most complex, of the value statements used in the questionnaire. Undoubtedly, it captures a number of important attitudes toward the resettlement process, such as "fitting in" and continuity with the past. "Ashamed to be Dependent on Welfare" contributed an additional 4% to the variance. "Willingness to Sacrifice the Present to the Future" also contributed 4% to the variance and suggests that the educational performance of the children represents a human capital investment in the future of the family.

The refugee families studied, both adults and children, see the potential for scholastic achievement to lie within themselves and their own efforts. Over 90% of them felt that what helped them to gain such success was the love of learning, the ability to work hard, and the capacity to persevere. Even "innate intelligence" fell slightly behind "effort" in their rating. Much agreement existed in the elements that were seen to hinder the children in their studies. More than two-thirds of the respondents recognized the need for better proficiency in English to attain high levels of scholastic achievement.

Disruptive behavior by non-Southeast Asian students was seen as a threat to achievement, reflecting the refugees' fear that their children will be affected by the materialistic and hedonistic values of the surrounding community. Other hindrances include problems of transportation, and family demands; on the other hand, the Southeast Asian students' physical and emotional problems and school deficiencies were seen as minor problems. Fate and luck were also ranked low as elements affecting performance.

When *all* available variables from *both* surveys were analyzed in relation to GPA, the first three items (accounting for an important 33% of the GPA variance) pertain to family roles and the relative influence of the husband and wife in decision-making. Children with higher GPAs came from homes where both parents were reported to participate in making a decision such as whether or not the husband should quit his job. By contrast, those students with lower GPAs came from homes where such a decision was made by the husband alone, or with minimal input from his wife. The item ranked third in accounting for GPA variance also relates to the relative equality of the husband and the wife in the home. Children with higher

GPAs came from homes that disagreed with the statement, "A wife should do whatever her husband wants."

The second most important factor in explaining GPA levels was whether parents read to the children at home. The children who did better in school came from homes where the parents read to them. Almost half of the parents reported they read to their children. Of those, twice as many read in their native language as in English. Those children read to in the native language had somewhat *higher* GPAs than those read to in English. While this difference in mean GPA is not statistically significant, the direction of the difference is, nonetheless, of interest. At a minimum, this finding suggests that the emotional aspect of reading to children may be as important as the cognitive aspect with respect to performance in school. It also suggests that skill gained in the native language may be transferred to English. Or, at least, the language barrier does not prevent the communication and transfer of other competencies or values that lead to academic achievement.

The next two items of importance, measured by independent contributions to the variance in GPA, involve a person's feelings of efficacy, or the degree of perceived control over external factors that affect one's life. In the fourth item, parents of the higher achievers expressed more confidence that their plans for the future would, in fact, materialize than did the parents of children with lower GPAs. Further, as indicated in the fifth item, they were more likely to believe that they could "live much the way they want," while the parents of the lesser achievers were more likely to believe that the problems of life were too great to allow certainty about the future.

There were some additional items of more modest importance. The parents of children who excel in school also value and seek new experiences. They are more likely to have come from urban backgrounds and to have had parents who themselves were relatively better educated. Their feelings of efficacy extend to their children, over whom they perceive themselves as having a relatively high level of influence. Also, they use withholding of privileges as a primary way of influencing the behavior of their children.

Thus, cultural values and social cohesion lie behind what will undoubtably be the long range success of the refugee community as a whole. The riches brought by these second-wave refugees from their homelands are not material, but rather the values and approaches to life advocated by their home cultures and societies.

Conclusions and Implications

Striking differences exist between the factors associated with achievement in the economic study conducted for ORR and those found to be associated with scholastic performance. The economic study found that the level of

English fluency upon arrival in the United States was the most powerful predictor of later economic standing. Minimal English proficiency—that is, *any* level beyond "none"—was found to enhance the likelihood of achieving economic self-sufficiency. In the educational study, however, neither the arrival nor the current English proficiency of the parents was found to be associated with the scholastic performance of the children. This is consistent with the finding that present economic standing was not associated with GPA.

There is, however, an important similarity between the findings of the two studies. Those households that achieved early economic independence were those in which both spouses were willing to participate in the work force. Thus, a high level of parental sharing of household responsibility is apparently critical for both economic achievement and children's scholastic achievement. Based on an extensive body of research on family size and school achievement, we would expect GPA to deteriorate with increased family size. Instead, we found families with five and six or more children doing as well or better than those with fewer children. In order for achievement to be roughly equal across different size families, a high level of reciprocal helping—one child teaching another and therefore learning more as well—goes on, especially where scholastic achievement is exceptional.

Also contradicting our expectations was the relationship of past socioeconomic standing to academic achievement. Past socioeconomic standing did not emerge as an important predictor for scholastic achievement in the United States. This is probably due to two factors. First, the children of less educated, low occupational level parents simply would not have had opportunity for schooling in Southeast Asia. In the United States, such opportunity is available to all children. Given that opportunity, these children, like their parents, are making the most of it, regardless of past socioeconomic status. Second, the basic cultural values, motivations, household factors, etc. that are required for scholastic success in the United States are broadly shared by the refugee families studied, regardless of past standing. That is, given the opportunity to succeed, they have the wherewithal to do so.

The refugees appear to have held fast to their values during the disruption of their lives. The pragmatic application of these values as operating principles has been to their advantage as they grappled with the problems of resettlement in a world vastly different from the one they left. The limited types of employment available to the parents of these children, however, restrict the adults' ability to use labor force participation to achieve economic and social mobility. Limitations in language proficiency and relevant skills preclude such achievements, notwithstanding the refugees' belief in hard work. Thus, in order to make the most of the family's human resources, energies are rechanneled and invested where the long-term payoff will be greatest, namely, opportunity for their children to excel in school.

Yet while the data suggest that the students in this study are excelling and, in the aggregate, their families are climbing out of poverty, these successes should not draw attention from the fact that many refugees remain in serious need of effective assistance if they are to make economic and social progress. Nuclear families with poor English are a major case in point. The refugees have important health, educational, and economic needs that still must be met to tide them over these rough spots and to help them move forward in American life. Such needs raise the question of the effectiveness of the programs designed for refugees. There is no question the refugees who are in programs value them, as Dunning too has pointed out in this volume, and they rank employment and language problems very high when asked what they see as necessary to getting ahead in life. On the other hand, it is difficult to point to specific program outcomes that relate to the attainment of economic self-sufficiency. We would caution any interpretation of these results to mean that the programs were ineffectual. The problem of testing program effects is one of methodology—unless a program produces a powerful and overriding effect, its outcome is difficult and often impossible to determine in the absence of a true experiment, e.g., the randomized assignment of persons to programs and the collection of data on the experimental and control groups before, during, and after the program change. And, even then, results often require a high level of equivocation, since such studies are usually conducted in an open community. On the basis of our data, we can say that vocational training (the most intensive type) does result in some benefits. But it is difficult to specify how much difference it makes, and what its potential would be if it were available to other than a select segment of the refugee population.

Perhaps it is the resourcefulness of the refugees themselves, both those who have access to service programs and those who do not, that makes program effects appear so weak. That is, the ability of the refugees to utilize their social resources has resulted in their ability to cope successfully with the adverse economic conditions and the other problems associated with resettlement. Friends and relations are the main sources of helpful employment information, and the reported increase in English proficiency after arrival is great, whether gained through ESL classes or picked up informally. While the service program data may raise some questions about targeting and appropriateness to refugee needs, there is no question about the perceived need for the programs or the great willingness of refugees to use them if available. Indeed, we would argue, these refugees are an ideal group for such programs. They use such help while and as long as they need it, then they move on to more profitable endeavors. That is how the system is supposed to work, and the refugees have benefitted greatly from it.

Our message is thus an upbeat one: despite a variety of existing problems, the Southeast Asian refugees are "making it." Yet the standard view continues to focus on difficulties. In the stories of the "ten years after" variety, published during 1985, the familiar strain was of a people lost in the traumas of the past and having difficulty in coping with the present, much less the future. Our first study, contracted and published by the Office of Refugee Resettlement, came out at that time but was not brought before the public eye. The size and quality of our data base indeed demand more attention. Agencies of the federal government too often have shown an inability to deal with the positive, which these data demonstrate, as opposed to the negative. They seem to be able to lay blame and try to deal with the resulting problems, but not to give credit and help guide the more positive aspects of a situation.

Curiously, some attention has been paid to the study from a different direction in the federal government. Secretary of Education William J. Bennett seized upon our results as confirming the soundness of his approach to American education—emphasis on the home, parental participation, and good character, i.e., individual responsibility.[3] In oral presentations he has drawn on our data to demonstrate the strength of his proposals, of what "ought to be." In so doing, he applies the ideals and values of a certain culture to the multicultural situation of the United States.

Considerations of others' uses of these data aside, one question that does arise concerns the data's implications about nonachievement. In that respect, two problems arise. First, factors related to success may not say much about failure. Second, our knowledge about why these children do so well is in itself limited. The evidence points to the possibility that these children (or more accurately, these households) behave so as to maximize what they bring with them by way of cultural background toward achievement. While our study provides evidence of empirical regularity with respect to the conditions that produce outstanding achievement, we still have very little knowledge of the daily operations within the home by which refugees grapple effectively with their problems. Yet neither the economically depressed conditions of the early 1980s nor any deficiencies of the schools their children attend have kept them from making progress.

Important to this progress is the compatibility of the refugees' values with the attitudes associated with success in the United States, including the "work ethic." The high level of motivation and willingness to face new experiences and endure hardships to become self-sufficient are reflected in the values expressed by the refugees. But it is critical that there be opportunity in order for the refugees' aspirations to materialize. Despite difficult circumstances, these families climbed out of welfare dependency rapidly, given their situation, and made the most of the available job opportunities. It would be safe to venture, though, that for long-term social and economic advancement, education is viewed as a more effective avenue to success than workforce participation. It is also worth pointing out that the opportunity for educational advancement in the United States is more egalitarian than in Southeast Asia. Thus, many families are able to provide their children with an education that would have been reserved for only an advantaged few there. This new opportunity for education may also be a motivating factor that helps explain academic achievement.

A final point deserves emphasis. Much of the past literature on refugee and immigrant groups has emphasized that successful resettlement occurs because refugees adopt the ways of their nonrefugee neighbors. The Southeast Asian refugees studied, however, appear to have gotten along as well as they have because of the cultural values they have brought with them—values they perceive as quite different from those of their nonrefugee neighbors. However, these values have helped them precisely because they are compatible with the requirements for success in the United States, even though the refugees face a vastly different social and economic landscape than what they knew in the past. It is thus not an "either-or" situation for the refugees, a choice between their "traditions" and American "modernity." Rather, we suggest that refugees can (and do) maintain "their proper normative stance" at the same time as they are coming to grips with American life. This bodes well both for refugee achievement and for the maintenance of cultural diversity in the United States.

Notes

1. The findings for the self-sufficiency study are presented in Caplan, Whitmore, and Bui (1985). The study on academic achievement is currently being prepared for publication.
2. The materials resulting from the surveys are kept at ISR, University of Michigan, as are copies of questionnaires (in all four languages) and reports dealing with the surveys. A public-use data tape is available for the survey on refugee self-sufficiency. For overviews of the two studies, see Caplan et al. (1985a, 1985b).
3. See his report, "What Works—Research about Teaching and Learning" (Washington, D.C., U.S. Department of Education, 1986) for these emphases.

8

Portraits, Patterns, and Predictors of the Refugee Adaptation Process: Results and Reflections from the IHARP Panel Study

Rubén G. Rumbaut

The Indochinese Health and Adaptation Research Project (IHARP) is a comprehensive longitudinal study of the migration and resettlement of Sino-Vietnamese, Hmong, Khmer, Lao, and Vietnamese refugees in San Diego County, California. IHARP is based on random samples of men, women, adolescents, and school-aged children from each of the five main Indochinese ethnic groups who were resettled in the United States between 1975 and 1983. Thus, unlike earlier studies carried out in the wake of the evacuation of the 1975 (mostly Vietnamese) refugees or subsequent research that has focused on specific aspects of the adaptation of some of the "second wave" ethnic groups, the IHARP study encompasses both of the major "waves" and all of the major ethnocultural groups of Southeast Asian refugee migrants to the United States; it distinguishes the sizable segment of ethnic Chinese from Vietnam (who constitute between a quarter and a third of all refugee admissions from Vietnam, and who differ in significant ways from the Vietnamese) as a separate sample for analysis; it focuses on refugee women (whose centrol role is often neglected in studies of migration and mobility) and their children, and not solely on male heads of household; it combines quantitative survey research with qualitative "oral histories" and in-depth open-ended interviews; and it allows for a longitudinal rather than cross-sectional analysis of the refugee "adaptation process," broadly con-ceived. The study, originally funded during 1982–1985 by NICHD[1] at the University of California, San Diego, was relocated thereafter to San Diego State University, where it continues to ramify into related quantitative and qualitative research projects based on the original IHARP data set. Cur-rently, ongoing projects include a qualitative-quantitative study of the educational and occupational attainment of refugee youth, funded by the U.S. Social Security Administration/Office of Refugee Resettlement; and a longitudinal analysis of infant mortality in the Indochinese population of San Diego County, funded by a Maternal and Child Health research grant from the U.S. Public Health Service.[2] Additional secondary analyses of the data set, and a possible "T3" follow-up of the original panel of adults and children several years later, are being planned into the 1990s.

Sampling Procedures and Survey Data Collection

As a first step in developing a representative sample of the Indochinese refugee population of San Diego County, an exhaustive effort was made to come as close as possible to the ideal of achieving a complete enumeration of the population universe of each of the five major ethnocultural groups— i.e., the Hmong, Khmer, Lao, Vietnamese and Sino-Vietnamese communities. Simple random samples would then be drawn from each of the five universe enumeration lists. Far from the dull and routine task of "counting heads" that is portrayed in some methodology textbooks, the effort at "enumerating the universe" proved to be an extraordinarily challenging, complicated, expensive, and time-consuming process. For example, access to basic but confidential records (names, addresses and telephone numbers of Indochinese refugees in San Diego County) posed legal questions that were addressed with the assistance of the General Counsel of the University of California. IHARP obtained legal opinions citing specific legislative authority granting access to needed information for *bona fide* research purposes—including section 10850(d) of the California Welfare and Institutions Code, and the Confidentiality of Medical Information Act (COMA) of the California Civil Code, which had become effective in January 1982— and, after several months of negotiations with appropriate government agencies, we gained legal access to pertinent records of the San Diego County Departments of Health and Social Services and other government records.

Similarly, the enumeration effort posed sociopolitical problems as well. Because access to and control of client lists provide refugee service organizations with competitive advantages for a number of purposes, and because of legitimate concerns about the confidentiality of such information, agencies were reluctant to share them and, in some cases, were adamantly opposed. Nor, once access to such data was successfully negotiated, were the technical data-gathering problems easily overcome: in most cases, lack of computerized records meant that lists had to be obtained by hand-copying thousands of records of Indochinese persons.

The enumeration process lasted from July 1982 through March 1983. In the end, IHARP was able to compile a confidential list of approximately

55,000 records (containing source dates, names, addresses, telephone numbers, and ethnicity of individuals and families in the Indochinese communities of San Diego) from thirty major public and private sources, including: (1) complete lists from the Welfare Department of all refugees who were currently receiving ("time-eligible") or had previously received ("time-expired") some form of public assistance (this source alone yielded about 30,000 separate entries); (2) lists from the Health Department of all refugees initially resettled in the San Diego metropolitan area ("primary arrivals"); (3) complete membership lists from several Indochinese mutual aid associations (with the Hmong and Cambodian records being by far the most exhaustive) and from a variety of Indochinese cultural and religious (e.g., Buddhist and Catholic) organizations, as well as subscription lists of ethnic newspapers and magazines; (4) patient lists from private health care providers, community clinics, and screening programs, and client lists from social service providers, community clinics, and screening programs, and client lists from social service programs; (5) a complete search of the County telephone directories for 1982 and 1983 (using inventories of all known Hmong, Khmer, Lao, and Vietnamese surnames); and (6) other miscellaneous sources of information (even including the 480 persons who applied for staff research positions in IHARP), which were updated through early 1983.

All this information was systematically processed and reduced to a listing of family units or heads of household, and then reduced again to eliminate all duplicate entries (double-checking throughout for the ubiquitous misspellings, miscoded ethnicity, and different name usages in these populations). This procedure yielded a total enumeration of over 9,000 "family" or sampling units in over 6,000 households,[3] distributed by ethnicity to form the five ethnic universe lists. Simple random samples of householders were then drawn from each of these five lists.[4] Based on this enumeration, and on the subsequent process of locating respondents and carrying out household censuses, we estimated a total Indochinese refugee population of nearly 40,000 persons in San Diego County as of April 1983—one of the four largest metropolitan Indochinese concentrations in the United States (the three other metropolitan areas, all also in California, are Los Angeles, Orange, and Santa Clara Counties). The IHARP data are thus based on probably the most complete enumeration of any large community of Indochinese refugees in the United States.

The resulting IHARP T1 sample includes 739 adults (366 men, 373 women) from the five major ethnic groups, residing in 437 households, as follows: 201 Vietnamese respondents (in 120 households); 140 Lao (in 82 households); 123 Khmer (in 81 households); 144 Hmong (in 80 households); and 131 Sino-Vietnamese (in 74 households). Complete household listings were obtained for each household, yielding basic demographic information on a total of 3,003 persons, ranging in age from birth to 89 (interviewers developed sufficient rapport with respondents to obtain their "true" age, which in many cases differed from the official or "green card" age (see Gordon's discussion in this volume of ORR's official statistics on the stated age of refugee admissions). Data from this larger household sample permit the calculation of child-woman ratios, sex ratios, age-dependency ratios, and related demographic indicators for the Indochinese population of San Diego County as a whole.

Respondents were selected for the IHARP adult sample if they were between the ages of 25 and 65, and their spouses were included even if they were under 25 or over 65. The T1 adult respondents ranged in age from 18 to 71 years, with a mean age of 37 years. In addition, using Kish random selection tables, an additional sample of school-age children was drawn; in-depth data (including complete educational histories, English proficiency levels, social integration, health status, and psychological well-being measures) were then collected from each family (via proxy interviews with the parents) on one child aged 6 to 11 and on one adolescent aged 12 to 17, yielding a T1 random sample of 351 school-age children, who were followed up in the T2 interviews as well. Thus, for certain purposes (e.g., analyses of physical health status, emotional well-being, English proficiency), the total T1 sample of respondents for whom we have detailed data is 1,090 persons, ranging in age from 6 to 71.

Structured, comprehensive T1 interviews (with many open-ended questions), lasting an average of nearly three hours, were conducted during mid-1983 with each of the adult respondents, and were repeated a year later in mid-1984 (T2) for all but the Lao sample.[5] Additionally, intensive qualitative interviews were also conducted midway between the two main surveys (at "T1.5") with a selected subsample of 10 persons from each ethnic group (again, except the Lao), which were audiotaped, translated, and transcribed, and which provide a rich complement of qualitative information to the quantitative data collected (cf. Rumbaut 1985a). The two main waves of interviews were conducted by skilled, extensively trained (over a three-month training program), co-ethnic interviewers in the home and language of the respondent. All interviews were audiotaped. Typically female respondents were interviewed by female interviewers, and male respondents by male interviewers. Occasionally arrangements were made to take a respondent to the university or other suitable locale to ensure privacy and minimize interruptions during the interviewing process. Only two (younger) respondents requested to have the interview in English; the other 737 respondents were interviewed in five different native languages, and in the case of the Sino-Vietnamese, in three different dialects of Chinese (most Sino-Vietnamese respondents did not speak Vietnamese well enough or preferred not to be interviewed in Vietnamese).[6]

The T1 refusal rate was about 6% for the sample as a whole, with the lowest refusal rates among the Hmong (2%), Lao (2%) and Khmer (3%), and somewhat higher refusal rates for the Vietnamese (7%) and Sino-Vietnamese

(13%). Four out of five of the persons refusing the interview were working (often at two jobs, plus going to school or participating in other training programs); two persons cited health reasons (one had active tuberculosis); and a few cited unspecified personal reasons. At T1.5, there were no refusals. At T2, refusal rates were lower for the Chinese and Vietnamese than they had been at T1, and refusal rates were zero for the Hmong and Khmer (i.e., 100% of those respondents located at T2 agreed to be reinterviewed).

By T2, however, there was an attrition of 99 persons from the T1 adult sample (a loss of 16.5%). That is, excluding the Lao sample, out of the 599 adults interviewed at T1 (300 men and 299 women, residing in 355 households), a total of 500 (248 men and 252 women, residing in 296 households) were reinterviewed at T2 to add a longitudinal dimension to the IHARP data base. Most of the 99 persons lost during that intervening year were Hmong (T1 N = 144, T2 N = 109) who moved out of San Diego to agricultural areas in Central California (as part of a remarkable migratory movement of Hmong clans from throughout the United States to those areas around Fresno and Merced Counties), and Vietnamese (T1 N = 201, T2 N = 157) who moved elsewhere in San Diego County but could not be located. The Khmer sample, by contrast, remained almost intact (T1 N = 123, T2 N = 120; the three persons lost moved to Santa Ana in the interim). Difference-of-means tests between respondents and nonrespondents at T2 over an extensive list of T1 variables were conducted, comparing key demographic, socioeconomic, health and mental health characteristics of the 99 persons who were not reinterviewed at T2 against those of the 500 persons who were interviewed at both T1 and T2. The results show no statistically significant differences between them (indeed, the characteristics of the two groups were virtually identical), suggesting that the sample mortality at T2 produced no significant bias in the follow-up sample. Accordingly, the results reported in this paper will be based primarily on the longitudinal T1-T2 adult sample (N = 500).

Portraits of Adaptation

The first decade of Southeast Asian refugee resettlement and adaptation to the United States presents a portrait in diversity. Only one in six of the approximately 800,000 refugees admitted during this period actually came in 1975, as part of a largely elite "first wave" of about 130,000. Most of the refugees arrived in the United States in or after 1980. These more recently-arrived refugees have been not only much more numerous but also much more heterogeneous. They include the Vietnamese and Sino-Vietnamese "boat people," the survivors of the Pol Pot period in Kampuchea, the lowland Lao, and almost all of the highland Hmong. Many of these latter groups came from rural backgrounds, with little education, knowledge of English, or transferable occupational skills—indeed, they arrived with comparatively fewer "human capital" resources than any other legal immigrants in recent U.S. history, and experienced much more traumatic migration histories. What is more, the size, suddenness, timing, and context of their entry into the United States further complicated their reception. They arrived *en masse* (fully 450,000 during 1979–82 alone), and at the worst possible time: the peak of their arrival (1980) coincided with the highest domestic inflation rates in memory, followed (during 1981–1983) by the most severe economic recession in nearly half a century, and by an accompanying sociopolitical climate of intensifying nativism, racism, xenophobia, and "compassion fatigue." Despite formal placement policies that have sought to disperse them throughout the United States, secondary migration (especially to California where 40% of the refugees now reside) has produced a number of areas with high Indochinese concentrations—notably in Los Angeles, Orange, and San Diego Counties in Southern California.

This section presents selected indicators from the IHARP data of the diversity of adaptational resources and outcomes characterizing the experience of these refugee groups at different points in time: from T0 (1975) to T1 (1983) and T2 (1984). These descriptive "portraits of adaptation" will be drawn by ethnicity, gender, level of premigration education (a rough proxy for social class of origin), and cohort of arrival, dealing in order with: social background characteristics; migration life events; English proficiency; occupational status; household composition and economic adaptation; health status; and psychological adaptation. Subsequent sections will then turn to multivariate analyses of selected outcome variables in order to identify principal predictors of these multidimensional adaptation processes.

Social Background

Table 8.1 presents a summary of key social background characteristics for IHARP's longitudinal adult sample (N = 500), broken down by ethnic group, gender, and cohort of arrival (i.e., the 1975 first wave, the 1976–1979 cohort, and the 1980–1983 arrivals, who are also the most numerous). In most respects, there are highly significant differences between all these groups. In terms of the age of the adults in the sample, the Sino-Vietnamese are noticeably older than the other groups, and "first wave" refugees were younger at arrival than those who came later. The Vietnamese have resided in the United States the longest (reflecting the fact that most of the first cohort of 1975 refugees were Vietnamese), whereas the Khmer are the most recent arrivals (averaging only 2.7 years in the United States at the time of the T1 interviews in 1983. The elite composition of the first wave (a typical phenomenon in refugee migrations) is apparent: three out of four were high school graduates, and over one-third had professional backgrounds. A disproportionate number of these were South Vietnamese urban Catholics

Table 8.1 Social Background Characteristics of Indochinese Refugees at T0 (1975) and T1 (1983) (IHARP Longitudinal Adult Sample, N = 500)

Social background characteristics	Time	Ethnicity					Gender			Time of Arrival			
		Hmong (N = 109)	Khmer (N = 120)	Chinese (N = 114)	Vietnam. (N = 157)	p	Male (N = 248)	Female (N = 252)	p	1975 (N = 39)	1976–79 (N = 172)	1980–83 (N = 289)	p
Age and Time													
Age at arrival in U.S.	T0/T1	33.4	32.9	38.7	32.1	*	34.7	33.5	NS	30.6	32.3	35.6	*
Age at interview	T1	37.0	35.5	42.2	36.1	*	38.3	36.8	NS	38.6	36.8	37.8	NS
Years in the U.S.	T1	3.7	2.7	4.4	4.9	*	4.5	4.2	NS	8.2	4.4	2.4	*
Education													
% Urban	T0	10.1	45.0	95.6	94.9	*	65.7	63.5	NS	94.9	64.0	60.9	*
Years of education	T0	1.7	4.9	6.6	9.8	*	7.4	4.8	*	11.9	6.5	5.1	*
% High school grad.	T0	1.8	13.3	19.3	46.5	*	29.0	16.3	*	74.4	23.8	14.9	*
% Writing illiteracy	T0	73.4	34.1	18.4	1.2	*	18.1	39.3	*	2.6	25.6	34.9	*
Occupation													
% White collar	T0	5.0	7.1	12.2	33.1	*	17.2	13.6	*	48.4	19.4	9.5	*
% Sales	T0	2.0	14.2	38.8	18.8	*	11.8	25.9	*	6.5	20.1	18.6	*
% Blue-collar	T0	2.0	8.0	27.6	10.5	*	13.4	9.8	*	3.2	7.4	15.2	*
% Military	T0	31.3	15.9	6.1	25.6	*	37.0	0.5	*	35.5	20.8	17.9	*
% Farmers, fishers	T0	59.6	54.0	14.3	10.5	*	19.3	49.8	*	3.2	32.2	37.6	*
Religion													
% Buddhist	T1	4.6	67.2	56.6	49.0	*	47.6	43.2	NS	48.7	45.0	45.1	NS
% Ancestor worship	T1	46.8	0.8	20.4	12.1	*	17.7	20.0	NS	5.1	21.1	19.4	*
% Catholic	T1	10.1	4.2	0.9	23.6	*	10.5	11.2	NS	30.8	8.2	9.7	*
% Protestant	T1	8.3	16.0	4.4	2.5	*	7.7	7.2	NS	5.1	5.3	9.0	*
% Other, mixed	T1	22.1	8.4	4.4	1.9	*	8.4	8.4	NS	10.3	8.2	8.3	NS
% No religion	T1	8.3	3.4	13.3	10.8	*	8.1	10.0	NS	0	12.3	8.3	*

*p < .01, NS = Not significant

(including a sizable number who had fled from the North to the South in 1954 after the defeat of the French), many of whom had worked in some capacity for the U.S. government or American companies. More recent cohorts are more rural in origin and are characterized by decreasing levels of education and native literacy, by decreasing proportions of professionals and other white-collar workers as well as of former military personnel, and by increasing proportions of farmers, fishers and production workers. In all of the groups there were wide gaps in premigration socioeconomic status between men and women. The Hmong were predominantly preliterate farmers or former guerilla fighters from the rural highlands of northern Laos. The Khmer (about 15% of whom are ethnic Chinese from Cambodia) provide a profile similar to the Lao—predominantly Theravada Buddhists, with an average of 5 years of premigration education—except that about 80% of the Lao came from urban areas, compared to about 45% of the Khmer. The Sino-Vietnamese were primarily "middleman minority" shopkeepers and production workers (very few were former ARVN military), drawn overwhelmingly from the Cholon area of Saigon.

Migration

As Table 8.2 shows, equally significant differences are apparent by ethnicity and cohort (but not by gender) in terms of the life events that characterized refugees' exodus from their homelands. All groups exhibit very high levels of family loss and separation. The Khmer, in particular, reflect the most traumatic migration histories, with significantly greater number of reported deaths of close family members—and more than 75% of Khmer refugees still did not know by T2 the fate or whereabouts of family members left behind in Cambodia. The Khmer, who spent an average of over two years in refugee camps in Thailand before being resettled, were most likely to have fled alone (especially males) and also reported the greatest number of "push" factors in their decision to leave.[7] The Hmong may rank next to the Khmer in the threatening and traumatic nature of their migration, a significantly greater proportion of them reported having feared that they would be killed during the escape (92.7%). Most went without food during what typically was a journey on foot through dense jungles over many days, and once they crossed the Mekong river into Thailand they languished in Thai refugee camps longer than any other group while awaiting resettlement (an average of nearly three years). In fact, a greater proportion of the Hmong actually fled their country in 1975 than any of the other refugee groups— including the Vietnamese—even though they were not resettled in the United States until much later. The Sino-Vietnamese in the sample, almost all "boat people," were much more likely (71.7%) to have bribed their way out of Vietnam (especially after the events of 1978–79 in Vietnam, including the border war with China), they were less likely to have fled alone without family members, and they were somewhat more likely to have been

Table 8.2   Stressful Life Events in the Migration of Indochinese Refugees at T0 (1975), T1 (1983), and T2 (1984) (IHARP Longitudinal Adult Sample, N = 500)

Migration life events	Time	Ethnicity					Gender			Time of Arrival			
		Hmong (N = 109)	Khmer (N = 120)	Chinese (N = 114)	Vietnam. (N = 157)	p	Male (N = 248)	Female (N = 252)	p	1975 (N = 39)	1976–79 (N = 172)	1980–83 (N = 289)	p
Decision to Leave													
Total push factors	T0/T1	4.3	7.1	3.2	3.5	*	4.8	4.1	*	2.6	4.2	4.9	*
Total pull factors	T0/T1	0.3	1.0	0.5	0.3	*	0.4	0.6	NS	0.3	0.4	0.6	*
Loss & separation													
Deaths in close family	T0/T1	1.1	1.6	0.5	0.7	*	0.9	1.0	NS	0.8	0.8	1.0	NS
% Family in prison	T0/T1	11.9	5.5	13.6	42.0	*	25.4	21.6	NS	44.1	23.1	20.4	*
% Fled without family	T0/T1	19.3	29.2	11.4	13.4	*	23.0	13.1	*	25.6	19.8	15.9	NS
% Family separation	T1	72.5	83.3	68.8	82.8	*	80.9	74.2	NS	82.1	76.6	77.4	NS
% Cannot communicate	T1	25.3	79.0	21.7	5.2	*	27.9	35.5	NS	17.9	24.2	38.1	NS
with family left behind	T2	18.4	76.3	16.1	4.1	*	26.1	26.9	NS	17.6	19.4	31.7	*
Migration process													
% Gave bribes to exit	T0/T1	21.3	19.3	71.7	32.7	*	49.8	50.2	NS	13.2	35.7	39.0	*
% Assaulted in escape	T0/T1	25.7	25.2	36.8	30.6	NS	30.8	28.6	NS	0	24.4	36.7	*
% Feared would be killed during escape	T0/T1	92.7	80.7	73.7	73.2	*	77.7	81.0	NS	18.4	86.6	83.0	*
% Went without food during escape	T0/T1	87.2	68.1	62.8	56.7	*	64.4	70.5	NS	15.8	70.3	72.6	*
Years in refugee camps	T0/T1	2.9	2.1	0.9	0.6	*	1.5	1.6	NS	0.2	1.2	1.9	*
% Secondary migrant to San Diego	T1	27.5	39.2	28.9	33.8	NS	35.5	29.8	NS	59.0	33.1	28.7	*

*p < .01, NS = Not Significant

assaulted during the escape process. The Vietnamese in general and the 1975 refugees in particular spent the least time in refugee camps, but both of those groups were significantly more likely to have family members imprisoned in the homeland.

English Proficiency

Although first-generation adult refugees may struggle to maintain their cultural traditions, they must nevertheless cope with the pressing demands of a new social and economic environment. Previous research and the IHARP data suggest that, in a bicultural setting, fluency in the dominant language is a central resource in the social and economic adaptation of these newcomers—affecting such areas as access to health care and social services, the possibility of communicating and developing relationships with dominant group members, the abilities to get a job or a driver's license and to learn basic information about U.S. society. Table 8.3 presents data on English proficiency levels both premigration at T0 (1975) and postarrival at T1 and T2, showing the gradual but steady gains in English speaking and writing ability over time, although at different rates, among all the ethnic groups, among men and women, and among groups of differing levels of education.[8] Still, even at T2, sizable proportions of the adult refugees could not yet speak or write in English, or could do so only poorly—especially women, the Chinese (who are older) and the Khmer (who are more recently arrived), and the least educated. The Hmong reflect a particular facility to pick up spoken English quickly, but they have great difficulty picking up English literacy skills (by T2, 77% still could not write in English). It is also worth noting that two-thirds of the 1975 cohort (compared to fewer than one sixth of the subsequent cohorts) reported some knowledge of English premigration, again reflecting the class composition of the first-wave refugees and adding to their human capital advantages. Our multivariate analyses show that proficiency in English is primarily a function of *age* and premigration *education:* older refugees pick up the new language much more slowly than the young, and proficiency in English reading and writing is especially aided by the degree of literacy already gained in other languages. Length of residence in the United States ranks a distant third as a predictor of English proficiency outcomes, and number of months of ESL instruction enters the regression equation as a weak but positive predictor of English proficiency only for respondents with less than a sixth grade education. Indeed, the number of months in ESL classes (attendance in which is required as a condition of eligibility for public assistance) varies inversely with level of education. Conversely, the greater the premigration level of education, the greater the number of months spent in vocational or academic training programs (which both presuppose some degree of English proficiency and enhance it in the process).

Table 8.3   English Proficiency and Occupational Adaptation at T0 (1975), T1 (1983), and T2 (1984) (IHARP Longitudinal Adult Sample, N = 500)

English and employment measures	Time	Ethnicity					Gender			Education (years)				
		Hmong (N=109)	Khmer (N=120)	Chinese (N=114)	Vietnam. (N=157)	p	Male (N=248)	Female (N=252)	p	None (N=119)	1-6 (N=167)	7-11 (N=101)	>12 Yrs. (N=113)	p
English ability														
% Could not speak ("Not at all" or "Poor")	T0	99.1	95.8	89.5	71.3	*	83.1	91.7	*	100.0	98.2	92.1	54.0	*
	T1	43.1	63.3	63.2	31.2	*	38.7	58.7	*	68.9	70.7	35.6	7.1	*
	T2	28.4	45.8	47.4	22.3	*	27.9	42.1	*	57.1	44.3	26.7	5.3	*
% Could not write ("Not at all" or "Poor")	T0	99.1	95.8	91.2	66.2	*	83.0	89.3	*	100.0	99.4	89.2	49.5	*
	T1	85.3	75.8	67.6	36.3	*	53.3	73.8	*	99.2	85.0	46.5	9.7	*
	T2	77.0	65.8	58.7	29.3	*	45.2	65.1	*	94.1	70.7	36.7	8.0	*
English literacy index (Read + write, 0 to 10)	T0	0.1	0.3	0.6	1.9	*	1.1	0.6	*	0	0.1	0.6	3.1	*
	T1	2.2	2.3	2.4	4.1	*	3.5	2.3	*	1.2	1.9	3.5	5.6	*
	T2	2.7	2.7	2.8	4.6	*	3.9	2.7	*	1.6	2.5	3.9	5.9	*
Training programs														
Months in ESL classes	T1	29.9	12.1	13.1	10.9	*	18.2	13.3	*	21.4	17.2	13.8	9.5	*
Months, job training	T1	1.5	2.2	2.1	4.2	*	4.0	1.3	*	0.4	1.8	3.0	6.0	*
Months, U.S. colleges	T1	1.7	2.3	3.8	8.3	*	6.4	2.4	*	0	0.9	4.2	14.3	*
Employment														
% Ever employed, U.S.	T1	33.0	30.0	40.4	55.4	*	55.6	26.6	*	10.1	35.3	48.5	75.2	*
	T2	36.7	34.2	52.6	65.0	*	63.7	33.7	*	15.1	43.1	60.4	81.4	*
% In the labor force	T1	34.9	23.3	35.1	58.0	*	60.1	19.0	*	10.9	31.8	49.6	71.7	*
	T2	35.8	29.2	38.6	59.9	*	62.5	22.6	*	11.7	33.6	55.4	76.1	*
% Currently employed	T1	17.5	16.7	21.0	35.6	*	31.8	15.9	*	0.8	15.6	29.8	54.9	*
	T2	18.4	21.7	30.7	46.5	*	41.6	20.3	*	2.5	20.4	38.6	69.0	*
Unemployment rate (%)	T1	49.9	47.2	39.9	38.4	*	46.9	16.8	*	92.6	50.9	39.9	23.4	*
	T2	48.6	37.5	20.5	22.4	*	33.6	10.6	*	78.6	39.3	30.3	9.3	*

*p < .01, NS = Not Significant

Occupational Adaptation

Table 8.3 also presents four measures of the occupational adaptation of these groups at T1 and T2: the percent ever employed and currently employed in the United States, and rates of labor force participation and unemployment (for a more detailed analysis, see Rumbaut 1986a). Unemployment rates were very high at T1 (in mid-1983, near the end of the recession), but declined substantially by T2 for the overall sample. Hmong unemployment rates scarcely changed during that period (from 49.9% to 48.6%), despite the fact that such measures conceal the very high level of Hmong discouraged workers (16%) who were not looking for work and who were therefore excluded from the unemployment rate. Nonetheless, strong gains in employment are evident for all the other groups—most notably for the 1975 cohort (whose T1 unemployment rate already stood at 12.5%) and for high school graduates (whose unemployment rate declined to 9.3% by T2). By comparison, during these two time periods (mid-1983 and mid-1984) the corresponding unemployment rates for the San Diego metropolitan area were 8.2% and 6.6% respectively, reflecting the recovery of the local economy from the 1981–83 recession. The low unemployment rates for women basically reflect a much lower rate of labor force participation than that of American women—most of the refugee women indicated their status as "homemaker," with considerable child-care obligations and a disadvantaged labor market position—although the data suggest the increasing entry of (especially Vietnamese and Chinese) women into the labor force, as well as the fact that 1975 cohort women have very high rates of labor force participation.

Table 8.4 switches the focus of attention from a concern with the occupational characteristics of individuals to a sketch of the characteristics of the jobs and employers of those respondents who were employed at T2 (N = 154). Those data show, first, the distribution of employed refugees in various employment sectors of the San Diego economy by ethnicity, gender, and cohort of arrival. The majority (over half) were employed in manufacturing work (the modal job was electronic assembly line work), to which many are channeled by refugee job training programs—even though the vast majority find their jobs informally (through self, family, or friends) rather than through formal or semiformal agencies or sponsors (cf. Forbes 1985). Note that almost one in six (14.3%) were employed in professional or paraprofessional jobs in the public sector, many of them working in refugee resettlement and related programs (e.g., as translators, job counselors, social service workers, interviewers—suggesting yet another impact of government funding on the labor force incorporation of these groups. The Vietnamese and the 1975 cohort predominated among private-sector professionals. Women were overrepresented among clerical workers and in nondurable manufacturing (especially in the garment industry). Sino-

Table 8.4 Characteristics of the Jobs of Employed Refugees, 1984 (IHARP Longitudinal Adult Sample, N = 154 Employees)

Employment sectors and job characteristics for employee subsample	Ethnicity					Gender			Time of Arrival			
	Hmong (N = 20)	Khmer (N = 26)	Chinese (N = 35)	Vietnam. (N = 73)	p	Male (N = 103)	Female (N = 51)	p	1975 (N = 26)	1976–79 (N = 78)	1980–83 (N = 50)	p
Employment sector												
% Professional, private sector	0	0	0	11.0	*	5.8	3.9	NS	23.1	1.3	2.0	*
% Professional, public sector	35.0	15.4	5.7	12.3	*	14.6	13.7	NS	26.9	16.7	4.0	*
% Clerical/office work	5.0	3.8	17.1	8.2	*	3.9	19.6	*	7.7	7.7	12.0	NS
% Trade and services	5.0	15.4	34.3	17.8	*	24.3	9.8	*	11.5	20.5	22.0	*
% Durable manufacturing	30.0	50.0	20.0	47.9	*	44.7	29.4	*	26.9	37.2	50.0	*
% Non-durable manufacturing	25.0	15.4	22.9	2.7	*	6.8	23.5	*	3.8	16.7	10.0	*
Job characteristics												
% Temporary jobs	45.0	11.5	25.7	15.5	*	20.8	21.6	NS	7.7	19.5	30.6	*
% No fringe benefits	60.0	26.9	52.9	29.2	*	34.3	46.0	*	11.5	41.6	46.9	*
% Cannot be promoted	90.0	84.6	66.7	45.7	*	62.0	65.3	*	37.5	69.7	65.3	*
% This is first job in U.S.	45.0	42.3	62.9	49.3	NS	42.7	66.7	*	11.5	46.2	78.0	*
% Indochinese Employer	0	11.5	54.3	15.1	*	21.4	21.6	NS	19.2	20.5	24.0	NS
% Size of enterprise is under 10 employees	30.0	19.2	51.4	27.4	*	31.1	33.3	NS	19.2	32.1	38.0	*
Ethnicity of coworkers												
% Indochinese mostly	25.0	23.1	51.4	17.8	*	26.2	29.4	NS	23.1	30.8	24.0	NS
% Other minorities	40.0	7.7	14.3	17.8	*	16.5	21.6	NS	3.8	23.1	18.0	*
% Anglos mostly	35.0	69.2	34.3	64.4	*	57.3	49.0	NS	73.1	46.2	58.0	*

*p < .01, NS = Not Significant

Vietnamese were concentrated in the petty bourgeois trades and service sectors, while the Khmer and Vietnamese predominated in the durable manufacturing sector.

The familiar contrast of primary versus secondary labor markets—with the latter encompassing most jobs in sales and service, clerical work and nondurable manufacturing—is also in evidence. Even among this subsample of employed Indochinese adults, it is clear that many (including over half of the Hmong and the Sino-Vietnamese) were in vulnerable, temporary, dead-end jobs offering few fringe benefits or avenues of advancement (including some of the public sector professionals, 27% of whom were in nonpermanent jobs). It should be noted that for over half of these employed respondents, their job at T2 was their first job ever in the United States. Although self-employment was relatively rare (only about 2.5% were self-employed), it is significant that over one in four of the employed respondents worked in jobs with mostly other co-ethnics, and that about one in five worked for typically small enterprises owned by an Indochinese employer—suggesting at least the beginning of an ethnic economic enclave option. The Sino-Vietnamese were disproportionately found within this small but developing enclave: more than half of them worked with or for co-ethnics.

Household Composition and Economic Adaptation

Table 8.5 presents data on the size, composition, and economic adaptation of Indochinese family/households. Of the 296 family/households in the longitudinal sample, 48 were headed by a woman, including 8.6% of the Vietnamese, 14.1% of the Sino-Vietnamese, 16.7% of the Hmong and 26.6% of the Khmer—this last high figure reflecting very high death rates of family members in Kampuchea in the late 1970s. Indeed, of all the women in the sample (N = 252), 22.6% of Khmer women were widowed, compared to only 5.1% of Hmong and Sino-Vietnamese women and but 1.4% of Vietnamese women; conversely, only 69.4% of Khmer women were married, compared to 88.1% of the Sino-Vietnamese, 91.5% of the Hmong and 94.4% of the Vietnamese. Household size was very large, ranging from 9.0 persons per Hmong household at T2, to 5.3 for the Vietnamese (by contrast, the mean U.S. household size is 2.7); household composition was complex, with a very high proportion of dependent children (reflecting high levels of fertility among these groups). The Khmer were much more likely to include unrelated individuals ("fictive kin") in their households as a support strategy, though the significant decrease in unrelated individuals between T1 and T2 suggests a trend toward traditional Khmer nuclear family arrangements. The Hmong, in particular, retain extended family arrangements, sometimes crowding 18 to 22 persons in small three-bedroom apartments.

Table 8.5 shows that the number of two-wage-earner families (which implies the entry of the second spouse into the labor force and is also strongly associated with lower fertility) is slowly increasing over time. The

Table 8.5 : Family/Household Composition and Economic Adaptation at T1 (1983) and T2 (1984) (IHARP Longitudinal Adult Sample, N = 296 Households)

Family/household composition and economic situation	Time	Ethnicity					Education (of Household Head)				
		Hmong (N = 60)	Khmer (N = 79)	Chinese (N = 64)	Vietnamese (N = 93)	p	(None (N = 48)	1-6 Yrs. (N = 99)	7-11 Yrs. (N = 70)	>12 Yrs. (N = 79)	p
Family/household											
Total household size	T1	8.8	8.7	5.8	5.5	*	8.6	8.0	6.5	5.6	*
	T2	9.0	7.5	5.9	5.3	*	8.2	7.6	6.3	5.3	*
Nuclear family size	T1	5.8	3.4	4.4	4.0	*	4.8	4.8	4.2	3.5	*
	T2	6.1	3.6	4.5	4.2	*	4.9	4.9	4.3	3.6	*
% Children under 18 (in household)	T1	58.2	44.0	45.3	44.0	*	52.9	51.2	48.6	37.3	*
	T2	56.5	45.4	44.7	42.4	*	51.7	51.7	46.8	36.7	*
Wage-earners											
% Families with two wage earners	T1	6.7	3.8	7.8	15.1	*	0	4.0	5.7	22.8	*
	T2	8.3	5.1	9.4	17.2	*	0	4.0	10.0	25.3	*
% Families with no wage earners	T1	65.0	64.6	60.9	46.2	*	93.8	65.7	57.1	27.8	*
	T2	73.3	64.6	51.6	38.7	*	95.8	66.7	48.6	22.8	*
Poverty status											
% Below poverty line	T1	93.3	82.3	81.3	57.0	*	93.8	91.8	77.9	44.3	*
	T2	88.3	81.0	76.6	61.3	*	97.9	88.9	74.3	45.6	*
Total family income, as % of poverty line	T1	67.1	100.3	79.6	130.5	*	65.9	72.1	83.5	164.1	*
	T2	71.9	92.2	86.4	129.1	*	55.0	77.7	91.7	156.7	*
Public assistance											
% Get no assistance (cash or non-cash)	T1	11.7	25.3	29.7	43.0	*	8.3	10.1	31.4	63.3	*
	T2	13.3	29.5	25.4	45.2	*	10.6	12.2	28.6	65.8	*
% Cash assistance (AFDC, SSI, RCA, GA)	T1	78.3	69.6	65.6	51.6	*	87.5	80.8	64.3	31.6	*
	T2	70.0	66.7	63.5	43.0	.05	85.1	74.5	55.7	27.8	*
Welfare dependency (Welfare/total income)	T1	.725	.752	.655	.563	*	.899	.803	.634	.379	*
	T2	.728	.690	.627	.483	*	.883	.767	.598	.291	*

*$p < .01$, NS = Not Significant

proportion of two-wage-earner families is highest among the Vietnamese and the 1975 cohort, and it is these groups who are the best off among the refugees. Still, more than half of Vietnamese households were below the federal poverty line at both T1 and T2. Poverty rates ranged up to about 90% for the Hmong—by far the highest among any group in San Diego County and six times higher than the 15% poverty rate for the United States in 1984. Total family income was often considerably below the poverty threshhold, as measured in Table 8.5 by an income-to-needs standard (i.e., the ratio of total family income to the poverty line standard, adjusted by nuclear family size). By this measure, Hmong family incomes averaged around 30% *below* the U.S. poverty standard. Only the Vietnamese and the most educated groups had family incomes exceeding the poverty threshhold. Finally, Table 8.5 presents data on the percentage of families receiving no public assistance of any kind, the percentage of families receiving cash assistance, and a "welfare dependency" measure, calculated as the ratio of welfare income to total family income from all sources.

Health Status

Table 8.6 presents selected indicators of refugee physical health status and health care utilization. Although physical/functional health status was assessed through various objective instruments as well as subjective self-report scales, the focus here is on self-rated health (which was found to correlate strongly with more objective measures). The Khmer (49%), women (42%), and the least educated (44%) were most likely to report "poor or fair" health at T2; by comparison, only 8% of American adults under 65 (and 32% of older Americans over 65) assessed their health as "poor or fair" in 1984. The Hmong were more likely to report chronic physical symptoms (persisting over six months), and to have had a major illness between T1 and T2. Smoking is overwhelmingly a male habit in the refugee communities: 56% of Indochinese men were smokers at that time, compared to only 4% of the women; by contrast, 1985 data show that 33% of American men and 28% of American women were smokers. Among Indochinese men, 70.7% of the Khmer were smokers (and they also smoked the most cigarettes daily and drank alcoholic beverages most often), followed by the Vietnamese (64.7%), the Sino-Vietnamese (54.5%) and the Hmong (26%); among the women, 12.9% of the Khmer were current smokers, compared to only 1.7% of the Hmong and the Chinese, and none of the Vietnamese. The refugees generally exhibited a pattern of health care underutilization in the area of preventive care: 44.5% of the respondents had never had a general check-up when not ill, and 21% said that they had never been to a dentist in the United States, partly reflecting limitations in publicly funded coverage for such services. The Indochinese were more likely to seek health services through community clinics located near their homes and through the private clinics of local Indochinese physicians. Among major problems experienced

Table 8.6 Health Status and Health Care Problems (1984) (IHARP Longitudinal Adult Sample, N = 500)

Health status and health care access problems	Ethnicity					Gender			Education (years)				
	Hmong (N=109)	Khmer (N=120)	Chinese (N=114)	Vietnam. (N=157)	p	Male (N=248)	Female (N=252)	p	None (N=119)	1-6 (N=167)	7-11 (N=101)	>12 Yrs. (N=113)	p
Self-rated health													
% Excellent	2.8	5.0	18.4	34.4	*	26.2	7.5	*	3.4	12.6	21.8	32.7	*
% Good	70.6	45.8	50.9	33.1	*	46.8	50.0	NS	52.9	48.5	45.5	46.0	NS
% Poor or fair	26.6	49.2	30.7	32.5	*	27.0	42.5	*	43.7	38.9	32.7	21.3	*
Health indicators													
Chronic (> 6 months) physical symptoms	1.04	0.68	0.70	0.50	*	0.62	0.80	NS	1.16	0.68	0.49	0.47	*
% Major illness, T1-T2	15.6	11.7	8.8	6.4	NS	8.1	12.3	*	19.3	10.8	4.0	5.3	*
% Current smoker	12.8	40.8	27.2	35.0	*	56.0	4.0	*	16.0	32.9	34.7	35.4	*
Health care use													
% Used clinic, hospital	56.5	44.2	22.8	22.3	*	25.1	44.8	*	55.9	37.1	27.7	16.8	*
% Saw M.D. past year	59.6	65.0	65.8	69.4	NS	59.7	71.0	*	65.5	73.1	61.4	57.5	.05
% Never seen dentist	29.2	28.0	16.1	10.2	*	23.0	16.8	NS	25.2	21.1	17.2	15.0	NS
% Never had general check-up when not ill	60.6	59.2	28.9	33.8	*	41.5	47.6	NS	62.2	46.1	38.6	29.2	*
Access problems													
% Language problem	82.6	85.0	53.5	28.0	*	50.4	68.3	*	85.7	68.9	51.5	24.8	*
% Fear MediCal cutoff	84.4	71.7	70.8	47.7	*	59.0	74.5	*	84.9	75.4	66.7	34.5	*
% Transportation	56.0	68.3	27.2	11.5	*	26.2	50.4	*	70.6	38.3	36.6	6.2	*
% Clinic too far away	52.3	25.8	21.2	3.8	*	14.3	32.7	*	51.3	22.9	12.9	5.4	*
% Lack of money	45.0	22.9	20.2	10.2	*	16.7	29.4	*	40.7	19.3	15.8	16.8	*
% No help from doctor	22.4	19.2	8.8	1.9	*	8.1	15.9	.05	28.0	10.2	5.9	3.5	*
% Too long wait in clinic or doctor's office	73.8	30.0	23.0	26.8	*	26.1	47.2	*	61.9	33.3	29.7	22.1	*

*p < .01, NS = Not Significant

in gaining access to health care, 60% of the respondents at T2 cited language problems, followed by lack of transportation (39%), long waiting in clinics (37%), lack of insurance (30%) and of money (23%), and getting no help from the doctor (12%); 67% also worried that MediCal coverage would be cut.

Psychological Adaptation

The mental health of the refugees was assessed through various quantitative and qualitative measures (see Rumbaut 1985a for a detailed discussion). Table 8.7 presents some selected indicators of their psychological adaptation by ethnicity, gender, and education. Note that over half of the Hmong and the Khmer respondents at T2 reported nightly problems getting to sleep, and many also indicated loss of appetite and other stress-related disturbances. We adapted a measure of psychological adjustment from the General Well-Being (GWB) Index developed and validated by the National Center for Health Statistics and used in the first national Health and Nutrition Examination Survey (HANES-I) of the general American population with a sample of nearly 7,000 adults aged 25–74. This instrument, composed of 18 items scored on a 0-to-5 scale, contains indicators of the presence, severity, and frequency of significant symptoms of psychological distress or well-being experienced by the respondent over the preceding month. It is a reliable measure of general and persistent *affective states* as reported by the person, rather than a clinical diagnosis as determined by psychiatric observation. Data at T1 and T2 for the refugee sample are presented in Table 8.7 for GWB scores classified into two main categories: "Positive Well-Being" and "Demoralization." While the prevalence of demoralization for the American population was 26% (a HANES finding confirmed by other national and regional studies using similar screening scales), the rate was *three times higher* (77.8%) for the Indochinese refugees at T1. A year later at T2 there was noticeable psychological improvement overall, but the refugee prevalence rate was still very high at 65.7%. Women were consistently more demoralized than men (as is also the case among American adults in the HANES sample). The Khmer exhibited the highest rates of demoralization and of depressive symptomatology at both T1 and T2, with little change over time. Interestingly, at T1 the most educated refugee group actually showed higher rates of demoralization than all but those refugees with no education at all, suggesting perhaps the psychological impact of status loss among the best educated. However, by T2, the best educated group had made a remarkable turn-around, with the data showing the same linear relationship between psychological well-being and education as found in the HANES data and in related studies of social class and mental illness.

A second measure used was a comparative Satisfaction with Life Areas (SLA) scale which had been previously used with samples of Indochinese refugees in Denver (Ossorio 1979). This scale asked for a *cognitive appraisal*

Table 8.7　Psychological Adaptation at T0 (1975), T1 (1983), T2 (1984), and T3 ("Next Year") (IHARP Longitudinal Adult Sample, N = 500)

Mental health variables	Time	Ethnicity					Gender			Education (years)				
		Hmong (N=109)	Khmer (N=120)	Chinese (N=114)	Vietnam. (N=157)	p	Male (N=248)	Female (N=252)	p	None (N=119)	1–6 (N=167)	7–11 (N=101)	>12 Yrs. (N=113)	p
Stress symptoms														
% Appetite problems	T2	22.0	42.5	11.4	14.6	*	17.7	26.6	*	31.9	24.6	15.8	14.2	*
% Sleep problems	T2	61.5	55.8	23.9	21.7	*	31.9	46.2	*	60.5	44.0	26.7	20.4	*
G.W.B. index														
% Positive well-being	T1	12.8	12.6	32.7	28.2	*	25.0	19.3	NS	16.1	23.5	29.0	20.4	NS
	T2	35.5	15.0	31.0	50.6	*	42.5	26.1	*	24.4	25.5	40.4	52.2	*
% Demoralization	T1	87.2	87.4	67.3	71.8	*	75.0	81.7	NS	83.9	76.8	71.0	79.1	NS
	T2	64.5	85.0	69.1	49.3	*	58.5	73.8	*	75.6	74.2	59.6	48.7	*
Depression measure														
(0 to 5 scale)	T1	1.88	2.18	1.33	1.29	*	1.62	1.66	NS	1.93	1.71	1.52	1.35	*
	T2	1.60	1.90	1.43	1.25	*	1.39	1.66	*	1.82	1.57	1.40	1.27	*
Life satisfaction														
(0 to 6 scale)	T0	5.05	5.18	4.86	4.99	*	5.14	4.90	*	5.08	4.96	5.05	5.00	NS
	T1	3.94	4.45	4.15	4.17	*	4.20	4.17	NS	3.96	4.20	4.33	4.26	*
	T2	3.92	4.71	4.21	4.48	*	4.42	4.29	NS	3.95	4.41	4.46	4.59	*
	T3	3.83	5.02	4.30	4.63	*	4.55	4.40	NS	4.04	4.50	4.62	4.77	*
Self-concept														
Actual self (1 to 7)	T2	3.06	4.66	4.16	4.88	*	4.33	4.20	NS	3.30	4.26	4.54	5.03	*
Ideal self (1 to 7)	T2	5.37	6.06	5.47	6.17	*	5.94	5.69	*	5.37	5.80	5.97	6.17	*
Ideal-actual differential	T2	2.31	1.40	1.31	1.29	*	1.61	1.49	NS	2.07	1.54	1.43	1.14	*

*p < .01, NS = Not Significant

from the respondent about nine areas of everyday life: work, money, homelife, children, neighborhood, social contacts, health, religion, and leisure. The scores are based on a 0 to 6 scale (where 0 = "very displeased," 6 = "very pleased," and 3 = neutral midpoint) and averaged to produce an overall SLA score. Table 8.7 presents SLA results for four points in time (T0, T1, T2, and "Next Year"), by ethnicity, gender, and education. Surprisingly, at each point in time the Khmer were the most satisfied and optimistic group, even though they were consistently the most demoralized and depressed group on the GWB affective measure. This distinctive (and even dissociative) Khmer pattern of both high depression and high satisfaction replicates earlier cross-sectional findings reported in Ossorio (1979) and Rumbaut (1985a), and here confirmed longitudinally as well. The Hmong are the least satisfied overall, and indeed they are the only group whose SLA scores *decrease* over time, reflecting a particularly pessimistic appraisal of their situation.

Finally, Table 8.7 reports results from a self-concept semantic differential measure that was employed in the T2 interviews to assess "internal" *self-appraisal* in the psychological adaptation process as opposed to the "external" appraisal of various life areas provided by the SLA measure. Here the respondents were asked to rate two concepts of themselves—their *actual self* ("what I really am") and *ideal self* ("what I would like to be")—along seven bipolar scales, each scored from 1 to 7. The seven scales were: "busy," "useful," "effective," "respected," "looking to the future," "satisfied with life," and "free to do things." In Table 8.7, three measures are presented: the overall "actual self" score, the overall "ideal self" score, and the difference or distance between the ideal self and the actual self scores—this last measure interpretable so that the greater the ideal-actual discrepancy, the greater the lack of self-esteem. There are significant differences especially by ethnicity and education, with higher self-esteem generally being associated with higher levels of education. The Vietnamese exhibit the highest self-ratings for both actual and ideal self, as well as the lowest ideal-actual differential—a strong self-esteem profile. The Sino-Vietnamese exhibit lower rankings than the Khmer or the Vietnamese on both the actual and ideal self-ratings, but also a lower ideal-actual differential than the Khmer (and one that is practically identical to the Vietnamese differential). The Khmer pattern reflects in part the curious satisfaction/depression combination noted above: a higher "cognitive" appraisal of actual and ideal selves combined with a greater "affective" gap in self-esteem. The Hmong, however, reflect both the lowest self-rankings on each scale as well as a far greater ideal-actual gap in self-esteem than any of the other groups.

Fertility and Adaptation

It is particularly important to understand the demography of this population in order to appreciate more fully the challenges and constraints of their resettlement and adaptation (cf. Rumbaut 1985b; Rumbaut and Weeks 1986). Results based on the T1 household sample (N = 3,003) show that this is a very young population, with an age and sex structure typical of the populations of developing countries, characterized by high fertility and dependency ratios. Of the total sample, 52.3% were males and 47.7% were females—a sex ratio of 110 males per 100 females. However, the sex ratio for the Vietnamese is about 120 (almost identical to the national data on admissions reported by Gordon in this volume), whereas for the other four groups the ratio of males to females is more even balanced. The median age for the Indochinese population as a whole is only 18 years—and the Hmong, astoundingly, have a median age of under 13 years—contrasted against a much older median age of 31 for the American population. The youthful, expansive age structure of the Indochinese reflects the high levels of current fertility in the refugee population. For example, we found child-woman ratios (CWRs)—i.e., the number of children under 5 per 1,000 women of childbearing age (defined as 15 to 44 years)—to range from 511 for the Sino-Vietnamese to an exceptionally high 1,769 for the Hmong, with the Khmer falling in between at 816; by contrast, the CWR for American women nationally is 309.

Data from the T1 subsample of women of childbearing age (N = 313) permitted a closer analysis of fertility levels and patterns. For example, age-specific birth rates (children born in the previous year) permitted us to estimate a corrected total fertility rate (TFR) of 5.7 children per Indochinese woman (weighted to reflect the different proportions of the ethnic groups in the United States), in contrast to the 1985 TFR of 1.8 children per American woman. Data on the number of children ever borne by women aged 45 to 49 in our sample, which may be taken as completed family size, confirmed our TFR findings that the Hmong have the highest fertility, followed by the Khmer, the Lao, the Sino-Vietnamese, and lastly the Vietnamese. Indeed, in the period of slightly less than one year between the T1 and T2 interviews, 22% of Hmong respondents of childbearing age had borne a child, as had 19% of the Khmer, 11% of the Chinese, and 7% of the Vietnamese. Moreover, at T2, 16% of the Hmong respondents indicated that they were pregnant, as were 9% of the Khmer, 4% of the Chinese, and 3% of the Vietnamese. At this time also, 41% of the Hmong women respondents of childbearing age reported that they planned to have more children, as did 33% of the Khmer (and 22% of the Lao at T1), 19% of the Chinese, and 27% of the Vietnamese.

The high levels of fertility within the Indochinese community have significant implications on several fronts. For example, the data suggest a substantial rate of natural increase for the immediately foreseeable future, and point out clearly the magnitude of need for maternal, child health, and family planning services to be made available to this population at least for the near term. Indeed, based on differential fertility rates of the various

Indochinese ethnic groups, the actual total Indochinese population in the United States was probably just over 1 million as of September 30, 1985—a 25% increase over the 800,000 who had been admitted as refugees or immigrants to the United States from 1975 to 1985 (Rumbaut and Weeks 1986). And finally, as will be discussed in more detail below, the data also underscore the relationship between fertility, poverty, and welfare dependency in the refugee communities.

In multivariate analyses of fertility and adaptation, we sought to identify the main determinants of refugee fertility within the United States (with the number of children born in the U.S. used as the criterion variable), and to measure the independent effect of antecedent (e.g., urban/rural background, ethnicity, education, time in the camps, deaths of children in the family) and intermediate factors (e.g., current English proficiency, employment, wage earners in the family and job income) on fertility, controlling for proximate determinants that would influence the number of children born in the United States (the number of years married [which is also a proxy for age], number of children born prior to arrival in the U.S., and length of residence in the U.S.). Multiple regression techniques were used to test this model, which accounted for nearly half (49.6%) of the variation in fertility levels in this population, and the results (which are discussed in detail in Rumbaut and Weeks 1986) may be briefly summarized as follows.

Net of the influence of years in the United States, years married, and number of children born prior to arrival (these three proximate covariates together accounted for nearly 30% of the explained variance in the dependent variable), several additional variables were found to be significantly related to current childbearing outcomes. Fertility was highest for respondents from rural backgrounds and varied inversely with premigration education and with time spent in refugee camps. Indeed, the fertility of women with less than six years of education was twice as high as that of women with twelve years or more of education. These background variables, however, did not enter the multiple regression equation; rather, their effects were mediated partly by ethnicity (Hmong ethnicity was a strong positive predictor and Chinese ethnicity a weak negative predictor, but otherwise the effect of ethnicity was accounted for by the effect of other variables in the model) and mainly by measures of present economic and cultural adaptation. The number of wage-earners in the family, English literacy level, and family job income emerged as significant predictors of lower fertility, together accounting for over 10% of the explained variance in the model. The number of families co-residing in the household had a modest *negative* effect on fertility, possibly indicating that the presence of grandparents or other adult kin relations in the household who are available to take care of preschool children serves to free women of childbearing age to enter the labor force— a decision that tends to have a depressive influence on fertility. Finally, the number of infant or child deaths in the family since 1975 had a modest positive effect on fertility net of all other determinants, possibly suggesting a (short-term) process of family rebuilding in reaction to family loss.

In general, then, these data highlight the relative importance of refugee economic and cultural adaptation processes as a downward pressure on fertility in the United States. Indeed, we found that the number of children born per year in the United States declines steadily and significantly with length of residence in and thus exposure to the United States. Only in part is this a function of the socioeconomic characteristics distinguishing the 1975 cohort from subsequent immigration waves: i.e., first-wave refugees were also more urban, educated, and prone to lower fertility than more recent arrivals. However, among second-wave refugees (including the Lao in this analysis), women who had lived three to five years in the United States were bearing children at a significantly lower rate (.20 per year) than those with less than three years of U.S. residence (.28 per year). This pattern of a general decline in childbearing over time in the receiving society is observable among all the ethnic groups and suggests a cumulative depressive impact on fertility as a result of economic and cultural adaptation processes. The next section turns to a closer analysis of these processes, focusing on findings concerning the determinants of refugee "economic self-sufficiency."

Earnings and Economic Self-Sufficiency

The promotion of "refugee economic self-sufficiency" is the principal goal of U.S. refugee resettlement policy, as enunciated in the Refugee Act of 1980. In practice this has meant a policy concern with (and an accompanying debate about) ensuring early employment and minimal reliance on transfer income. In this regard, multivariate analyses of IHARP panel data (Rumbaut 1986a) have focused on two dependent variables: (1) *personal job earnings* (measured as the total income earned by an individual from all jobs held in the previous calendar year), and (2) *welfare dependency* (measured as the proportion of total annual family income coming from public cash assistance programs). The sample for the analysis of earnings included all individuals with previous occupational experience in the homeland in order to test for the effect of transferable job skills (N = 449, since 51 persons in the longitudinal sample reported having had no premigration occupation). The sample for the analysis of welfare dependency was restricted to heads of household with premigration occupational experience, since the dependent variable here refers to the proportion of family welfare income rather than individual earnings (N = 283, since 13 female heads of household reported no prearrival labor force participation).

The multivariate model tested sought to examine the independent contributions at both T1 and T2 of selected human capital variables, household size and composition, and other key demographic and situational predictors of earnings and welfare dependency. A dummy variable for the 1975 cohort was inserted in the model to avoid confounding time and cohort effects (cf. Bach and Carroll-Seguin 1986; and Gordon in this volume). Because of colinearity with the measure of prearrival English literacy, years of premigration education were dropped in these runs; a dummy variable for high school graduate was included, however. Dichotomous dummy variables were also included for gender, marital status, Vietnamese (vs. non-Vietnamese) ethnicity, and car ownership. Continuous variables included the age of the respondent (in years); months in the United States; premigration occupation prestige [Treiman] scores; English literacy level prearrival and English literacy gain postarrival in the United States (measured at T0, T1, and T2, as noted earlier, by summing a 0-to-5 English *reading* proficiency scale and a 0-to-5 English *writing* proficiency scale to form a composite 0-to-10 literacy index); number of interstate moves (as a measure of secondary migration into San Diego County); months completed in job training programs as of T1; and both the number of children born in the United States (providing an approximate measure of pre-school-age children in the family/household) and the number of dependent children under 18 born before arrival in the United States. The ordinary least squares regression results accounted for about half of the explained variance (adjusted R squared ranged from 0.46 to 0.54), and may be summarized as follows.

Turning first to the multivariate analyses predicting refugee *earnings,* at both T1 and T2 the number of months in the United States remained the strongest predictor of earnings; that is, controlling for all other independent variables in the model, earnings were shown to increase significantly over time in the United States, although the magnitude of the effect decreased from T1 to T2 (from 33% to 27% of the explained variance). Nonetheless, the value of being a member of the 1975 cohort was also clear and consistent at both T1 and T2, worth over $3,000 in annual earnings net of other effects. It is not the passage of time alone (which presumably serves as a proxy for processes not otherwise measured by variables in the model), nor is it solely the characteristics and context of arrival of the first wave, but both time *and* cohort effects (among other factors) that shape economic outcomes. Human capital variables are also significant predictors of personal earnings, accounting for about 15% of the explained variance at both T1 and T2. The strongest of these variables—replicating earlier findings of other researchers (Bach 1984; Caplan, Whitmore, and Bui 1985)—is the level of prearrival English literacy (which is strongly associated with level of education but superior as a predictor of earnings in the U.S.). Other significant human capital predictors were degree of English literacy gain after arrival in the United States, premigration occupational prestige, and being a high school graduate. Interestingly, from T1 to T2, we found that postarrival gain in English proficiency grows in significance as a predictor of earnings while prearrival English declines by comparison—suggesting that prearrival English literacy is indeed a crucial resource (as cross-sectional studies of Indochinese refugee economic adaptation have found), but one whose relative value will decline over time (as the IHARP longitudinal data suggest).

Turning to a consideration of the situational variables in the model, the data show that having a car makes a substantial difference in earnings, as other studies have found to be the case at least for Southern California (cf. Strand 1984); the value of having a car was cut in half by T2, however, perhaps reflecting the fact that by T2 the great majority of employed refugees already owned a car. Secondary migration, on the other hand, is associated with reduced earnings. Perhaps surprisingly, the value of partici- pation in job training programs was found to be negative (at T1) to negligible (at T2) for earnings, possibly suggesting that job placements obtained through such programs may be less stable and less remunerative than jobs located through informal contacts or personal initiative (see also the recent critical evaluation by Berkeley Planning Associates et al. 1986). The effect of household variables and marital status on earnings is relatively weak, but earnings are negatively affected especially by pre-school-age children in the household. Controlling for all other variables in the model, refugee women were found to be at a very significant earnings disadvantage—as are nonre- fugee women in the labor market generally. Age had a weak but negative effect: the older the refugee, the lower the level of earnings. Finally and surprisingly (though replicating the earlier findings of Bach [1984] using ORR national data), Vietnamese ethnicity was found to be significantly and negatively associated with earnings at T1 (the effect was not significant though still negative at T2) when other variables were controlled, even though bivariate relationships show the Vietnamese as a group doing best occupationally and economically.

Comparing these findings to the results of multivariate analyses of *welfare dependency*, again number of months in the United States was a strong predictor variable, showing that welfare dependency significantly decreases over time even when all other variables in the model are controlled—though the effect is reduced considerably between T1 and T2. Indeed, by T2, the most significant predictor of welfare dependency for our San Diego sample was that of family/household composition, especially the number of depend- ent children in the family—born both pre- and post-arrival in the U.S.. By T2 these two latter variables accounted for about 20% of the explained variance, as much as that explained by months in the United States. Indeed, T2 partial regression coefficients in this analysis suggested that the percent- age of family income coming from public assistance would be increased by about 10% for each dependent child in the family born in the United States and by another 6% for each dependent child in the family born before arrival in the United States. Moreover, being married also added to the proportion of family income coming from public assistance—underscoring in particular the importance of eligibility rules in the AFDC-Unemployed

Parent program in California, which (as do 25 other states) provides assistance for indigent but intact two-parent families.

In contrast to our findings on earnings, these results showed further that English proficiency was *not* significantly associated with welfare dependency, nor was being a high school graduate likely to reduce dependency net of other variables. Months in job training programs also showed no effect either way. The only human capital variable that was significantly and negatively associated with welfare dependency was premigration occupational prestige, but it accounted for only 2.5 percent of the variance. Car ownership was strongly and negatively associated with the dependent variable, suggesting in part the positive relationship between car ownership and employment/earnings, though in part the effect may also be an artifact of eligibility rules for public assistance (which permit a welfare recipient to own a car only if the value of the car is less than $1,500). Gender and ethnicity of the head of household were not significantly associated with welfare dependency, but dependency did increase significantly with age and also with poor health status (which is itself in part a function of age).

Of considerable interest was the finding that secondary migration was positively associated with welfare dependency net of other variables ($p < .05$), although the effect explains just over one percent of the variance. The possibility that Indochinese secondary migrants to California moved there at least in part because of the less restrictive welfare system in that state has long been speculated about by policy makers and resettlement workers (see Forbes 1985 for an excellent review of the argument), but that had not been demonstrated by systematic evidence. Available bivariate data were inconclusive; if anything, as is the case with other internal migrants generally, the characteristics of secondary migrants to California in the IHARP sample (comprising fully one-third of the respondents) reflected a group somewhat younger, more educated, more English-proficient, as likely or more likely to be employed, and of longer residence in the United States than primary migrants who had been sponsored directly for resettlement in San Diego. However, controlling for the other variables in the model, the multivariate results indicate that secondary migration to California has tended to decrease earnings and increase reliance on transfer income. Overall, then, these analyses carry the implication that refugee welfare dependency is not so much a function of human capital or related variables such as job training, but rather that it is principally a function of the interaction of family/household composition (and accompanying refugee needs) with the structure of the available system of public assistance (see also Bach, Carrol-Seguin, and Howell 1986)—although, in accord with the findings of the ISR "self-sufficiency" study, the data also strongly show that reliance on transfer income as a transitional survival strategy does continue to decline over time. This latter finding, like earlier reported data showing a general interrelated (though by no means "automatic") decline in fertility, unemployment and psychological depression over time, again points to the fact that adaptation processes are *temporally* as well as *socially* patterned.

The analyses of the effect of adaptation processes on both fertility and welfare dependency outcomes dovetail at this point. The data (based on a California sample) lead to the conclusion that for most of those refugee families who already have a large number of children, poverty and dependence on public assistance may well remain a fact of life until the children are grown and economically self-sufficient; but for those with small families, or those who have not yet begun family-building activity, it seems clear that motivation to limit family size will be positively associated with an ability to avoid later dependence on welfare. In this respect, then, the IHARP findings suggest the need to take family planning services—and related support services such as child care—into account as part of a larger policy aimed at economic self-sufficiency. In another respect, the youthfulness of the Indochinese population additionally underscores the fact that the future of these communities will hinge heavily and increasingly on the educational, occupational and economic attainment of the sizable generation of young people who are now completing their education in the United States and reaching employment age. Before discussing findings on the educational attainment of refugee youth, however, this chapter turns to a related multivariate analysis of another central dimension of the refugee experience: the process of psychological adaptation.

Depression and Adaptation

The research literature on migration and mental health has repeatedly suggested that refugees experience significantly greater psychological distress and dysfunction than other immigrants. It is axiomatic to observe that unhappiness is a natural (if not necessary) consequence of human misfortune, and refugees by definition tend to experience a much greater share of such misfortune. What has not been so clear are the specific dimensions, duration, and distribution of psychological distress and dysfunction among different refugee groups, and their impact on other facets of cultural and economic adaptation. Based on the comparable IHARP and HANES measures already discussed, Indochinese refugees as a whole do experience significantly greater levels of distress than the non-refugee population. To be sure, the Indochinese are a culturally heterogeneous population whose migration histories have differed sharply in many respects. But while the psychological experience of exile is complex and multidimensional, it is also socially and temporally patterned and predictable. This section focuses on one aspect of that experience, based on a measure of depressive symptomatology derived from the items composing the General Well-Being (GWB) index (for a more detailed discussion, see Rumbaut 1985a, Rumbaut and Rumbaut 1986, and Rumbaut 1986b).

Factor analyses of the GWB items in the IHARP sample revealed two principal factors, each composed of 8 items (loading on the factor above a 0.50 criterion), which together accounted for more than 50% of the variance in the GWB data.[9] One factor reflects dysphoric symptoms and a sad, anxious, and depressed mood, here labeled *Depression;* this factor alone accounted for 40% of the variance in the GWB items at T2.[10] The other factor is composed of items reflecting a vital, cheerful sense of positive affect and well-being, here labeled *Happiness.* The data show these two subscales to be highly reliable and internally consistent measures. While the two are inversely correlated (-.469 at T1 and -.497 at T2), they tap different and more discriminatory psychological dimensions of the broader GWB measure, which tend to be concealed when the two components are aggregated into a single GWB score. For example, there were different psychocultural profiles among the four ethnic groups for each of the two factors; and certain stressful life events (e.g., deaths in the family) were significant predictors of one factor (*Depression*) but not of the other, while the fulfillment of basic gender roles by men and women were significant predictors of *Happiness* outcomes[11] but not of *Depression*. It is the findings pertaining to the *Depression* factor that will be discussed here.

Mean depression scores for the sample as a whole were 1.64 at T1 and 1.53 at T2 (interpretable on the 0-to-5 scale on which they were based), suggesting some amelioration of depressive symptoms for the overall sample between T1 and T2. It should be pointed out that T1 depression scores were significantly and strongly correlated a year later with T2 depression scores for both men and women ($r = .430, p < .0001$)—the strongest such intercorrelation obtained among any of the health and mental health measures over time. This finding suggests that what is being measured here is not an acute or transient mood state, but a chronic and persistent affective condition. (By contrast, the intercorrelation of the overall GWB scores at T1 and T2 was only .165.) In fact, when the T1 depression score was entered as an independent variable in multivariate analyses of T2 depression scores, the T1 score emerged as the principal predictor of the T2 score—accounting for nearly 20% of the explained variance in T2 depression levels by itself. Moreover, depression scores were also significantly ($p < .0001$) and strongly correlated with key stress-related somatic symptoms, notably with sleep ($r = .474$) and appetite ($r = .342$) disturbances—evidence suggestive of the validity of the measure.

In general, bivariate results show that depressive symptoms are *socially* patterned. For example, there were significantly more elevated depression scores for the Khmer and the Hmong; for women; for respondents over 50 years of age; for persons from rural backgrounds with little education; for those in maritally disrupted statuses and with the most traumatic migration histories, who reported the most deaths of close family members, who escaped without their families or who cannot now communicate with them, and who spent the longest time in refugee camps. Depression scores were also significantly higher for the least acculturated, those most desirous of returning to the homeland, the least English proficient, the unemployed, those below the poverty line and dependent on welfare assistance, those who did not own a car, and those reporting more chronic physical symptoms and poor physical health status. Interestingly, those reporting no religion had significantly lower depression scores than any of those who adhered to a religion, and this effect persisted, though weakly, when other possibly confounding factors were controlled (cf. Rumbaut 1986b).

In addition, the psychological adaptation process appears to be *temporally* patterned as well. In a paper reporting T1 results (Rumbaut 1985a), it was observed that the first year in the United States tends to be a relatively euphoric period for the refugee, and it was during the first year that refugees had the lowest *Depression* scores and the highest *Happiness* and *Life Satisfaction* scores; by contrast, it was during the second year that they had the highest depression scores and the lowest measures of well-being. That second year is thus a period of "psychological arrival" and "exile shock," involving the helpless/hopeless realization that everything that matters seems utterly unattainable and beyond control. After the third year, however, there appeared to be a psychological rebound and relative stabilization. T2 data permitted a longitudinal test of this hypothesis, and the results (based on t-tests of statistical significance) confirm the original prediction: those who had been in the United States for one year or less at T1 experienced a significant *increase* in depressive symptoms by T2, whereas those who had been in the United States between 13 and 23 months at T1 reflected a significant *decrease* in depression scores, as did those who had been in the country for over 48 months.

Given the multiplicity of variables that were significantly related to depressive outcomes, and the possibility of confounding factors and spurious relationships, multivariate analyses were performed to identify the principal predictors of *Depression* at both T1 and T2 while controlling for a wide range of potentially related variables. The results are of considerable interest. In all models tested, for the sample as a whole and separately for both men and women, the first variable entering the stepwise regression equation was an objective measure of physical health status—the poorer the health status, the higher the level of depression.[12] With physical health status controlled, as well as in all runs that excluded health status from the model, it turns out that the strongest predictor of depression at both T1 and T2 was our measure (derived from the T1 interview) of total "push" factors in the decision to leave the homeland. A related though weaker predictor entering the regression equation at T1 was the number of years since migration from the homeland, which was positively associated with depression net of the effect of other variables. This finding points to the very essence of the refugee experience—the coerced nature of their homelessness—as a determinant of depressive symptomatology even years after the migration process was set in motion. It also supports the view of the refugee as not merely another class of immigrant, but, at least on psychosocial grounds, as a qualitatively different social type—even though it is possible to measure differences among the refugees themselves in their degree of "refugeeness," of perceived "push" or coercion along a continuum from voluntary to involuntary decision-making in the critical, fateful, and often sudden choice of going into an uncertain exile—typically with little planning or preparation and with no realistic possibility of return.

Other significant positive predictors of depression at T1 underscored the impact of life events (deaths of children, death of spouse, having escaped unaccompanied by one's immediate family, total person-months of family separation and of family imprisonment) involving family loss and separation—not surprisingly especially in a population where the family is the central institution of social life. Among these stressors, there were different effects for men and for women. Deaths of close family members were significant predictors of depression for men, whereas separation from and imprisonment of close family members were significant predictors of depression for women. In addition to these differences by gender, we found that for women (but not for men), depression decreased significantly as the number of (nuclear and nonnuclear) family members currently residing in the household increased—underscoring the buffering effect of familial social supports for women, who have been frequently home-bound in this population. For men (but not for women), depression decreased significantly for those who were married (a finding that parallels other research with the general American population) and it varied inversely with the number of close Indochinese (but not American) friends—underscoring the buffering effects of marriage and co-ethnic friendships for men.

Finally, for the sample as a whole, three other variables in the regression equation were significantly associated with higher depression scores at T1 (and all but the third at T2 as well): a rural background; a low level of American acculturation (as measured by a cultural values scale, identified through factor analytic techniques, composed of items similar to those used by Roberts and Starr in the research reported in this volume); and not owning a car—all indicative of problems of sociocultural isolation and resourcelessness, and of the role of cultural and economic adaptation in shaping psychological outcomes. Indeed, by T2, multivariate results suggest that the impact of earlier life events on depression, though still significant, tends to recede in importance over time, while contemporary stressors and socioeconomic adaptive processes (particularly unemployment status) tend to become increasingly salient in predicting depressive outcomes.

The Educational Attainment of Refugee Youth

In the Fall of 1986, as part of the Southeast Asian Refugee Youth Study (SARYS) [see note 2], a subsequent investigation was begun into the educational and occupational attainments and aspirations of a distinctive cohort that can be labelled the "1.5" generation of refugee youth. These "1.5ers" are young people who were born in their countries of origin but who are being formed in the United States, where they are completing their education during the key formative periods of adolescence and young adulthood—in the interstices of two societies and cultures, between the "first" and "second" generations, between being "refugees" and being "ethnics" (or "hyphenated Americans"). The original IHARP data set did not include objective measures of the educational attainment of such school-age youth, such as grade point averages (GPAs) or standardized achievement test scores. However, under a collaborative arrangement with the San Diego Unified School District, it was possible to obtain complete academic histories for all Indochinese youth in the IHARP random sample who had been enrolled in any of the San Diego City Schools (K–12) at any point between 1983 and the 1986–87 school year. Complete longitudinal records (in some cases going back ten years) were collected for each such student, including transcripts of all courses ever taken, grades received, and scores attained for all standardized achievement tests. The resulting sample (N = 579) forms what will be referred to as the IHARP-SARYS sample (cf. Rumbaut and Ima 1987).[13] While it is beyond the scope here to attempt to summarize the extensive SARYS study, a few selected findings will be highlighted below.

Table 8.8 presents official San Diego City Schools (SDCS) data on cumulative grade point averages (excluding physical education courses) for all 12th grade students enrolled during the 1986–87 academic year in local high schools (N = 6,377 seniors), broken down by ethnic/racial category. (The data, by definition, exclude all students who may have dropped out of school before the 12th grade—whose grades are known to be much lower than those of students who do not drop out. It is also the case in San Diego that drop-out rates for Indochinese students are significantly lower than for other students—not least, incidentally, because AFDC eligibility rules for children under 18 require that they be enrolled full-time in school.) The results show that "Asians" (an SDCS category that includes mainly U.S.-born Chinese, Japanese, and Korean students) have the highest percentage of students with GPAs above 3.0 (52.1%), followed by Indochinese students (39.6%), Filipinos (38.3%), whites (34.6%), Pacific Islanders (24.2%), Hispanics (13.8%), and Blacks (9.4%). Remarkably, despite their recent arrival in the United States, Indochinese seniors were outperforming all but a small group of other Asian students in San Diego's high schools—including majority white students.

Since the SDCS data do not permit a further breakdown by the five main

Table 8.8 Cumulative Grade Point Averages (GPAs) of Students in San Diego City
Schools, by Ethnicity* (SDCS High School Seniors, N = 6,377; IHARP-SARYS
Sample, N = 239)

Ethnic group	3.0 or above		2.9 to 2.0		Below 2.0		Total
	%	(N)	%	(N)	%	(N)	(N)
SDCS Seniors							
Asian	52.1	88	37.3	63	10.7	18	169
Indochinese	39.6	182	48.0	221	12.4	57	460
Filipino	38.4	134	45.4	159	16.3	57	350
White	34.6	1,232	46.5	1,656	18.9	673	3,561
Hispanic	13.8	122	50.7	448	35.5	314	884
Black	9.4	81	47.7	409	42.9	368	858
IHARP-SARYS							
Indochinese	40.4	96	45.2	108	14.6	35	239
Vietnamese	53.4	29	33.3	18	13.0	7	54
Chinese-Viet.	48.9	22	33.3	15	17.8	8	45
Hmong	40.4	19	55.3	26	4.3	2	47
Khmer	20.0	7	68.6	24	11.4	4	35
Lao	32.8	19	43.1	25	24.1	14	58

*GPAs excluding Physical Education courses. SDCS data are for all 12th graders in city high
schools during the 1986–87 academic year; IHARP-SARYS data are for 7th–12 graders.

Indochinese ethnic groups, we relied on our IHARP-SARYS sample of
Indochinese secondary school students (N = 239) to provide such a comparison. As Table 8.8 shows, the cumulative GPA profiles of the IHARP-SARYS
Indochinese sample are nearly identical to the SDCS totals for Indochinese
seniors—a fact that adds to confidence about the generalizability of findings
based on our sample. The results are illuminating and intriguing. We had
hypothesized that the greater the level of education of refugee parents, the
greater would be the educational attainment of their children in American
schools—i.e., a social class explanation for the process of refugee youth
achievement. As predicted, the Vietnamese exhibit the highest GPAs of any
of the Indochinese groups; what is more, a greater proportion of Vietnamese
students (53.7%) had GPAs above 3.0 than any other group in the city. Also
as predicted, the Sino-Vietnamese follow, with 48.9% having GPAs above
3.0. What is quite surprising is that the next-ranked group is the Hmong:
40.4% of Hmong students had GPAs above 3.0, a higher proportion than for
the Khmer and the Lao, and higher also than for majority white students,
Filipinos, Hispanics, and Blacks. Specifically, the mean cumulative GPA of
the Vietnamese sample was 2.97, followed by the Sino-Vietnamese (2.88),
the Hmong (2.78), the Khmer (2.64), and lastly the Lao (2.57); these

differences by ethnic group are statistically significant, although they are not significant by gender for the overall sample.[14]

The Comprehensive Test of Basic Skills (CTBS) is the nationally standard-ized instrument used by the San Diego City Schools to measure the educational achievement of (K–12) students. Based on the CTBS scores, we found that Indochinese students as a group were in the top quartile nationally in mathematics computation, but in the lowest quartile nationally in reading vocabulary. In general, achievement test scores show a typical low-to-high progression from vocabulary and reading comprehension skills, up through language expression, spelling, language mechanics, application of math concepts, and math computation—that is, a sequence of achieve-ment that moves from the most "subjective" culture- and language-bound basic skills tested to the most "objective" rule-bound and universally appli-cable skills. While math scores were remaining fairly stable over time, there was evidence of rapid improvement in reading and language skills over time as the refugee students increasingly come to learn and master the English language. Intergroup differences in achievement scores generally confirm the above GPA rankings: the Vietnamese did best (in fact, 49% of the Vietnamese were in the top 10% nationally in math skills), followed by the Sino-Vietnamese and the Hmong. However, the Lao reflected higher skill scores than the Khmer (especially in math), even though the Lao had lower GPAs than the Khmer—a fact that deserves explanation, and may reflect motivational dynamics.[15]

We next linked the IHARP data set (covering a wide range of independent variables, including household size and composition, the parents' premigra-tion characteristics and all major postarrival adaptation variables) with the SARYS data on educational outcomes; multivariate analyses were then conducted to identify the principal predictors of the children's GPAs and CTBS achievement test scores. The multiple regression models tested are more explanatory of CTBS scores (explaining about 50% of the variance in the dependent variable) than of GPAs (explaining about 25% of the variance in GPAs), a finding that suggests that GPA attainment may be more influ-enced by individual and contextual factors that were not directly measured in this data set.[16]

Briefly, the following results may be highlighted:

(1) Measures of educational achievement increase with length of time in U.S. schools, and the younger refugee students appear to be achieving at a higher level than their older siblings or peers. This reflects the fact that, at least in the short run, the more recently-arrived, older students are more handicapped by language deficiencies and have less time to "learn the ropes" of the new system; whereas the younger ones (a greater proportion of whose lives has now been spent in the United States) are not so handicapped.[17]

(2) In general, multivariate results confirm the effect of ethnocultural

background on academic success: being Vietnamese, Chinese, and Hmong has a positive effect on outcomes, while being Lao or Khmer does not, when the analysis is controlled for the effects of age or length of time in the schools.

(3) Household size per se is not correlated with academic outcomes, but the number of adults residing in the household is positively associated with higher GPAs and achievement test scores—emphasizing the importance of two-parent families for student educational attainment. Moreover, high-GPA-attaining students (>3.0) are much more likely to live in two-wage-earner families whereas not a single student with a low GPA (<2.0) lived in a two-wage-earner family.

(4) With regard to the effect of the adaptive resources of the parents, it is the mother's (not the father's) socioeconomic resources as well as psychological status that most significantly influence student performance in the schools. This finding suggests that it is the mother who plays the principal role in the socialization and supervision of the children within these households.

(5) The number of years of residence in the United States is a significant predictor of CTBS reading and language scores, as might be expected, but not of GPAs or math achievement scores.

(6) Finally, measures of cultural attitudes held by the parents are also associated with student attainment patterns. The more strongly held were traditional values and a sense of ethnic pride and identity, and the more convinced were the parents (both mothers and fathers) that as Asians they would never have equal status with Americans in the United States, the higher the GPAs attained by their children. These results (which in part parallel those of the ISR study, as summarized by Whitmore, Trautmann, and Caplan in this volume; cf. Portes and Bach 1985) may suggest the motivational role of ethnic pride and resilience, self-justification, and determined effort exemplified consensually by both parents within a cohesive, duty-bound family structure. Such results also undermine the familiar notion that "Americanization" in cultural attitudes and values is a prerequisite for success in American society. Ironically, the opposite may be the case.

The Pivotal Role of Women

The preceding analyses have touched on only a few of the multiple, interrelated dimensions of Southeast Asian refugee adaptation to the American economy and society. One key theme that recurs is the importance of looking at *the refugee family/household as a unit of analysis* (rather than simply focusing on the characteristics of individuals), and in particular the need to better understand *the pivotal role of women* in the adaptation of refugee families. Indeed, within refugee families, the role of women emerges as a central underlying variable in the determination of each of the main adaptation outcomes that have been examined in this chapter: fertility, earnings and economic self-sufficiency, mental health, and the educational attainment of refugee children.

Thus, for example, the role of women is basic to the reproduction of the group. Fertility patterns are intricately linked not only to present levels of poverty and dependency on public assistance, and to health and mental health concerns, but also to the likelihood of women's participation in the labor force and thus to the family's prospects for economic self-sufficiency. It is women who enter the labor force who supply the essential second income that tends to lift the refugee family/household out of a cycle of poverty and dependency—a process that itself has a depressive effect on fertility. As well, women's psychological status at T1 was predictive of their husbands' level of depression at T2, but the reverse is not true—a finding that seems to point to significant contribution of the wife to the emotional support of her spouse. Finally, with respect to the future of refugee communities, given that the education of the children is relied upon as perhaps the principal strategy for socioeconomic mobility, it is the mother's (not the father's) resources that are most predictive of the children's educational attainment—a finding that underscores the woman's central role in the supervision, motivation, and socialization of the children within the family.

Despite their pivotal role in ensuring the well-being of their families amidst conditions of relative poverty and acculturative stress, these refugee women arrived with a significant disadvantage in social status and basic human capital resources relative to their male counterparts, reflecting a legacy of subordination in their countries of origin, and their traditional domestic responsibilities within the household in the United States have often served only to widen the "adaptive gap" between the genders in the competitive American context. It is women who shoulder the burdens of child-bearing and child-rearing within the family, who are most discriminated against in the job market when they work outside the home, and who—not surprisingly—also show significantly greater levels of poor health, chronic depression, and distress over time relative to the men in the IHARP panel. Yet the process of resettlement in the United States has also opened new possibilities for women that had been previously unavailable or traditionally suppressed. Their adaptation to these new situational demands is producing, in turn, very rapid sociocultural changes in gender roles within all of the Indochinese ethnic groups—changes that, while accompanied by and at the cost of considerable marital and intrafamilial conflict in the short run, may, in the future, elevate the status of women in these groups and enhance their and their families' socioeconomic prospects. Indeed, the IHARP series of qualitative interviews suggests that the issue of gender stratification and status/role change is extraordinarily complex in both public and private spheres of social life. To achieve an understanding of this issue, and to better appreciate its implications for both social theory and social policy, much more research will be needed—particularly research that departs from the traditional ways of studying the adaptation of immigrant groups.

The neglect of the role of immigrant women is only beginning to be rectified by recent scholarship.[18] In an essay originally published over a decade ago, Maxine Seller observed that the relative lack of systematic knowledge about immigrant women was due to the persistence of negative stereotypes that imply that "women did little worth writing about" (Seller 1987:197). Regarding studies of turn-of-the-century "forgotten" immigrant women from Southern and Eastern Europe, she cites early twentieth-century stereotypes that may continue to influence some contemporary views of the matter, such as one librarian's observation that "[immigrant] women are left behind in intelligence by the father and children. They do not learn English; they do not keep up with other members of the family" (ibid.:197). Indeed, the cases Seller studied provide some remarkable parallels to the experience of Southeast Asian refugees we have observed—including a depiction of the ways in which traditional gender patterns break up as the mix of economic pressures and opportunities produce new bases of economic, legal, and social power among immigrant women. For instance, in a quotation directly mirroring statements heard from male Hmong refugees in San Diego, Seller notes that male Ukrainian immigrants to the United States felt that "the laws here are made for women" (ibid.:201)—because traditionally permissible practices such as wife-beating could now be reported to police and challenged in American courts. And the following observation applies as well to the conclusions in IHARP: "Undoubtedly life was too much for some immigrant women. Broken homes, physical and mental illness, despair, even suicide were all too often present in the ethnic ghetto. The amazing thing is that, given the cultural shock of immigration and the problems of poverty, discrimination, and survival in urban slums, so many women were able to keep themselves and their families from being defeated" (ibid.:202).

Reflections on the Research Process

In reflecting on the past research on Southeast Asian refugee resettlement, one is struck by how little is known about the actual process of conducting complex research undertakings, such as the ones reported in this volume, which typically involve several languages and dialects with groups of widely varying economic and ethnocultural backgrounds. Methodological issues of validity, reliability, and generalizability are fundamental to the proper conduct of any research study, but these issues become much more problematic in the context of comparative multicultural survey research. Published reports of research studies (as well as final reports to funding agencies) often convey a purified, reified, "frontstage" version of the research activity as a scientific product. It is rare to gain from such reports a fuller "backstage" understanding of the research activity itself—not just as a set of technical procedures, but as a social and moral process, and as an organizational and political accomplishment—to get a look, in short, at the "human element" in survey research, and at the range of questions and concerns that are raised especially with regard to the conduct of survey research among cultural minorities. Yet the technical and methodological requirements of such research hinge on the sociopolitical and organizational arrangements of the project; and what is more, the events that constitute the research activity as a social process are frequently more telling and interesting than the final tabulations of results.

Consider, for instance, the interviewing process itself. In IHARP, while the interviewer was duly trained to follow the requisite technical procedures for data collection, the interview also involved at least two persons communicating with each other, often about painful and problematic experiences, within a defined social context. The interview situation sometimes created stress (though the goal was to study it!); sometimes it served in part as a cathartic, quasi-therapeutic occasion that allowed respondents to discuss many aspects of their resettlement with a supportive, active listener; sometimes it served too as an opportunity for guided, systematic reflection on the respondent's life experiences—in effect, a "life review" of the experience of exile. In the process, a number of problems often came to light that put the skilled interviewer in a position (which we had encouraged during the training program) of actually assisting the respondent at the end of the interview. In many cases, that assistance took the form of providing advice and referral information, or active intervention and follow-up. Among dozens of such cases were, for example: an IHARP interviewer following up with a caseworker to obtain SSI benefits for an eligible mentally retarded Hmong boy whose family was not receiving the assistance to which he was entitled (the family received a retroactive "golden check" for $2,838.50 and began receiving the higher SSI rate of $350/month); successfully contacting the Indonesian Red Cross and ultimately locating in Canada relatives of a Khmer respondent from whom they had been separated in the Galang refugee camp; effectively intervening in a case involving a seven-car accident caused by a refugee respondent without insurance (who was subsequently being hounded by collection agencies and insurance companies to pay for the damage caused to the other vehicles, and who was despairing to the point of threatening suicide at the time the IHARP interview took place); and helping respondents to find a job, make funeral arrangements, resolve a dispute involving school transcripts, assist a family to set in motion a search process for lost family members in Cambodia, and contact the property management company and the local gas-and-electric company to fix a gas leak that was posing a serious threat. In one instance, staff arranged through a local priest for an exorcism to "chase the spirits away" in a Hmong household where the respondent wanted to "become a Christian family," but where the father maintained animist practices and the mother was "always bothered by evil spirits during night time"—the ceremonial healing helped, and she was thereafter able to sleep at night. All such cases revealed the dual technical-social character of the interviewing process, and helped develop goodwill relationships that enhanced (not "contaminated") both the quality of the data being collected and the cooperation of the respondents in the T2 reinterviews.

On a more theoretical level, reflection on the research to date underlines the need to connect theories of adaptation with theories of international migration and of so-called "race and ethnic relations" generally, thus placing the study of refugee migration and adaptation in its larger context and grasping the process holistically; that is, encompassing the process of migration and adaptation in its totality, from an examination of conditions and contexts in the countries of origin, to the nature and characteristics of the migration flows, to the stages, types, and dimensions of the process of incorporation into a new society. In addition, the "process of refugee adaptation" needs to be addressed multidimensionally—both "horizontally," covering a variety of adaptation "realms" (of which only a few have been touched upon in this paper), and "vertically," focusing on different units of analysis (from the individual to the household to the community). A brief inventory of topics emerging from such a matrix might include: the psychological adaptation of refugees to their "coerced homelessness" and to the crisis of exile; the phenomenology of alienation and estrangement; the segmented labor markets into which they are incorporated and the "segmented welfare systems" that may provide them with an alternative mode of subsistence outside of the secondary low-wage labor market; the "mode of reproduction" (and not just the "mode of production") that structures the adaptive contexts of refugee groups; the social ecology of their spatial settlement patterns and the development of ethnic communities; their cultural adaptation (which will require both a sophisticated understanding of refugees' cultural backgrounds and a more explicit appreciation of the complexity and contradictions of American cultural contexts than is typically assumed in homogenized conceptualization of "acculturation"); and the varieties of adaptive "careers" and coping strategies shaped by such key independent variables as *age* (e.g., the differential adaptation of young and old), *gender* (especially a much needed focus on the situation of women both within and outside their families), *social class* (especially the range of class-linked motivations that distinguish what Egon Kunz [1973] once called different "vintages" and not just "waves" of refugees from the same country of origin); and *time* itself (especially the issue of generations). All of these aspects and dimensions of adaptation need to be addressed far more systematically in our studies and research than they have been. That such an agenda will deepen the understanding of adaptive phenomena and human complexity should be apparent. What we should not underestimate, in the process, is the importance that such theoretical and analytical contributions can have for social policies, public education and practical action.

Notes

1. Grant No. R01–HD15699 from the National Institute of Child Health and Human Development ($747,000, including indirect costs).
2. The first of these, the Southeast Asian Refugee Youth Study (SARYS), was conducted during 1986–87 in collaboration with Professor Kenji Ima of the department of sociology at San Diego State University. The study of Southeast Asian infant mortality commenced in 1987 in collaboration with Professor John R. Weeks and the International Population Center of San Diego State University.
3. A sampling unit, or householder, may consist of: married couples without children; married couples with children under 18; unmarried adult siblings residing in the same household; single parents with children under 18; or a related or unrelated adult individual householder (e.g., an elderly widowed mother, a single man or woman, a boarder).
4. Actually, six universe lists were prepared: (1) Hmong, N = 849 sampling units or "families"; (2) Khmer, N = 1,503; (3) Lao, N = 1,686; (4) Sino-Vietnamese, N = 1,023; (5) Vietnamese, N = 4,597; and (6) a special list of N = 151 persons who could not be identified as either Chinese or Vietnamese. (Indeed, the identification of ethnic Chinese from Vietnam was particularly difficult because, unlike the other groups, they could not be distinguished by unique surnames, and occasionally we found cases of intermarriages between Chinese and Vietnamese—all of which necessitated specifying rules for random selection and sample assignment.) In a few instances, an attempt to contact an individual on the sampling list turned up a person or persons who were not in the universe list, though they had arrived in San Diego prior to April 1983—indicating that our best efforts at complete enumeration had not yet produced an entirely exhaustive list. Such "unenumerated" sampling units were living in the same household with an "enumerated" sampling unit or had moved into a dwelling unit that had been recently vacated by an enumerated sampling unit. Those unenumerated sampling units were placed on a separate "unenumerated list" and several were selected by random procedures and subsequently interviewed. This subset is regarded as a simple random sample of the detected unenumerated units. In several other instances (particularly among the Vietnamese, where husbands and wives typically retain separate family surnames), we found that two members of the same sampling or enumeration unit were kept in the universe list, increasing the probability of their selection in the random sample. And of course not all persons in the sample were ultimately located: some were found to have moved out of the County, others moved within the County but could not be located, and in still other cases (usually a disconnected telephone number, and no forwarding address) cases were unlocatable. Within-ethnic-group *sampling weights* were developed, therefore, to equalize the sampling

probability of both enumerated and unenumerated locatable units. Differences in population characteristics between weighted and unweighted results proved to be negligible; in fact, weighted results across a wide range of independent and dependent variables were virtually identical. Thus, *unweighted* results are used in the data and analyses reported herein.

5. The loss of a longitudinal frame for the Lao sample is itself a story that reveals much about the nature of intra- and interethnic rivalries, factionalism, and coalitions in the Indochinese refugee community, and underscores the political and not merely technical dimensions of survey research as a social process. The NICHD grant initially provided funding only for three fulltime Staff Research Associates (SRAs) in IHARP. These positions came to be widely perceived as highly prestigious and well-paying within the refugee community, and were sought after by dozens of well qualified applicants. After a lengthy and intensive process of screening and interviewing many finalists for these positions, the project's personnel committee chose a Vietnamese, a Khmer, and a Hmong applicant as the best qualified to fill the three SRA positions. Despite the presence and assistance of respected members of the Lao community in the IHARP Advisory Board, a fledgling "Coalition" of Lao community "leaders" and cultural brokers (which was later disbanded) objected to the selection of a Hmong over any Lao candidate (the Lao generally look down on the Hmong as a racially "inferior" group), and a "spurned" Lao candidate anonymously wrote and distributed a flyer printed in Lao accusing the project of "corruption" and of forcing the Lao to defer to Hmong "boys," and urging a Lao boycott of the study. (A Vietnamese finalist who was not offered the SRA position also reacted in a similar fashion in a local Vietnamese newspaper that he edited, and considerable organized opposition was also temporarily expressed against the selection of the IHARP Vietnamese SRA by opposing factions of Vietnamese and their American patrons within social service and resettlement agencies who compete for control of available personnel and funding sources.) Extensive meetings and discussions with this Lao Coalition to explain fully both the SRA selection process and to consider mutually acceptable alternatives led to our commitment to seek (as it turned out, successfully) additional funding from NICHD to retain fulltime Lao (as well as Sino-Vietnamese) SRAs for years two and three of the project—the politics of the situation aside, there was a clear need for such additional research assistance in order to achieve successfully the scientific goals of the project. In addition, separate teams of Lao consultants, translators, and interviewers were hired by IHARP; they reported directly to the Principal Investigator, and were paid for their participation during the lengthy three-month training program and related project activities through March 1983. At that time, when all other teams were completing their rehearsal interviews and beginning T1 interviewing in the field, three of the four Lao interviewers (who were also members of the Coalition) began what in time was recognized and admitted to be an organized "boycott" of the project, with the express purpose of refusing to begin any data collection until funding was secured to pay for a separate Lao SRA, despite the prior contractual and other agreements that had been reached to the contrary. Repeated efforts and entreaties to secure their participation were deflected, though it was clearly understood that both the T1.5 and T2 phases of the longitudinal study would be jeopardized by any further delay. (Later we learned of other instances of programs in the San Diego area that had been delayed or cancelled because of similar conflicts involving Lao positions, possibly reflecting, in retrospect, the misconceived application to American "sponsors" of sets of expectations that

traditionally guide what have been called "patron-client" relationships in the Lao community [cf. Van Esterik 1985].) By the time all other groups had completed the T1 phase of data collection, not a single Lao pre-test interview had yet been carried out. As late as July, a representative of the Lao Coalition proposed as a "solution" to the impasse caused by their "community resistance" the idea that the Lao portion of the research study be "subcontracted" out to the Lao Coalition—a curious blending, to say the least, of Lao "patron-client" cultural patterns with American-style "pork barrel." Following discussions with Lao members of our Community Advisory Board, IHARP requested and obtained the resignations of the boycotters in Summer 1983. By September 1983, NICHD funding was approved to retain both Lao and Sino-Vietnamese SRAs. (For the latter, we simply promoted a Sino-Vietnamese interviewer who had already completed the T1 phase, and the T1.5 and T2 Chinese portions of the study went off without a hitch.) Two new, exceptionally well-qualified Lao applicants were selected for these positions, went through a special training program designed separately for them, and completed the T1 phase of the Lao portion of the study during early 1984, around the time when the other groups were beginning T2 data collection. (No problem related to this situation was ever actually encountered in the field, incidentally, and no Lao respondent in the random sample indicated ever having heard of the conflict; in fact, the Lao refusal rate of 2% matched the Hmong rate as the lowest of any group.) As a result, only T1 cross-sectional data were able to be collected for the Lao sample, and the opportunity of enhancing the Lao part of the study through subsequent longitudinal interviews was lost.

6. Survey questions and instruments were developed over a period of several months in close consultation with a 22-person Community Advisory Board from all of the five ethnic groups, as well as with input from a variety of social service and health care agencies involved in refugee resettlement. As is customary in cross-cultural surveys, the interview schedules were translated into each of the five Indochinese languages by one team of translators, and then independently back-translated into English by another team of translators. The resulting translations were carefully examined by IHARP staff research associates, and then again collectively during the training program with all project interviewers, to resolve discrepancies and ensure that the intended meaning of the English original carried over comparatively and as exactly as possible into all of the five languages. Finally, the questionnaires were pretested both in English and in each native language with convenience samples of respondents, then refined again prior to their use in the field. [Note: Copies of both the T1 and T2 questionnaires are available in English, Chinese, Hmong, Khmer, and Vietnamese—and copies of the T1 questionnaire in Lao. Also available are copies of the T1 and T2 codebooks, a detailed "IHARP Research Interviewer's Training Manual," periodic IHARP Status Reports written during the course of the original 1982–85 project, fact sheets and data tables, and other supplementary materials. Most of these materials may be obtained at cost through IHARP, Department of Sociology, San Diego State University.]

7. Respondents were asked at T1 an extended open-ended question about the reasons for their decision to leave, and all these responses were later coded and quantified. Factor analyses identified a number of discrete political, economic, and social "push" *and* "pull" factors—ranging from imprisonment and persecution to a desire for family reunification and a better life. A variety of indices were constructed and examined for their association with a wide range of dependent variables. The most useful proved to be not indices of "political" vs.

"economic" motivations, but rather of perceived "push" vs. "pull." Contrary to popular notions and debates about these issues, we found that these are *not* mutually exclusive, zero-sum dimensions, but may often be additive or mutually reinforcing—e.g., the Khmer reported a greater number of both "push" and "pull" (and both economic and noneconomic) motives for fleeing. A total push index (PUSHALL) was created by summing across all factors reflecting fear or force/coercion in the decision to leave (e.g., fear of the consequences of their past association with the former government or military, fear of harm or harassment, fear of or ideological opposition to communism, imprisonment in re-education camps, forced displacement to new economic zones, famine conditions, inability to make a living, etc.) Similarly, a total pull index (PULLALL) was created by summing across all reported reasons that positively attracted the person to leave and seek resettlement in the United States (e.g., desires to get a better job, improve their standard of living, seek better education for their children, find more "freedom," reunite with family). The PUSHALL measure (regardless of the "political" vs. the "economic" content of the "push") turned out to the be the principal predictor of depressive symptomatology at both T1 and T2. The PULLALL measure consistently washed out in multivariate analyses of psychological adaptation outcomes.

8. Speaking, reading, and writing ability in English as well as in all other languages known by the respondent were measured comparatively at each interview on a 0 to 5 scale, where 0 = "not at all," 1 = "a little or poor," 2 = "some," 3 = "fair," 4 = "well," and 5 = "fluently, like a native." In addition, overall English literacy level was measured by summing the reading and writing scale scores to produce a 0-to-10 index—with the T0, T1 and T2 results shown in Table 8.3. The validity of these respondent self-reports was assessed through various methods, and separately by the interviewer whenever (as happened in many cases) the respondent's use of English was known to the interviewer. In most such cases, the interviewer agreed with the reported proficiency score, though in a few instances the interviewer observed that the score seemed exaggerated; if so, the interviewer's assessment was substituted as the more accurate score. Nevertheless, we noticed a curious phenomenom at T2: 96 out of the 500 respondents in the longitudinal sample (19%) rated their English proficiency level one notch *below* the score which they had reported at T1. (A similar phenomenon has recently been observed by Robert Bach [personal communication] in his review of national panel data from the ORR annual refugee survey.) In order to examine this effect, we split the sample into three groups—those whose reported English proficiency improved by T2 (the "increasers"), those who stayed the same (the "stayers"), and the 96 who rated their English lower at T2 than they had at T1 (the "decreasers")—and then conducted one-way analyses of variance on a broad range of variables in the IHARP data set. The results are quite interesting. We found no significant differences between these groups in their length of residence in the United States, premigration education or occupational prestige, poverty level, household size or composition, close American friends, level of acculturation, or psychological well-being—nor was there any relationship by ethnicity or gender. However, relative to the others, the decreasers were significantly younger (p < .0001) and less dependent on welfare (p < .01), had been employed for a greater percent of the time in the U.S. (in American jobs where they are more exposed to English usage by native speakers), were more likely to live in two-wage-earner households (p < .05), and reported being less satisfied with their progress in learning English (p < .05). This profile suggests that the decreasers may have been more achievement-

    oriented and have set higher evaluation standards for themselves (and hence were less satisfied with their English progress). On this basis, we have called the observed phenomenom the "Socrates effect" (to reflect the wisdom attributed to Socrates, which is evidently shared by the decreasers, that the more he knew, the more he knew how little he knew). The results shown in Table 8.3, consequently, have adjusted the decreasers' T1 English proficiency score downward to match the reported T2 score.

9. Nearly identical results were obtained by using both VARIMAX and oblique rotation methods, and at both T1 and T2, providing evidence for the stability of the factors. Reliability coefficients (Cronbach's alpha) for each of the two factors ranged from .834 at T1 to .873 at T2—particularly impressive given the multilingual, multicultural Indochinese respondent groups. A third, two-item minor factor was also identified, reflecting somatic concerns. We later obtained the data tape for the original HANES survey from the National Center for Health Statistics, and conducted a separate factor analysis of the GWB items for the large American national sample (N = 6,913). The results confirmed the same underlying three-factor structure of the GWB instrument, with a negative factor composed of "distress" items, another of "positive well-being" items, and a third of "somatic" items. In most (but not all) cases, the items loading on each factor were the same ones identified based on the IHARP data.

10. Items loading on the "Depression" factor included, for example, the following: How often during the past month have you . . . (1) felt so sad, discouraged, hopeless, or had so many problems that you wondered if anything was worthwhile? (2) felt down-hearted or blue? (3) been anxious, worried, or upset? (4) been under or felt you were under any strain, stress, or pressure? (5) been bothered by nervousness or your "nerves"? (6) felt tired, worn out, used-up, or exhausted? Descriptive results, scored on a 0-to-5 frequency scale, are provided in Table 8.7.

11. For instance, in multivariate analyses of "Happiness" scores, we found that for women, the number of children born in the United States is predictive of higher happiness, whereas for men it is exactly the opposite (the more children, the unhappier the men). Similarly, the greater the level of welfare income, the unhappier the men—whereas for women the effect again is the opposite. It seems likely that these data reflect culturally prescribed norms validating the gender roles of "mother" for women and of "provider" for men. While children may be a source of self-esteem and self-validation for women, they may add (as does dependency on welfare income) to the perceived burden of the "provider" role for men and undermine the men's perception of their self-worth.

12. We used the Quality of Well-Being (QWB) Scale, an instrument developed by a University of California, San Diego, team which included IHARP co-investigator John P. Anderson, to measure health status (for data on the validity and reliability of this instrument, see Kaplan and Bush 1982). The measure produces an overall weighted QWB score based on all physical symptoms experienced by the interviewee over the last six days, as well as any health-related limitations on mobility and on physical and social activities.

13. One-third of the respondents in the original IHARP T1 sample had no school-age children; only one in six had school-age children who were not attending school within the San Diego Unified School District (although the IHARP sample covered all of San Diego County, 84% of the Indochinese were found to reside within the city of San Diego). Thus, half (49.1%) of the total sample (including 60% of the Hmong, and about 45% of the other groups) did have children in the city schools and entered the IHARP-SARYS sample. There were no differences

in length of residence in the United States or in measures of cultural values or psychological well-being between the families in the SARYS subsample and those who did not enter the SARYS subsample. However, as might be expected of refugee families with dependent children in city schools, the adults (parents) in the IHARP-SARYS sample tended on average to be older, less English proficient, less likely to be employed, more welfare-dependent, poorer, and residing in larger households than the non-SARYS group (those adults without children or with children in suburban schools in the County).

14. A useful comparison may be made between our results and those of the ISR study reported by Caplan et al. 1985b (see also Whitmore, Trautmann, and Caplan, this volume). Overall, the ISR sample (of Vietnamese, Sino-Vietnamese and Lao students in five U.S. metropolitan areas) reflects a somewhat higher level of scholastic achievement than that found in the IHARP-SARYS sample. The mean GPA for the ISR sample as a whole was 3.05, compared to 2.77 for our sample; and 27% of students in the ISR sample had GPAs above 3.5, compared to 18% in our sample. This difference is largely explained by the absence of Khmer and Hmong (and evidently the presence of only a few Lao) in the ISR sample. The comparison with ISR results becomes much closer when we look only at the Vietnamese students in our sample: 26% of the latter had GPAs above 3.5 (almost identical to the 27% figure reported by the ISR study), while only 3.7% had GPAs below 1.5 (a figure identical to ISR results). These data suggest that our findings are not regionally specific and that they may be reasonably generalized to a larger refugee student population.

15. These findings, like those on GPAs, require that the original hypothesis be modified: while social class differences still explain much of the patterns of achievement that are observable among Indochinese refugee youth, both between and within ethnic groups, other factors need to be taken into account to explain the reasons for the lower Lao and Khmer levels of attainment, and for the much higher than expected patterns of educational achievement among the Hmong youth—and indeed, for the general levels of Indochinese student performance relative to those of American students. The principal factors being examined through our qualitative research are cultural and structural patterns of family organization, and culturally patterned coping strategies. For example, the Vietnamese, Chinese and Hmong (the "VCH") all share patriarchal, hierarchical, highly disciplined extended family systems (and the Hmong, clan systems) built on a Chinese cultural model that instills deeply felt norms of filial piety and ancestor worship; an adaptive style that is active and pragmatic and oriented to a work ethic of personal effort; and collective, family-based economic strategies for "self-sufficiency." These forms of social organization not only provide a strong sense of historical and cultural continuity (and hence stability) that pervades social life, but they also create a structure of pressures (e.g., constant parental push, supervision, and control) that undergirds high educational achievement outcomes among the young—and that also serves to control expressions of juvenile deviance, except in those cases (such as unaccompanied minors, non-intact families) where the family organization is weakened or absent as a function of the post-1975 refugee diaspora. By contrast, the Lao and Khmer (the "LK") have common sociocultural roots that reflect more the influence of India than of China, including the same form of Theravada Buddhism, similar language and customs, and looser neolocal, bilateral systems of nuclear family organization; an adaptive style that is more passive and reactive, comparatively less pragmatic and more fatalistic; and more individualistic than collective adjustment strategies (including separate nuclear households and budgets). In

general, there tends to be a looser sense of discipline and obligation that
pervades all social life—not only outside the family (as in brittle Lao "patron-
client" relationships, based on ever-shifting, contingent, and negotiable notions
of "loyalty"), but within the family as well, including parent-child and husband-
wife relationships. The combination of these sociocultural elements—which for
the VCH confer relative advantages within the competitive American educational and economic systems—seem to explain in part many of our quantitative
findings on comparative educational attainment among Indochinese students,
net of social class differences. (For a detailed analysis, see Rumbaut and Ima
1987.)

16. We also looked at the effect of CTBS skill scores on GPAs. The Total Math score
on the CTBS is the principal predictor of GPA by far, accounting by itself for
44% of the explained variance in GPAs. The Total Language CTBS score·
contributes an additional 3% to the explained variance, but the Total Reading
score, which measures the skill areas where the refugee youth do worst, has no
effect on GPA outcomes.

17. This finding, however, cannot be projected indefinitely into the future. Rather,
we predict, based on our qualitative analyses, that this effect will soon plateau
and begin to diminish as the younger family members become more imbued
with prevailing American values and expectations—a process that will be dys-
functional for educational attainment. The exact transition will depend on the
structural ability of families to maintain traditional values and norms (pressures)
that lead to higher achievement, net of the social class advantages of parents (see
Rumbaut and Ima 1987).

18. This despite the fact that among legal immigrants to the United States, women
have outnumbered men each year since 1930. The common stereotype that
international migrants are preponderantly young men of working age has not
applied to the U.S. experience for over half a century (see Houston et al. 1984).

References

Aames, Jacqueline, Ronald Ames, John Jung, and Edward Karabenick. 1977. *Indochinese Refugee Self-sufficiency in California: A Survey and Analysis of the Vietnamese, Cambodians and Lao and the Agencies That Serve Them*. Report submitted to the State Department of Health, State of California.

A.P.W.A. (American Public Welfare Association). 1979. *Indochinese Refugee Report*, Vol. 1, No. 4 (October 30).

Ashmun, Lawrence F. 1983. *Resettlement of Indochinese Refugees in the United States: A Selective and Annotated Bibliography*. DeKalb, Ill.: Northern Illinois University, Center for Southeast Asian Studies, Occasional Paper No. 10.

Babbie, Earl. 1983. *The Practice of Social Research*. Belmont, Calif.: Wadsworth.

Bach, Robert L. 1984. "Labor Force Participation and Employment of Southeast Asian Refugees in the United States." In *Aspects of Refugee Resettlement in the United States*. U.S. Department of Health and Human Services: Office of Refugee Resettlement.

Bach, Robert L., and Jennifer B. Bach. 1980. "Employment Patterns of Southeast Asian Refugees." *Monthly Labor Review* 103(10):31–38.

Bach, Robert L., and Rita Carroll-Seguin. 1986. "Labor Force Participation, Household Composition, and Sponsorship among Southeast Asian Refugees." *International Migration Review* 20(2):381–404.

Bach, Robert L., Rita Carroll-Seguin, and David Howell. 1986. "State-Sponsored Immigrants: Southeast Asian Refugees and the Use of Public Assistance." Report prepared for the U.S. Office of Refugee Resettlement.

Baker, Reginald P., and David S. North. 1984. *The 1975 Refugees: Their First Five Years in America*. Washington, D.C.: New TransCentury Foundation.

Barger, W. K., and Tham V. Truong. 1978. "Community Action Work Among the Vietnamese." *Human Organization* 37(1):95–100.

Berkeley Planning Associates, Refugee Policy Group, and American Institutes for Research. 1986. "Evaluation of ORR's Discretionary Grant Support for Enhanced Skills Training and Multiple Wage Earners: Final Report." Report prepared for the U.S. Office of Refugee Resettlement.

Berry, J. 1980. "Acculturation as Varieties of Adaptation". In *Acculturation: Theory, Models and Some New Findings*. Edited by A. Padilla. Boulder, Colo.: Westview Press.

Blalock, Hubert M., Jr. 1979. "Measurement and Conceptualization Problems: The Major Obstacle to Integrating Theory and Research." *American Sociological Review* 44:881–94.

———. 1982. *Conceptualization and Measurement in the Social Sciences*. Beverly Hills, Calif.: Sage.

Caplan, Nathan, John K. Whitmore, and Quang L. Bui. 1985. *Southeast Asian Refugee Self-sufficiency Study: Final Report*. Ann Arbor, Mich.: The Institute for Social Research.

Caplan, Nathan, John K. Whitmore, Quang Bui, and Marcella Trautmann. 1985a. "Economic Self-Sufficiency Among Recently Arrived Refugees from Southeast Asia." *Economic Outlook, U.S.A.* 12(3):60–63.

———. 1985b. "Study Shows Boat Refugees' Children Achieve Academic Success." *Refugee Reports* 6(10):1–6.

Chance, N. A. 1965. "Acculturation, Self-Identification, and Personality Adjustment." *American Anthropologist* 67:373–93.

Chase-Dunn, Christopher. 1975. "The Effects of International Economics Dependence on Development and Inequality: A Cross-National Study." *American Sociological Review* 40:720–38.

Church World Service. 1980. *Selected Bibliography: Refugees and Refugee Migration*. New York.

Cichon, Donald J., Elzbieta M. Gozdziak, and Jane G. Grover. 1986. *The Economic and Social Adjustment of Non-Southeast Asian Refugees*. Washington, D.C.: Research Management Corporation.

Cooper, Roger G. 1978. "Dynamic Tension: Symbiosis and Contradiction in Hmong Social Relations." *The New Economic Anthropology*. Edited by John Clammer. New York: St. Martin's Press.

Cronbach, L. J. 1951. "Coefficient Alpha and the Internal Structure of Tests." *Psychometrika* 16:297–334.

Desbarats, Jacqueline. 1984. "Response to Paul Ong." *Amerasia* 11(2):133–40.

Desbarats, Jacqueline, and Linda Holland. 1983. "Indochinese Settlement Patterns in Orange County." *Amerasia* 10(1):23–46

Dillman, Don A. 1978. *Mail and Telephone Surveys: The Total Design Method*. New York: Wiley.

Downing, Bruce T., and Douglas P. Olney. 1982. *The Hmong in the West: Observations and Reports* (Papers of the 1981 Hmong Research Conference). University of Minnesota: Southeast Asian Refugee Studies Project.

Duncan, Greg J. 1984. *Years of Poverty, Years of Plenty*. Ann Arbor: The University of Michigan, Institute for Social Research.

Dunning, Bruce B. 1982. *A Systematic Survey of the Social, Psychological and Economic Adaptation of Vietnamese Refugees Representing Five Entry Cohorts, 1975–1979*. Washington, D.C.: Bureau of Social Science Research, Inc.

Durkheim, Émile. 1933. *The Division of Labor in Society*. Translated by George Simpson. New York: Free Press.

Eichenbaum, Jacob. 1975. "A Matrix of Human Movement." *International Migration Review* 7(Winter):21–41.

Eisenstadt, S. N. 1954. "Studies in Reference Group Behavior: 1. Reference Norms and Social Structure." *Human Relations* 7:191–216.

———. 1975. *The Absorption of Immigrants*. Westport, Conn.: Greenwood Press.

Ex, J. 1966. *Adjustment After Migration: A Longitudinal Study of the Process of Adjustment by Refugees to a New Environment*. The Hague: Martinus Niehoff.

Fairchild, Henry P. 1926. *The Melting Pot Mistake*. Boston: Little Brown.

Finnan, Christine R., and Rhonda Ann Cooperstein. 1983. *Southeast Asian Refugee Resettlement at the Local Level: The Role of the Ethnic Community and the Nature of Refugee Impact*. Menlo Park, Calif.: SRI International.

Forbes, Susan S. 1985. *Adaptation and Integration of Recent Refugees to the United States*. Washington, D.C.: Refugee Policy Group.

Frankel, Robert. 1980. *The Resettlement of Indochinese Refugees in the United States: A Selected Bibliography*. Washington, D.C.: Indochina Refugee Action Center.

Fuchs, Lawrence H. 1983. "Immigration, Pluralism and Public Policy: The Challenge of Pluralism to the Union." In *U.S. Immigration and Refugee Policies*. Edited by Mary Kritz. Lexington, Mass.: Lexington Books.

Gardner, Robert W., Bryant Robey, and Peter C. Smith. 1985. "Asian Americans: Growth, Change, and Diversity." *Population Bulletin* 40(4).

Goldbust, John, and Anthony H. Richmond. 1974. "A Multivariate Model of Immigrant Adaptation." *International Migration Review* 8(Spring):195–210.

Gordon, Linda W. 1980. "Settlement Patterns of Indochinese Refugees in the United States." *INS Reporter* 28(3):6–10.

———. 1985. "Age Structure and Fertility among Southeast Asian Refugees: Recent Findings and Implications." Paper presented at the national conference: Southeast Asian Refugees in the United States: The First Decade 1975–1985. San Francisco, Calif.

———. 1987. "Southeast Asian Refugee Migration to the United States." In *Pacific Bridges: The New Immigration from Asia and the Pacific Islands*. Edited by James T. Fawcett and Benjamin V. Carino. Staten Island, N.Y.: Center for Migration Studies. Pp. 153–74.

Gordon, Milton M. 1964. *Assimilation in American Life*. New York: Oxford University Press.

Grant, Bruce, et al. 1979. *The Boat People: An 'Age' Investigation*. New York: Penguin Books.

Graves, T. D. 1967. "Acculturation, Access, Alcohol in a Tri-Ethnic Community." *American Anthropologist* 59:306–21.

HEW Refugee Task Force. 1976. *Report to the Congress*. Washington, D.C.

Haines, David W. 1983. "Southeast Asian Refugees in the United States: An Overview." *Migration Today*. 11(2/3):8–13.

———, ed. 1985. *Refugees in the United States: A Reference Handbook*. Westport, Conn.: Greenwood Press.

———. 1986. "Vietnamese Refugee Women in the U.S. Labor Force: Continuity or Change?" In *International Migration: The Female Experience*. Edited by Rita Simon and Caroline Brettell. Totowa, N.J.: Rowman and Allenheld. Pp. 62–75.

Harding, Richard K., and John G. Looney. 1977. "Problems of Southeast Asian Children in a Refugee Camp". *American Journal of Psychiatry* 134(4):407–11.

Hendricks, Glenn L., Bruce T. Downing, and Amos S. Deinard, eds. 1986. *The Hmong in Transition*. Staten Island, N.Y.: Center for Migration Studies.

Hollingshead, August B. 1957. *Two Factor Index of Social Position*. New Haven: Yale Press.

Homans, George C. 1961. *Social Behavior: Its Elementary Forms*. New York: Harcourt.

Houstoun, Marion F., Roger G. Kramer, and Joan Mackin Barrett. 1984. "Female Predominance in Immigration to the United States Since 1930: A First Look". *International Migration Review* 18(4):908–63.

Howell, David R., ed. 1982. "Southeast Asian Refugees in the U.S.A.: Case Studies of Adjustment and Policy Implications". *Anthropological Quarterly* 55(3), special issue.

Human Resources Corporation. 1979. *An Evaluation of the Indochinese Refugee Assistance Program in California*. San Francisco, Calif.

Hyman, Herbert H. 1942. "The Psychology of Status". *Archives of Psychology* 269 (Columbia University).

IHARP (Indochinese Health and Adaptation Research Project). 1984. "Southeast Asian Refugees in San Diego Country: A Statistical Profile". University of California, San Diego: Department of Sociology.

Johnson, Patricia A., Deborah L. Burgess, et al. 1983. *Asian and Pacific Islander*

Population by State: 1980. Washington, D.C.: U.S. Government Printing Office. (1980 Census of Population Supplementary Report PC80-S1-12.)

Justus, Joyce Bennett. 1976. "Processing Indochinese Refugees." In *Exploratory Fieldwork on Latino Migrants and Indochinese Refugees*. Edited by Roy S. Bryce-Laporte and Stephen R. Couch. Washington, D.C.: Smithsonian. Pp. 76–100.

Kaplan, Robert M., and J. W. Bush. 1982. "Health-Related Quality of Life Measurement for Evaluation Research and Policy Analysis". *Health Psychology* 1:61–80.

Kelly, Gail P. 1977. *From Vietnam to America: A Chronicle of the Vietnamese Immigration to the United States*. Boulder, Colo.: Westview Press.

Khoa, Le Xuan, and John Van Duesen. 1981. "Social and Cultural Customs: Their Contribution to Resettlement". *Journal of Refugee Resettlement* 1(2):48–51.

Kim, Young Yun. 1977. "Communication Patterns of Foreign Immigrants in the Process of Acculturation." *Human Communication Research* 4:66–77.

———. 1979. "Toward an Interactive Theory of Communication-Acculturation". In *Communication Yearbook 3*. New Brunswick, New York: Transaction Books.

———. 1980. *Population Characteristics and Service Needs of Indochinese Refugees*. Volume 3 of the Research Project on Indochinese Refugees in the State of Illinois. Chicago: Travelers Aid Society of Metropolitan Chicago.

———. 1982. "Communication and Acculturation". In *Intercultural Communication: A Reader*, 3rd ed. Edited by Larry A. Samovar and Richard Porter. Belmont, Calif.: Wadsworth.

———. In press. *Communication and Cross-Cultural Adaptation: An Interdisciplinary Theory*. Clevendon, England: Multilingual Matters.

Kim, Young Yun, and Perry M. Nicassio. 1980. *Psychological, Social, and Cultural Adjustment of Indochinese Refugees* (Volume 4 of the Research Project on Indochinese Refugees in the State of Illinois). Chicago: Travelers Aid Society of Metropolitan Chicago.

Kogan, Deborah, Patricia Jenny, Mary Vencill, and Lois Greenwood. 1982. *Study of the State Administration of the Refugee Resettlement Program: Final Report*. Berkeley, Calif.: Berkeley Planning Associates.

Kunz, Egon. 1973. "The Refugee in Flight: Kinetic Models and Forms of Displacement". *International Migration Review* 7(2):125–46.

———. 1981. "Exile and Resettlement: Refugee Theory". *International Migration Review* 15:42–51.

Kuo, W. H., and Nan Lin. 1977. "Assimilation of Chinese-Americans in Washington, D.C." *Sociological Quarterly* 18:340–52.

Lazarsfeld, P. F., and R. K. Merton. 1964. "Friendship as a Social Process: A Substantive and Methodological Analysis". In *Freedom and Control in Modern Society*. Edited by Morroe Berger et al. New York: Octagon Books. Pp. 18–66.

LeBar, Frank M., and Adrienne Suddard. 1967. *Laos: Its People, Its Society, Its Culture*. New Haven: Human Relations Area Files Press.

Levine, Gene, and Colbert Rhodes. 1981. *The Japanese American Community*. New York: Praeger Press.

Lin, Keh-Ming, Laurie Tazuma, and Minoru Masuda. 1979. "Adaptational Problems of Vietnamese Refugees: Health and Mental Health Status". *Archives of General Psychiatry* 36(August):955–61.

Liu, William T., Maryanne Lamanna, and Alice Murata. 1979. *Transition to Nowhere: Vietnamese Refugees in America*. Nashville: Charter House.

Marsh, Robert E. 1980. "Socioeconomic Status of Indochinese Refugees in the United States: Progress and Problems". *Social Security Bulletin* 43(10):11–20.

Masuda, Minoru, Keh-Ming Lin, and Laurie Tazuma. 1980. "Adaptation Problems of Vietnamese Refugees: Life Changes and Perception of Life Events". *Archives of General Psychiatry* 37(April):447–50.

Mattson, Roger A., and Dang Dinh Ky. 1978. "Vietnamese Refugee Care: Psychiatric Observations". *Minnesota Medicine* 61(1):33–36.

McClelland, D. C. 1965. "Toward a Theory of Motive Acquisition." *American Psychologist* 20:321–33.

Merton, Robert K. 1957. *Social Theory and Social Structure*. Glencoe, Ill.: Free Press.

Montero, Darrel. 1979. *Vietnamese-Americans: Patterns of Resettlement and Socioeconomic Adaptation in the United States*. Boulder, Colo.: Westview Press.

————. 1981. "The Japanese Americans: Changing Patterns of Assimilation Over Three Generations". *American Sociological Review* 46:829–39.

Nachimias, David, and Chava Nachimias. 1981. *Research Methods in the Social Sciences*. New York: St. Martin's Press.

Nagata, K. 1969. "A Statistical Approach to the Study of Acculturation of an Ethnic Group based on Communication-Oriented Variables: The Case of Japanese Americans in Chicago". Ph.D. dissertation, University of Illinois, Urbana.

Newcomb, Theodore M. 1952. "Attitude Development as a Function of Reference Groups: The Bennington Study". *Readings in Social Psychology*. Edited by G. E. Swanson, T. M. Newcomb, and E. L. Hartley. New York: Holt.

Nguyen Manh Hung. 1984. "Refugee Scholars and Vietnamese Studies in the United States: 1975–1982". *Amerasia* 11(1):89–99.

Niewoehner, G. 1979. "Federal Policy Regarding the Indochinese Refugee Resettlement Program: An Overview". Paper presented at the American Psychological Association Annual Convention, September 3, New York, N.Y.

Office of Refugee Resettlement (ORR).

 1981a. *Report to the Congress: Refugee Resettlement Program*. Washington, D.C.: U.S. Department of Health and Human Services.

 1981b. *Refugee Resettlement in the United States: An Annotated Bibliography*. Washington, D.C.: U.S. Department of Health and Human Services.

 1982. *Report to the Congress: Refugee Resettlement Program*. Washington, D.C.: U.S. Department of Health and Human Services.

 1983. *Report to the Congress: Refugee Resettlement Program*. Washington, D.C.: U.S. Department of Health and Human Services.

 1984. *Report to the Congress: Refugee Resettlement Program*. Washington, D.C.: U.S. Department of Health and Human Services.

 1985. *Report to the Congress: Refugee Resettlement Program*. Washington, D.C.: U.S. Department of Health and Human Services.

 1986. *Report to the Congress: Refugee Resettlement Program*. Washington, D.C.: U.S. Department of Health and Human Services.

 1987a. *Report to the Congress: Refugee Resettlement Program*. Washington, D.C.: U.S. Department of Health and Human Services.

 1987b. *Monthly Data Reports*. Washington, D.C.: U.S. Department of Health and Human Services.

Okura, K. Patrick. 1980. "Indochina Refugees: Mental Health Needs and Considerations". Paper presented at the annual meeting of the American Public Health Association, Detroit, Michigan.

Ong, Paul. 1984. "A Discussion on 'On Indochinese Settlement Patterns'." *Amerasia* 11(2):127–33.

Opportunity Systems, Inc. (OSI).

 1975. *First Wave Report: Vietnam Resettlement Operational Feedback*. Washington, D.C.

1976a. *Second Wave Report: Vietnam Resettlement Operational Feedback*. Washington, D.C.

1976b. *Third Wave Report: Vietnam Resettlement Operational Feedback*. Washington, D.C.

1977a. *Fourth Wave Report: Vietnam Resettlement Operational Feedback*. Washington, D.C.

1977b. *Fifth Wave Report: Vietnam Resettlement Operational Feedback*. Washington, D.C.

1979a. *Sixth Wave Report: Indochinese Resettlement Operational Feedback*. Washington, D.C.

1979b. *Seventh Wave Report: Indochinese Resettlement Operational Feedback*. Washington, D.C.

1979c. *Eighth Wave Report: Indochinese Resettlement Operational Feedback*. Washington, D.C.

1981. *Ninth Wave Report: Indochinese Resettlement Operational Feedback*. Washington, D.C.

Ossorio, Peter G. 1979. "An Assessment of Mental Health-Related Needs Among the Indochinese Refugees in the Denver Metropolitan Area". Longmont, Colo.: Linguistic Research Institute.

Owan, Tom Choken, ed. 1985. *Southeast Asian Mental Health: Treatment, Prevention, Services, Training, and Research*. U.S. Department of Health and Human Services: National Institute of Mental Health.

Park, Robert E. 1964. *Race and Culture*. New York: Free Press.

Pearce, W. B., and K. R. Stamm. 1972. "Co-orientational States and Interpersonal Communication". In *New Models of Mass Communication Research*. Edited by Peter Clarke. Beverly Hills, Calif.: Sage. Pp. 197–204.

Pennsylvania Department of Public Welfare. 1979. "National Mental Health Needs Assessment of Indochinese Refugee Populations". Philadelphia: Office of Mental Health, Bureau of Research and Training.

Peters, Heather, B. Schieffelin, L. Sexton, and D. Feingold. 1983. "Who are the Sino-Vietnamese? Culture, Ethnicity, and Social Categories". Philadelphia: Institute for the Study of Human Issues.

Portes, A. 1968. "Dilemmas of a Golden Exile: Integration of Cuban Refugee Families in Milwaukee". *American Sociological Review* 34:505–18.

Portes, Alejandro, and Robert L. Bach. 1985. *Latin Journey: Cuban and Mexican Immigrants in the United States*. Berkeley: University of California Press.

Rahe, Richard, J. Looney, H. Ward, Tran Minh Tung, and W. Liu. 1978. "Psychiatric Consultation in a Vietnamese Refugee Camp". *American Journal of Psychiatry* 135(2):185–90.

Roberts, Alden E. 1983. "Social Mobility and Mental Health Among Vietnamese Refugees". Paper presented at the annual Southern Sociological Society meetings, Atlanta, Ga.

Rossi, Peter H., James D. Wright, and Andy B. Anderson. 1983. *Handbook of Survey Research*. Orlando, Fla.: Academic Press.

Rumbaut, Ruben D., and Ruben G. Rumbaut. 1984. "The Refugee: A Piece of the American Mosaic". Paper presented at the annual meeting of the American Psychiatric Association, Los Angeles.

———. 1986. "Refugees in the United States: A Mental Health Research Challenge". Paper presented at the 40th anniversary meeting of the Menninger School of Psychiatry, Topeka, Kans.

Rumbaut, Ruben G. 1985a. "Mental Health and the Refugee Experience: A Comparative Study of Southeast Asian Refugees". In *Southeast Asian Mental Health:*

Treatment, Prevention, Services, Training and Research. Edited by Tom C. Owan. National Institute of Mental Health. Pp. 433–86.

————. 1985b. "How Well are Southeast Asian Refugees Adapting?" *Business Forum* 10(4):26–32.

————. 1986a. "The Structure of Refuge and Southeast Asian Refugees in the United States: A Portrait of a Decade of Migration and Resettlement, 1975–1985". Paper presented at the annual meeting of the American Sociological Association, New York.

————. 1986b. "Patterns, Prevalence, and Predictors of Psychological Distress Among Southeast Asian Refugees: A Longitudinal Perspective". Paper presented to Psychiatry Grand Rounds, Baylor College of Medicine, Houston.

Rumbaut, Ruben G., Leo R. Chavez, Robert K. Moser, Sheila M. Pickwell, and Samuel M. Wishik. 1987. "The Politics of Migrant Health Care: A Comparative Study of Mexican Immigrants and Indochinese Refugees". In *Research in the Sociology of Health Care*, vol. 7. Edited by Dorothy C. Wertz. JAI Press (in press).

Rumbaut, Ruben G., and Kenji Ima. 1987. *Southeast Asian Refugee Youth Study: Final Report*. Report prepared for the U.S. Office of Refugee Resettlement.

Rumbaut, Ruben G., and John R. Weeks. 1986. "Fertility and Adaptation: Indochinese Refugees in the United States". *International Migration Review* 20(2):428–66.

Rynearson, Ann M., and Pamela A. DeVoe. 1984. "Refugee Women in a Vertical Village: Lowland Laotians in St. Louis". *Social Thought* 10(3):33–48.

Sedanko, Carol, and Terrence R. Tutchings. 1978. "Needs Assessment of the Texas Indochinese Refugee Population: Phase I Report". Austin: Texas Department of Human Resources.

Seller, Maxine S. 1987. "Beyond the Stereotype: A New Look at the Immigrant Woman". In *From Different Shores: Perspectives on Race and Ethnicity in America*. Edited by Ronald Takaki. New York: Oxford University Press. Pp. 197–203.

Selltiz, Claire, Lawrence S. Wrightman, and Stuart W. Cook. 1976. *Research Methods in Social Relations*. New York: Holt, Rinehart and Winston.

Shaw, Robert, Jr., 1977. "Preventive Medicine in the Vietnamese Refugee Camps on Guam". *Military Medicine* 142(1):19–28.

Shibutani, T. 1955. "Reference Groups as Perspective". *American Journal of Sociology* 60:562–69.

Silverman, Marsha. 1977. United States Health Care in Cross-Cultural Perspective: The Vietnamese in Denver. M.A. Thesis, University of Denver.

Simon, Julian L., and Paul Burnstein. 1985. *Basic Research Methods in Social Science*. New York: Random House.

Skinner, Kenneth A., and Glenn L. Hendricks. 1977. "A New Minority: Indochinese Refugees in Higher Education". University of Minnesota, *OSA Research Bulletin* 18(4).

————. 1979. "The Shaping of Ethnic Self-identity Among Indochinese Refugees". *Journal of Ethnic Studies* 7(3):25–41.

Smith, Hansen, and Anthony Oliver-Smith. 1982. *Involuntary Migration and Resettlement: The Problems and Responses of Dislocated People*. Boulder, Colo.: Westview Press.

Smith, Harvey H. 1967. *Area Handbook for South Vietnam*. Washington, D.C.: U.S. Government Printing Office.

Starr, Paul D., and Alden E. Roberts. 1982a. "Community Structure and Vietnamese Refugee Adaptation: The Significance of Context". *International Migration Review* 16(Fall):595–610.

———. 1982b. "Attitudes Toward New Americans: Perceptions of Indochinese in Nine Cities". In *Research in Race and Ethnic Relations*, vol. III. Edited by C. B. Marrett and C. Leggon. Greenwich, Conn.: JAI Press.

Starr, Paul D., Alden E. Roberts, Rebecca LeNoir, and Thai Ngoc Nguyen. 1979. "Adaptation and Stress Among Vietnamese Refugees: Preliminary Results from Two Regions". Paper presented at the Conference on Indochinese Refugees, George Mason University.

Stein, Barry N. 1979. "Occupational Adjustment of Refugees: The Vietnamese in the United States". *International Migration Review* 13(1):25–45.

———. 1980. "A Bibliography on Refugees". (Geneva) *News from the United Nations High Commissioner for Refugees* No. 4 (October/November).

Steinberg, Stephen. 1981. *The Ethnic Myth: Race, Ethnicity, and Class in America*. New York: Atheneum.

Strand, Paul J. 1984. "Employment Predictors Among Indochinese Refugees". *International Migration Review* 18(1):50–64.

Strand, Paul J., and Woodrow Jones, Jr. 1985. *Indochinese Refugees in America: Problems of Adaptation and Assimilation*. Durham, N.C.: Duke University Press.

Taft, Julia Vadala, David S. North, and David A. Ford. 1979. *Refugee Resettlement in the U.S.: Time for a New Focus*. Washington, D.C.: New TransCentury Foundation.

Taft, R. 1957. "A Psychological Model for the Study of Social Assimilation." *Human Relations* 2:141–56.

Thompson, Virginia, and Richard Adloft. 1955. *Minority Problems in Southeast Asia*. Stanford: Stanford University Press.

Trczinski, Eileen. 1981. *A Review of the Problems of Limited English Competence of Survey Respondents*. Ann Arbor: University of Michigan, Survey Research Center.

Turner, R. H. 1956. "Role-Taking, Role Standpoint, and Reference Behavior". *American Journal of Sociology* 61:316–28.

Tutchings, Terrence R. 1979. "Needs Assessment of the Texas Indochinese Refugee Population: Phase II Report". Austin: Texas Department of Human Resources.

U. S. Bureau of the Census. 1979. *Population Characteristics: Household and Family Characteristics, March 1978* (Current population report series P–20). P. 43.

U. S. Employment Service. 1977. *Dictionary of Occupational Titles*, 4th Edition. Washington, D.C.: U.S. Department of Labor, Employment and Training Administration.

Van den Berghe, Pierre L. 1981. *The Ethnic Phenomena*. New York: Oxford Press.

Van Esterik, John L. 1985. "Lao." In *Refugees in the United States*. Edited by David W. Haines. Westport, Conn.: Greenwood Press. Pp. 149–65.

Werner, O., and D. Campbell. 1970. "Translating, Working through Interpreters, and the Problem of Decentering". *A Handbook of Method in Cultural Anthropology*. Edited by R. Naroll and R. Cohen. New York: Columbia University Press, pp. 398–420.

Contributors

David W. Haines received an M.A. in Southeast Asian studies and a Ph.D. in social anthropology, both from the American University. He has published widely on refugee adjustment, as well as on American and Vietnamese society. He has recently completed social historical research on household structure in South Vietnam during the 1954 to 1975 period, and is currently conducting cross-national research on refugee resettlement programs in Western Europe under a Fulbright Scholar Grant. He is the editor of the 1985 volume *Refugees in the United States*.

Nathan Caplan is Professor Emeritus in psychology and Program Director for Social Research at the University of Michigan, where he has been for the past twenty-five years. His work has focussed on the application of research methodology to large-scale studies of social issues such as the causative factors of riots (for the Turner Commission); the effect of legal reforms on the prosecution of rapists; and the use of social science data and methods among cabinet- and ministerial-level government officials in various industrial countries, and in China.

Bruce B. Dunning retired from the U.S. Navy in 1969 after an extended career that included service in Vietnam. Following retirement, he earned an M.A. in sociology from George Washington University. He subsequently worked as a research analyst, then as a research associate, for the Bureau of Social Science Research, Inc., where he was initially project manager and then project director of its study of Vietnamese refugees. For the last five years, he has worked in Washington, D.C. as a writer, leatherworker, and artist.

Linda W. Gordon received a Ph.D. in sociology from Ohio State University, with a specialization in demography. She has worked as a demographic statistician for both the Immigration and Naturalization Service (1978–1980) and the Office of Refugee Resettlement (1980–present), where her responsibilities include development of basic program statistics and direction of the government's annual survey of refugees. Her publications focus on the demographic characteristics, geographic distribution, and adjustment patterns of refugees, and the place of refugees in the larger context of Asian immigration.

191

Young Yun Kim received a Ph.D. in communication studies from Northwestern University, where her research focused on the communication patterns of foreign immigrants. Since 1977, she has taught and conducted research at Governors State University in Illinois, where she is a professor of communication. She has published widely in the areas of interethnic and intercultural communication, has edited and written several books in those fields, and, since 1984, has been the editor of the *International and Intercultural Communication Annual*.

Alden E. Roberts received a Ph.D. in sociology from the University of Washington and is currently an associate professor of sociology at Texas Tech University. His other publications on Vietnamese refugees have appeared in *Research in Race and Ethnic Relations, International Migration Review*, and *Journal of Refugee Resettlement*. Work on other topics has appeared in such journals as *Quantity and Quality, Population Review, Sociology and Social Research, Pacific Sociological Review, Social Science Review*, and the *Journal of Social Psychology*.

Rubén G. Rumbaut received a Ph.D. in sociology from Brandeis University. He has since taught and conducted research at the University of California, San Diego and is now associate professor of sociology at San Diego State University. His most recent work on refugee adaptation has focussed on the situation of refugee youth and on the extent and causes of infant mortality. He has published widely on refugee adaptation to the United States, and on criminal justice, with particular emphasis on the role and organization of the police.

Paul D. Starr received a Ph.D. from the University of California at Santa Barbara and is currently a professor of sociology at Auburn University. Some of his publications on Vietnamese refugees have appeared in *International Migration Review, Journal of Refugee Resettlement*, and *Research in Race and Ethnic Relations*. He has also published on other topics in *Social Forces, Human Relations, Journal of Social Psychology*, and *Sociology and Social Research*.

Paul J. Strand received a Ph.D. in political science from Ohio State University. Since 1977, he has been at San Diego State University where he is now Director of the Social Science Research Laboratory and a professor in the department of political science. His research has included a broad range of issues in criminal justice, health services, and economic development, as well as extensive legal research. He is the author, with Woodrow Jones, of the 1985 volume *Indochinese Refugees in America*.

Marcella Trautmann has, since 1983, worked for the Institute for Social Research at the University of Michigan, where she became involved in research on Southeast Asian refugees. She also works as a counsellor at the university's medical school, aiding first- and second-year medical students toward the goal of ensuring their retention in the program. Her dissertation in social psychology, on which she is currently working, involves the comparative analysis of Southeast Asian refugee acculturation.

John K. Whitmore received an M.A. in cultural anthropology and a Ph.D in Southeast Asian history from Cornell University. He has taught Southeast Asian and Vietnamese history at both Yale University and the University of Michigan, and has conducted research on various aspects of early Vietnamese history, subjects on which he has published widely. He continues his work on the analysis of refugee surveys at the Institute for Social Research at the University of Michigan, and the investigation of Vietnam's society and politics during the fifteenth and sixteenth centuries.

Index